T0245732

Advance Praise for
More Than We Expected

"Nothing is worse than losing a child. How does a family go on? In this heartbreaking memoir, James Robinson writes beautifully about his son Nadav, a radiant child with a damaged heart. Robinson does not have all the answers, but he does show how family, faith, science and love can sustain people even at the worst of times."
—Ari L. Goldman,
Author of *The Search for God at Harvard*

"The tragically short life and death of Nadav Robinson is almost too much to bear. But the powerful, positive, passionate way that his father, James, tells the story of how he, his wife, Nadav's twin and older brother navigated that precious life—and death—is too compelling to put down.
"For parents paddling the treacherous waters of raising children with serious health challenges, it is an inspiring guide. For the rest of us, it is a lesson in the meaning of family, of living in the present, and of how Jewish faith and culture can cradle the most difficult of choices.
"This is a rare memoir that demonstrates how to find light in the darkest places."
—Jodi Rudoren,
Editor-in-Chief, *The Forward*

MORE THAN WE EXPECTED

FIVE YEARS WITH A REMARKABLE CHILD

JAMES G. ROBINSON

Post Hill
PRESS

A POST HILL PRESS BOOK
ISBN: 978-1-63758-822-2
ISBN (eBook): 978-1-63758-823-9

Post Hill Press
New York • Nashville
posthillpress.com

Published in the United States of America
1 2 3 4 5 6 7 8 9 10

"We do not leave the shore of the known in search of adventure or suspense or because of the failure of reason to answer our questions.

"We sail because our mind is like a fantastic seashell, and when applying our ear to its lips we hear a perpetual murmur from the waves beyond the shore.

"Citizens of two realms, we all must sustain a dual allegiance: we sense the ineffable in one realm, we name and exploit reality in another…

"They are as far and as close to each other as time and calendar, as violin and melody, as life and what lies beyond the last breath."

—*Abraham Joshua Heschel*

Yaniv, Nadav, and Gilad
Ages three and seven

෨෬

For our sons.

W hen we were expecting our first child, I heard about an old tradition at one of New York's most exclusive restaurants. To celebrate the birth of a son, the proud father would bring a special bottle of wine to the restaurant for cellaring. Twenty-one years later, on the son's birthday, they would share it together over lunch.

Even though I'd never be a regular at such a fancy restaurant, I thought this was a touching tradition. So when we found out we were expecting our first son, I asked a knowledgeable friend to suggest some affordable but cellar-worthy wines I could stow away until his twenty-first birthday. When his twin brothers were born four years later, I did the same with a few special bottles of vintage port.

I think of this now—sixteen years after our first child was born, twelve years after his twin brothers arrived, and six years after one of them died—because I feel the need to set down some precious thoughts. Like the bottles of wine buried in our basement, this bundle of paper—my memories and impressions of all we went through—will be there for them when they are old enough to appreciate it.

This isn't to say our family keeps things hidden. Quite the opposite. We share emotions freely and often, bursting out in sadness, or anger, or frustration, or love. Amidst these eruptions, life persists—awesome and baffling and confusing. Writing helps me make sense of it.

So I am leaving this for our sons in the hopes that it might help them too. Perhaps by the time they read these words, we all might understand things a little better.

ঙ০ঙ

I wonder what memories our sons will have of their brother years from now. Or myself—six years after his passing, I still find it hard to conjure up images from his brief life. Perhaps something in my brain is preventing those memories from emerging, protecting me from the aching sadness of his loss.

His name was Nadav; and he was one of a kind, born with a congenital heart defect so complicated that the diagnosis required three sentences to explain. From the beginning, the odds were against him; at some point, more likely than not, we'd have to bid him goodbye.

We have thousands of photos and videos cataloging our five years together—including one taken by an overeager anesthesiologist in the operating room, halfway through his birth. Whenever I find the courage to look at them, I'm overwhelmed by the emotions that come flooding back: the joy we felt when he was alive, and the sadness we endure now.

But this book is not a eulogy, nor a meditation on grief. The thoughts I share here are less about the tragedy of a truncated life, and more about what we learned during our time together—the lucky parents of an extraordinary child.

ഇന്ദ്ര

It is a terrible thing to know that you will probably outlive your child. But staring at that intense reality long enough, wrestling with its possibility, eventually offered me a glimpse of the profound; a deep and vivid sense of what it really means to live, grow, and heal.

We were blessed to witness countless miracles during Nadav's short life, precious moments of intense pride. There is something about a sick child that brings out the best in everyone, and we were lucky to see that too. We formed deep, enduring bonds with doctors, nurses, and other healers; with other parents faced with similar challenges; and with each other.

This book is our story, as I remember it.

ഇന്ദ്ര

A few years after Nadav died, I found myself at a school reunion, catching up with old friends I hadn't seen in years. We traded stories of the times we'd shared, comparing notes on what had happened since, until someone asked the inevitable question: "How many kids do you have?"

It's an innocent question, the parenting small-talk equivalent of "so, what do you do?" But for those of us who've lost a child, it's tricky to answer honestly.

The correct answer is "three"—but it's one that guarantees a difficult conversation ahead. Because the next question, of course, is, "How old are they?"

Well, I'd answer honestly, eleven and fifteen.

Of course, that's only two kids, and anyone really interested will raise an eyebrow (even if they don't) and in that moment—a slightly awkward pause—you need to decide: "Do I explain, or leave it alone?"

෨෬

In that quick, weird moment, that decision is all mine.

Often, I'll leave it alone—if I'm not in the mood to talk, or if I don't sense the potential intimacy that such a conversation demands. But if I choose to explain, I'll need to closely gauge their reaction to sense whether it's a story they really want to hear.

"It's a sad story," I say. "Just warning you."

And then, I let the hammer fall: "One of our sons died a few years ago, at the age of five."

And then: an instinctive, revealing reaction that tells me instantly whether our story is one they want to hear. If it's not there, I drop it.

They'll never honestly say they don't want to hear it. But you can tell.

෨෬

That night, at the reunion, I chose to explain. "It's a sad story," I said. "Just warning you."

And yet, as I explained the winding strands of Nadav's life—his malformed heart and charming smile; the fateful trip that stranded us on the other side of the world; the unexpected revelation of what caused his condition—I realized it wasn't a sad story after all.

Certainly, losing a child is a terrible tragedy. But the reason I needed to tell it, to share his life and death with others, was to explain why his life was such a profound privilege—something to be proud of, something worth sharing.

His life—like any life—was a unique, inexplicable blessing.

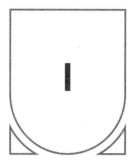

THE PATHS
UNFURL

Chapter 1

TERMINAL 8

On November 10, 2015—my fortieth birthday—I found myself in a dilapidated departure gate at JFK Airport, waiting to board a Qantas flight to Sydney, Australia with my family.

The airport was a lousy place to spend a birthday. There was no champagne, no friends, no drunken toasts—just the florescent glow of an aging terminal, reflecting the weary patience of countless long-haul travelers. My wife Tali and I had already celebrated in fine style a few days before, a surprise party at a rooftop bar filled with cold drinks and old friends. Now, as late afternoon approached dinnertime, we spent our energy trying to entertain our three sons—Gilad, eight, and his twin brothers Yaniv and Nadav, who'd just turned four.

It had only been an hour since we'd arrived at the airport, but the adrenaline of a new adventure was already wearing off. Much of the terminal was under construction, the food options were limited, and our sons were getting cranky. I felt for the boys; it wasn't much fun sitting around in an empty terminal with nothing to do.

But I had every reason to be excited. Tali and I loved to travel, and Australia was one of our favorite places. My mother is from Sydney, and much of my family was still there; Tali had worked there for four years before we knew each other. That small intersection eventually led to us meeting and then, inevitably, falling in love. And now, for the first time, all five of us would be able to experience that part of our shared history together.

⮞⮜

Still, the decision to go was not an easy one.

One of our sons—Nadav—had been born with a complicated heart defect, serious enough to require three surgeries by the age of four. Even then, there was no guarantee that he'd pull through; our hope was that he'd eventually be able to get a transplant as a teenager.

We'd spent the first four years of his life diligently doing our best to give him—and his brothers—the best life we could. For us, this required a little more effort, a little more patience, and a little more faith. We discovered an inner strength that I suspect all parents have, even if they don't always realize it. And we found ourselves faced with some hard truths about the things we can—and can't—control.

When the opportunity to travel to Australia presented itself, we'd consulted with his doctors. They didn't object, as long as we took some precautions. And so, after much deliberation…

(to Tali's eternal regret)

…we decided to go.

Chapter 2

THE FOUR CORNERS
OF THE EARTH

When my ancestors left Eastern Europe, long before the Holocaust, their paths led them to the other side of the world. My mother's family came to Australia in the mid-1800s; my father's forebears arrived in New Zealand around the turn of the twentieth century.

My father often joked that his grandparents actually wanted to go to New York. But since they spoke only Yiddish (he'd insist with a wry smile) the only word they recognized when they arrived at the docks was the word "NEW." And so, they ended up in New Zealand instead.

Their family name was "Vorobeichik," which means "little sparrow." In English, this became "Robinson," the first of many adjustments to their new life in the Southern Hemisphere.

୫୦୯ଷ

As Jewish citizens of the Commonwealth, my parents were raised as "British Orthodox"—outwardly assimilated, but inwardly traditional, if not always strictly observant. As a famous aphorism puts it: "dress British, think Yiddish." So, like my siblings, I had an English name (James, after my mother's grandfather John) and a Hebrew name (Zelig, son of Yeshia Yaakov, son of Michoyel, son of my namesake Zelig—my father's grandfather).

We were raised to feel a strong attachment with our past. Although the details were sometimes garbled—*Did they come from Tels, or Telsai? Was it Latvia, or Lithuania?*—it was always important that we knew where we came from. This ever-present connection to our ancestors could veer into the ridiculous; I have a vivid memory of my father and a visiting cousin during one late-night booze-up in our back garden, cold-calling random Vorobeichiks from the Brooklyn phone book.

Many years later, I traveled to Belarus and Lithuania, looking for the small town my great-grandparents had left a century earlier. I was spending a year in Russia for my junior year abroad, and some of the people I met there—knowing nothing about my past—told me that my poorly spoken Russian had an unmistakable Litvak accent. That small part of my heritage, at least, had persisted through the generations.

When I reached the town, the only thing I found was a small Jewish cemetery and dozens of chickens. No Vorobeichiks.

ℰℭ

My parents moved to New York the year before I was born (correcting his grandparents' mistake at the docks, my father explained) leaving most of my family—three grandparents, nearly a dozen aunts and uncles, and countless cousins—back in the Southern Hemisphere.

Every year during our summer vacation, our growing family would fly back to visit them all, leaving the heat and humidity for an extra month of winter's chill. My grandmother would always present us with newly knit woolen sweaters, still smelling faintly of lanolin, as we huddled next to space heaters to keep warm.

Despite the cold, I was never jealous of our friends back in the States. I loved everything about the trip—the long flight filled with silvery-blue cans of otherwise forbidden lemonade soda, the warm welcome from my grandparents at the Sydney airport, the gifts and treats foisted on us by our relatives, every meal a special event.

ᘒᘖ

I never knew my grandfather on my father's side—he'd died relatively young, long before I was born, when my father was just sixteen. Apparently, I inherited his temper—or so my father would tell me, smiling, whenever I got angry as a teenager, enraging me even more. (A small patch of plaster in my parents' kitchen marks the spot where I once put my hand through a wall.)

My father's mother, since remarried, lived in a high-rise apartment in the Auckland suburbs. She was a lovely woman, always laughing at something or another, fiddling with her hearing aid when she couldn't quite hear something, or turning it off when the conversation turned dull.

I had a great deal of affection for my grandmother in New Zealand, but most of our time was spent with my maternal grandparents, who lived in Sydney.

My Australian grandmother had no tolerance for nonsense, lecturing us sternly when we misbehaved, but she was full of wisdom and kindness. She had a potter's wheel in the basement, kitchen cabinets filled with hand-turned mugs and bowls, and her hands were strong from years of kneading clay. After the Friday night *Shabbat* prayers, she would place them firmly on each of our heads as she said the special blessing:

May the Lord bless you and keep you;
May the Lord shine his countenance upon
you and be gracious unto you;
May the Lord look kindly on you and give you peace.

My grandfather was a respected gastroenterologist, gentle and patient, tall and long-limbed, with a deep affection for children. For someone so polite, nurtured with the nuances of appropriate behavior, he could be a mischievous tweaker of what others considered "proper," quietly relishing his role as a clever and subtle contrarian. When I once loudly announced at the dinner table that oxtail stew was disgusting, he quite agreed, and conspiratorially suggested it should be named "yucktail stew" instead.

He'd served as a regimental doctor during the Second World War, part of a legendary unit that survived an infamous siege in North Africa, but he rarely spoke of what he'd seen. Instead, he preferred to share funny stories and light-hearted poems from his imagination. One long-running saga detailed the adventures of tiny composers who spent their days rehearsing symphonies in the squeaky bathroom tap.

Even from afar, we shared a special bond. Every few months, a new light blue aerogramme would arrive in the mail, full of stories and verse in his characteristic doctor's scrawl. I still have the composition books my mother used to collect them all, pasted in with yellowing tape. They are the most treasured mementoes of all my family heirlooms, along with the wallet my grandfather carried through the war, and my great-grandfather's prayer books, bound in blue leather and gold leaf.

૪)૦૪

Whenever we came to visit, Grandpa would always give us a tour of his garden—elegant orchids in a backyard hothouse, a rubbery banana tree in the side garden, carefully tended rose bushes out front. He'd show me the latest arrivals in the stamp collection he'd started for me when I was born, kneeling on a special ergonomic office chair, surrounded by his beloved books and the faint scent of Imperial Leather soap.

But Grandpa always seemed happiest in motion. We'd go for long walks around the neighborhood, his lanky strides setting a brisk pace. And then we'd head out for all sorts of special excursions—ferry rides to the Taronga Zoo, Gilbert and Sullivan operettas at the Opera House, shopping excursions for rugby jerseys downtown.

It was a special thrill to take the train, so different from the subway back home—the double-decker cars winding through the hilly neighborhoods of the North Shore, eventually emerging at the majestic Harbour Bridge with the gleaming city beyond.

The worst part, of course, was when these few precious weeks came to an end, and we'd have to pack up to go back home. I took comfort knowing that we'd be back soon enough, that everything I loved about the city would be waiting for me when we returned.

But by the time I'd grown old enough to visit my grandparents on my own, I began to realize that they'd changed too. Our walks became slower, their bodies increasingly frail. Instead of driving me to the airport, they'd bid me farewell from the front garden. I started to wonder if it would be my last time seeing them, and returning home, I was often left with a ghostly sense of premature grief.

I never quite knew how to say goodbye.

༄ඏ

actually met my wife, Tali, through my Australian family, our paths intertwined on the branches of my family tree.

She had moved to Sydney for work after college, living in a shared house in the shadow of the Harbour Bridge, and fell in love with the city. She lived there for four years, fully immersed in a world I only glimpsed—and while navigating the relatively small Jewish community there, she met my relatives, who became her adopted Jewish family. She joined them for Friday night dinners and Shabbat services, on occasion even sitting in my grandmother's seat in the Great Synagogue downtown.

Tali had moved back to the States by the time we met. I had been playing tennis with my cousin, who told me he needed to meet her at a bar that evening to return a book his brother had borrowed. "A friend of the family," he sighed, indicating a quick, obligatory drink, and I came along to keep him company. As it turned out, Tali and I spent the entire evening talking, even after my cousin called it a night.

We soon discovered that my family wasn't the only thing we had in common. We both liked the same type of yogurt; our fathers were both schmoozers, fond of starting random conversations with strangers; and her family had also migrated to the Southern Hemisphere from Eastern Europe.

Her father's parents moved from Russia to Argentina before the madness of the Holocaust began, but her mother's family, who'd stayed in Poland, was not as lucky. Her grandmother spent three years in hiding after her entire family was murdered; her grandfather spent four years fighting Nazis as a partisan in the Belarusian woods. They met just before the war ended, when a drunk Russian officer accidentally shot her in the foot. After a stop in Italy, they moved to Brazil, and then to Israel, where Tali's parents met—and married—in the mid-1960s.

ಹಃ

A few months after Tali and I met, my grandmother fell gravely ill. I decided to go visit her in Australia one last time and asked Tali to come with me. Although we were not officially engaged, it was pretty obvious to everyone that we soon would be.

During the trip, we went to see my grandfather's older brother; a sharp-witted former surgeon, slowed but still driving at the age of ninety-seven. Tali and I sat with him in his sunroom overlooking Sydney Harbour, sipping cups of tea, when he suddenly asked, "How many children do you want to have?"

It was a funny question, considering we weren't even engaged, but a good one.

"Two," said Tali, glancing at me.

"Four," I said, glancing at her.

"Three," he said, nodding his head. "Three is the right number."

ಹಃ

Our last visit with my grandmother turned out to be all I'd feared in my hesitant farewells. It was terrible seeing her in her bed, so weak and frail. I gave her a kiss on the forehead as she dozed; and for the first time, I said goodbye to someone I loved.

This time, knowing that I would never see my grandmother again, I didn't know exactly how to feel.

ಹಃ

When my grandmother died, she left me some money, which I resolved to put toward an engagement ring.

It took me a while to propose to Tali, but it had been clear for some time that we fit well together. I remember the moment I knew for sure, after just a few dates; we'd been invited to a friend's house on a Friday night, and they lit the Shabbat candles, her smiling face reflected in the glow. I wanted to share that moment with her over and over again, and a few months later, I told her so.

This was not news to Tali. She already knew that we'd get married, and insists, to this day, that I really didn't have any say in it.

ଧଓଃ

The following summer, we were married in a nearby park—a sunny day, just a little too warm; a brightly colored *tallis* hoisted above; surrounded by family and friends in a wide, happy circle.

On the front of our wedding invitation was a map of the world, labeled with all of the meaningful places from our past— my parents, from Australia and New Zealand, married in London; her parents, from Poland and Russia by way of Argentina and Brazil, married in Israel.

My grandfather flew to New York to be with us, along with many of our friends and family from around the globe. We made sure that each guest's name card had the appropriate flag on it, and the table on which they stood had the pageantry of an Olympic procession.

New York was our home, but the four corners of the earth tugged at our hearts.

Chapter 3

A WHIRLWIND OF MOVEMENT

When Tali became pregnant two years later, we consulted an obstetrician who lived not far from our home in Brooklyn. His practice, on the ground floor of an apartment building, was inherited from his father, decorated with family heirlooms, and his cheerful, unfussy demeanor always put us at ease.

The old-school office, full of relics, was devoid of any advanced equipment—so for anatomy scans we were sent to a busy clinic at the other end of town, packed with nervous parents-to-be. Our only worry then was that we'd accidentally learn the baby's gender. We'd gaze at the black-and-white sonogram, careful to close our eyes whenever the technician warned us, lest we accidentally glimpse a tell-tale clue.

‽‽‽

We somehow managed to avoid finding out until the baby arrived in late summer—on a Friday, three days early.

A boy.

Having heard the news, our families arrived to share the *simcha*—big smiles all around, hugs freely shared, no shortage of cheer. I took my father to the nursery to meet his first grandson, lying sleepy and swaddled behind a large glass window. He beamed.

Next to us were a half-dozen cops in full uniform, excitedly pointing in the same direction. One of New York's Finest had become a new dad as well—our sons were neighbors in the nursery—and his pals from the precinct had come off the beat to cluck and coo.

Exhausted and happy, I left the hospital in the early evening, floating in my own joy, along a busy avenue packed with bars and the drunken laughter of a late-summer's night. Walking past, I could not fathom what everyone was celebrating. How could they know happiness? My joy—the joy of new fatherhood—was the only joy; everything else seemed trivial and silly. I had welcomed another life into the world, and nothing else compared.

₧)℣

We named him Gilad, in memory of my grandmother.

He spent ten precautionary days in the NICU, diagnosed with a respiratory ailment; but we were assured that this was something minor, and we had no reason for concern. They found some fluid in his lungs, but the doctors suggested it was simply an after-effect of the c-section, and that it would clear up soon enough.

Tali went home after two days, and as she recovered, I went back to the hospital to care for Gilad. I still have happy memories of delivering still-warm breast milk on my bike each evening, nursing him from a bottle in the near-silent calm of the after-hours hospital ward. Those were quiet, special moments. And as the doctors had predicted, he came home healthy.

୨୦୧୫

Before Gilad was born, I had asked other dads for any words of wisdom about fatherhood. The best advice came from a colleague at work: "Take every day you're entitled to—paid and unpaid," he told me. "That time is priceless, and you'll never regret it."

So, I took three months of leave—the first two with Tali, right after he was born, and the last one after she'd returned to work, spending my days looking after Gilad all by myself. It was a wonderful month, just the two of us, getting to know each other. My friend was right—it was a real gift.

It was also really hard work—completely exhausting, in fact— but I was perhaps the most efficient I've ever been, particularly in the hour or so when Gilad napped, around midday. I couldn't believe how much I managed to get done in that hour—dishes, laundry, emails—a burst of productivity that left me breathless, always feeling that he was just about to start crying, the window of opportunity slamming shut until bedtime.

୨୦୧୫

At five months old, we brought Gilad to Sydney to meet his great-grandfather, who was now living alone. The long flight was easy enough, a grand adventure. Tali and I had done it enough times to not only endure the length but enjoy it. At the first drinks service, I asked for a lemonade soda—and when they pulled out the silvery-blue can, with a cup of ice and a little napkin tucked underneath, I felt right at home.

Gilad didn't mind the flight either. When he wasn't sleeping, he charmed the crew, poking his head above the edges of his little bassinet. To entertain him, I invented a game called "Sneak

Peeks"—hoisting him above our seat, popping up like a jack-in-the-box to smile at the passengers behind us. He loved it.

I felt so happy to be heading back—this time in the service of happiness, not grief.

ℬℭ

When we arrived, my grandfather was waiting for us in the driveway. After the usual exhausted hugs, we headed inside to the home where we'd shared so many memories. Tali and I sipped cups of tea, piping hot in my grandmother's mugs, while Gilad bounced up and down on Grandpa's lap. They had a grand old time together, goofing off and sharing giggles, ninety-two years and three generations apart.

Trying to hold off the inevitable jetlag—sunshine a tried-and-true antidote for post-flight drowsiness—we soon headed back out to the garden. An expert pruner of roses, Grandpa was always trying new things: one year, a collection of native Australian plants; another, a hothouse full of orchids. This time, we noticed that he'd lined one entire wall with eggplants.

"You must really like eggplants," I said, surprised.

"No, I can't stand them," he answered.

Then why did you plant them? I wondered, out loud.

"Well, I like *growing* them!" he replied, with a laugh.

It was characteristic of his joyful approach to life. The fate of the eggplants was irrelevant; simply tending to them was pleasure enough.

ℬℭ

As we stood outside, taking in the sweet Sydney air, I realized how amazing it was for my grandfather to meet Gilad. It would be amazing enough to see your toddler grow, graduate college, get married, and have kids. But to also live long enough to meet your *great*-grandkids—well, that was something. What a blessing, what an achievement, what pride.

We spent a month Down Under, introducing Gilad to his extended family in both Australia and New Zealand. He was far too young to enjoy the many things that I'd grown to love about the place—rugby matches, fish and chips wrapped in newspaper, and meat pies with mushy peas. But everyone loved giving him cuddles and pinching his cheeks.

This time, for some reason, it wasn't quite as hard to say goodbye.

ಬಿಂಚ

The next few years were a whirlwind of movement.

Gilad needed a proper bedroom, so we moved into a larger apartment. We bought a used car—a ten-year-old red Subaru Outback that got us where we needed to go with no complaints—and whenever the opportunity to travel presented itself, we took it. It was a worthy splurge, Tali always believing that experiences outweighed possessions.

It was the stage of life when friends were getting married, and we said yes to as many invitations as we could—a convenient excuse to show Gilad the world. We traveled to Europe for two weddings, jokingly giving him a local name in each country. In Scotland, decked out in a little tartan kilt, we dubbed him, "Gil MacRobin." In Greece, lugged around ancient ruins in a clever carrier backpack, he became "Giladakis Robinopolous." We even bought him a little blue soccer jersey to celebrate his new nationality.

Gilad, who'd just turned one, was an early riser, so Tali and I—both night owls—kept him on Eastern Daylight Time. Five hours ahead of an otherwise torturous sleep cycle, he stayed awake until midnight and slept in until midmorning, allowing us to enjoy the evening festivities. One night, a bevy of smitten Greek girls kept him company in a jam-packed club, *rembetika* blaring, leaving us to grab a few minutes for ourselves.

After the wedding in Athens, we spent a week on a beautiful island called Kythera—famous, as we found out, for its relationship to Australia. There had been a mass emigration from Kythera to the Southern Hemisphere at the turn of the century; even now, a fair number of Greek Australians trace their roots back to the island.

The owner of the small B&B we stayed in perked up when I mentioned that my mother was from Sydney too. "What's her name?" she asked, prompting me to sheepishly admit that she was not, in fact, Greek.

Our flight back to the mainland was unexpectedly canceled the day before we were due to leave. The island's only air traffic controller had taken ill, and nobody knew when he might recover. ("He's never been sick before," the hotel owner admitted. "It could be weeks!") So, we took the midnight ferry instead. Gilad had fallen asleep in his stroller by the time we boarded, and we decided to wedge him into a cabin closet to keep him steady. Otherwise, we worried, he'd pitch and roll as the ship chugged through the night.

When we arrived at the port of Piraeus at dawn, the closet seemed to have shrunk; it took us fifteen frustrating minutes to get him out. But despite all of the jolting and jostling—and a bumpy train ride bracketed by endless stairs—he didn't wake up until we arrived at the airport to check in. "We missed our flight," I told the gate agent apologetically, just as Gilad opened his eyes with a yawn, blinking in the terminal's bright lights.

Traveling with small children was challenging, but we were getting pretty good at it.

ଽଠଔ

W edding invitations gave us a good reason to explore new places, but we didn't need any special excuses to return to Sydney. After Gilad's second birthday, we flew down again. He was still too young for lemonade soda, but this time, he was old enough to have his own seat. He even took a turn wearing the captain's hat in a visit to the 747's cockpit.

When we landed, Sydney still felt like home. My grandfather was noticeably older; he had started using a cane, and his memory was getting worse. But of course, he still enjoyed seeing his great-grandson, who by this time was able to explore the world on his own two feet. Gilad toddled around the garden, smelling the famous roses, feeding scraps of his lunch to the colorful lorikeets on the porch.

Just before we left, my grandfather spent a lovely afternoon tossing a ball with Gilad on the couch, giving it stern orders to *Behave!* whenever it rolled away. Gilad was overcome with giggles, an honest moment of delight; each of them having as much fun, it seemed, as I had during any of the ambitious outings we'd done when I was young.

ଽଠଔ

Our departure the next day was tinged with sadness. My grandfather put on a good show, but in a private moment he admitted that it was almost "his time to go." I'd always feared that our curbside farewell would be for good. Now, I knew for sure that this goodbye would be our last.

Gilad would never know my grandfather as I had; he was too young, my grandfather too old. They would never go to the zoo together, or shop for sports jerseys downtown, or share a bowl of pasta before an evening at the Opera House. Just playing with a ball would have to be enough.

But we were so very lucky to have made those trips; to be able to traverse the world, connecting our family across generations—and ever so briefly—pass a little bit of light from the past into the future.

Chapter 4

UNEXPECTED SWERVES

Sometimes, when I got especially tired, I would joke that I would rather have adopted grandkids than become a parent—skip straight to the days when a new toddler could be a part-time hobby instead of a full-time job.

But I loved being a father. It gave me a chance to emulate my grandfather's sense of joy—crafting silly songs out of thin air and creating goofy games out of everyday objects. And I finally understood my own father's beaming smiles in the fading Kodachrome snapshots taken when I was a toddler—the giddy happiness of a new parent. I loved introducing Gilad to the world and eagerly anticipated every milestone—his first words, his first steps. It brought out the best of who I wanted to be.

And yet, no matter how much I enjoyed parenthood, I found myself having to accept its fundamental truth: nothing ever turns out quite as you'd expect. There is another life in the mix, after all, and with it comes an unavoidable unpredictability—no matter how hard you might try to keep things under control.

৪৩৫৪

Every year, I looked forward to planning Gilad's birthday parties. Other parents deferred to play spaces to provide out-of-the-box celebrations—a precise procession of pizza and presents, carefully choreographed to the minute; everyone out the door, party favors in hand, in exactly two hours.

I took a different approach. About a month before each birthday, I picked a theme, did some online research (*Wow, you can get TWO DOZEN of those for just five bucks?*), and went a little nuts. As a result, our parties were completely original, if somewhat strange, and always bordered on chaos. And I took pride that they always lasted longer than two hours.

Gilad's first birthday was somewhat normal: a dozen one-year-olds, squirming in their parents' laps, rolling soft balls around an empty yoga studio. But his second birthday was a little looser. We gathered with our friends in a nearby park, large enough for the toddlers to freely roam as us parents relaxed over coffee and bagels.

The theme was "golf," and we brought plastic clubs and balls for the kids to play with. But despite my attempts to harness their energy in some sort of coordinated activity, they seemed happy enough flinging little plastic golf balls in random directions. I started to realize that a good birthday party just needed a prompt and a boundary—a blank canvas on which the kids could create their own fun.

The following year, in the aftermath of World Cup mania, we settled on soccer, asking friends to wear their favorite team's jersey. Clad in his little Greek soccer shirt, we'd planned for the famous "Giladakis" to make a repeat appearance—for old time's sake. But when rain appeared, our plans for a grand match in the park were derailed. We told people to come to our apartment instead and let Gilad's friends loose in our narrow hallway with a bunch of balls. The neighbors couldn't have been too pleased with the noise, but the kids didn't have any trouble having fun.

It had become clear to me that despite everything I did to prepare, I usually had very little say in how things turned out. Sometimes it was just best to yield to chaos, and let the little ones figure it out on their own.

ᎥᏟᎶ

Our daily lives were not immune from unexpected swerves. Gilad's pediatrician had noticed that he seemed unusually congested, his ears persistently clogged with fluid— echoes of his NICU stay at birth. A specialist recommended that we consider a common childhood procedure to remove his adenoids and put tiny tubes in his ears. By draining the fluid that built up there, the thinking was, he'd avoid nasty ear infections in the future.

The doctor assured us that it was perfectly routine: lots of kids had them, nothing to worry about. And so, a month after his third birthday, Gilad went to the hospital for what we were told would be a minor operation.

I drove him there in our red Subaru, the clinic a lonely brick building far from our home. The procedure required an IV and general anesthesia, but I believed what I'd been told—there was no reason to worry. And an hour later, when Gilad was wheeled out into the recovery room, the nurse told me that everything had gone well. He woke up slowly, working his way through a foam cup full of ice chips, and after an hour or so, we were discharged into the cool fall air.

ᎥᏟᎶ

I barely considered what might happen if there had been complications. Gilad's pediatric care had been built on reassuring routines—height and weight duly noted, vaccines administered like clockwork, unexpected fevers quickly solved with chicken soup or antibiotics. Each check-up marked another milestone: everything on track and working properly.

I'd had a few minor medical crises as a kid, all sports-related: a hyperextended elbow playing tag in an overwaxed school gym; a broken wrist when my ice skates went out from under me; a fractured finger when a handstand went too far. The worst was when I tripped over a soccer ball and seriously busted my nose. Rushed to the emergency room, I needed general anesthesia and a dozen stitches below my upper lip.

But my memories of these injuries are mostly of thankful convalescence. The doctor who set my broken bones had known many of the Brooklyn Dodgers; his office was warm and familiar, decorated with black and white locker-room photos autographed by ballplayers. Even my hospitalization had a happy ending: sipping warm, homemade soup through a straw, presented with a favorite Transformer toy to help me ignore the throbbing pain. A few broken bones here and there seemed par for the course.

So as a parent, I trusted our doctor to tell us what was going on. If something wasn't quite right—a sniffle, a rash, a cough— she'd know what to do.

ᏚᎤᏣ

The following spring, we discovered to our joy that Tali was pregnant again—this time with twins.

To announce the pregnancy, we bought a four-pack of mini champagne bottles, delivering them to our parents along with the good news. Gilad gave two to my mother and father at Sunday brunch, with a simple declaration: "BABIES!" And that evening we made the hour's drive to tell Tali's parents, unexpectedly showing up on their doorstep at dusk, bottles in hand. All of them were overjoyed, their happiness mingling with our pride.

I was less direct in breaking the news to my siblings, sending them random pictures of famous Minnesota Twins baseball players. This prompted some confused emails; they probably wondered if my account had been hacked. But they hooted and hollered once I called to explain—"Twins? Oh, *twins*!" After that, the word spread quickly. "All of Sydney is abuzz!" one cousin reported from Australia. Another, who'd had twins of her own, wrote to Tali offering detailed advice on feeding techniques.

Now that our secret was out, it was suddenly real. Just as we were getting used to having one child, we'd soon have three.

ဆဝလ

When my grandfather heard, he emailed us immediately. "I am delighted to hear that you are pregnant with twins," he wrote. "A big lift for the family tree!" But it would be the last email he ever sent me. He died a few months before the twins arrived—one of our tree's most solid roots suddenly gone, as if yielding to the next generation.

My mother had called to let me know of my grandfather's death, expecting me to be devastated by the news. But although I'd feared this moment for years, I was surprised by my reaction. "Now that he has died," I wrote to my siblings soon afterward, "I have been strangely calm, hardly upset at all."

I'd learned, somehow, how to cope with the reality of his death.

His was a full life, I reasoned; he lived well into his nineties. But it was more than that. Now that I'd become a father, I was beginning to realize why he so enjoyed seeing the world through children's eyes. He not only tolerated their chaos, their imaginations, their utter unpredictability; he welcomed and encouraged it.

For someone who had seen men die in war, watching new lives emerge must have felt an incomparable blessing. Perhaps he saw in their unwritten lives an answer to the riddle of our own mortality, their unbounded energy an antidote to the inevitability of growing old.

Soon, we would be welcoming two new lives into our own family. They would never know their great-grandfather, but I hoped that—like my Lithuanian accent, passed down through generations, emerging somehow in my halting Russian—I might be able to carry his spirit along, as best I could.

Ⅎℴℭ

The early days of our second pregnancy were not particularly stressful. We'd been through this before; we knew what to expect.

To guide us through, we'd returned to our family obstetrician, cheerful as ever. He still hadn't upgraded his equipment, so again we were sent across town for anatomy scans. It was here that we got our first glimpse of the twins. As before, our only worry was that we would accidentally learn their gender, and so we once again averted our eyes whenever the sonographer told us to. Tali and I had agreed that we didn't want to know the sexes until they were born.

We had become so relaxed that I'd begun taking Gilad to a nearby playground to pass the time during the ultrasound. And yet, after one seemingly routine visit, Tali emerged to meet us in the blinding sun, her eyes watery with tears.

"We need to make an appointment," she said in a soft voice. "They noticed an issue with one of the twins. There's something wrong with the heart."

Chapter 5

THE PLAN

There's something wrong with the heart. A vague diagnosis; an inexplicable observation; six simple words that left us stunned, fearing the worst.

I spent the rest of the day online, frantically researching congenital heart issues—what the possible defects might be, which hospitals had the best ratings, and the long-term prognosis for kids with heart issues.

When I'd finished, I sent what I'd found to Tali—a bundle of copy-and-pasted links, topped with the only optimism I could muster. "The good news," I wrote, "is that we live in an era of medical miracles, and not the Middle Ages."

ഇരൂ

The next day, still reeling, we found ourselves in the pediatric cardiology department of Mount Sinai Hospital, Tali lying on a bed, twenty-six weeks pregnant, as a fellow meticulously scans her belly. The echocardiogram took hours, with the supervising cardiologist taking over toward the end. She was quiet and focused, looking intently at the screen—red and blue dots flowing every which way—trying to avoid the healthy twin to get the best view of the other's abnormal heart.

Afterward, the cardiologist introduced herself properly. "My name is Shubhika," she said, "but everyone calls me Shubhi." We sat in her small office as she explained the situation as best she could. It was her birthday, and the scent of fragrant Indian food wafted in from the break room; her colleagues waiting patiently, curries slowly getting cold.

I marked the date on our calendar, and we'd remember it for years to come: Shubhi's birthday—the day of diagnosis, the day we met.

₨⁡℣

Shubhi walked us through what she'd seen in simple, direct terms. One of the twins had a malformed heart. There was no wall separating the two ventricles—just a single chamber, with red and blue blood mixing inside. And there was no connection between the heart and the lungs.

These defects, Shubhi told us, were a symptom of a rare but well-known condition called "heterotaxy." Futhermore, the problems were likely not limited to the heart; other organs might be affected as well. In particular, there was a good chance the baby would be missing a spleen.

But we'd deal with that later. For now, the big worry was the heart.

₨℣

s Shubhi talked, she sketched the heart with a ballpoint pen: a three-fingered blob, leaning slightly to the left.

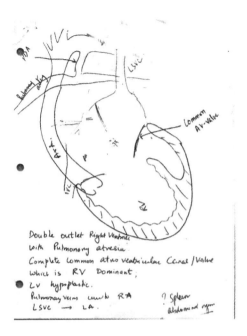

Double outlet Right Ventricle
with Pulmonary atresia.
Complete common atrio ventricular Canal / Valve
which is RV Dominant;
LV hypoplastic.
Pulmonary veins comb to RA
LSVC ⟶ LA.
? Spleen
abdominal organ

Whenever we met, she always started with the same diagram. No matter how complicated her drawings became, the fundamental anatomy never changed.

But there was some reason for hope, Shubhi explained. Over the years, pediatric cardiologists had devised an approach to helping children in these situations. They'd developed a sequence of three surgeries, all palliative, that could give our child a chance to live.

Still, even if successful, these surgeries would do nothing to address the heart's unusual anatomy. Although surgeons could work wonders, there was no fixing the heart itself. It was beyond repair.

೮೦೮೮

Shubhi patiently walked us through the plan.

Our twins didn't have names yet—we still didn't even know their gender—so for the time being, she referred to them with simple aliases. Twin A was the healthy one; Twin B was the reason we were here.

The first priority would be to reconnect Twin B's heart and lungs—no more than a week after the twins were born.

All newborns are born with an extra connecting blood vessel—the ductus arteriosus—that would keep the circulation flowing properly after birth. But even with the help of medication, that tenuous connection would naturally close. We'd need to find another way for the blood to flow.

The answer was a procedure called a "BT shunt." The surgeon would temporarily stop the heart, putting it on bypass, and then they'd implant a tiny conduit between two arteries—just millimeters in diameter—to create a more permanent pathway for red blood to move, roughly approximating its proper flow.

ಬಾ

Even if that first surgery was successful, Shubhi told us, living with a single ventricle would eventually become unsustainable. Red and blue blood would continue to mix in the single chamber, causing low oxygen saturations in the bloodstream, and those levels would continue to decrease as the body grew.

To address this, Twin B would need two more operations.

Stuck with a single chamber, surgeons would rework Twin B's circulation so that the body's blue blood would be diverted directly into the lungs. This would happen in two stages: the Glenn, at five months, would divert blue blood returning from the upper half of the body, and the Fontan, at three or four years, would divert blue blood from the lower half.

If successful, these surgeries would transform the malformed heart into a pump for red blood only, rendering the missing ventricle moot and keeping Twin B's oxygen levels high enough to lead a relatively normal childhood.

෴

There were no guarantees that this approach would work. Not only were the surgeries risky in and of themselves, but convincing blue blood to flow passively to the lungs would depend on a delicate and unpredictable balance of pressures.

The hope was to get Twin B to teenage years—somehow dodging the countless things that might go wrong—and eventually be a candidate to inherit a new, full-size heart via transplant. That was the plan.

෴

Tali and I discussed whether it was worth asking for a second opinion. We'd decided to go to Mount Sinai first, but it was just one of New York's many prestigious hospitals. In one of our meetings, Tali asked Shubhi point-blank, "Is this the best place for us to be?"

To Shubhi's credit, she gave us an honest answer. "If it wasn't," she said, "I'd tell you. I'd send you somewhere else." There were some congenital heart issues that other places were better equipped to treat, she admitted. But in her opinion, our situation was something that Mount Sinai was well-prepared to handle.

And by that point, we'd come to feel comfortable with Shubhi. We could already sense her humble expertise; it was obvious that she would do everything she could to help our child. It felt right, and even more so after the appointment, when I noticed a familiar name on the list of attending pediatric cardiologists at the front desk. It was someone I'd gone to high school with eighteen years ago, and we shared a hug on our next visit, amazed at our unexpected reunion.

It was the first of many strange coincidences we would encounter, and I took it as a sign that we should trust our instincts. We were in good hands; this was the right place to be.

၂၀၀၃

Tali and I can be quite different in how we approach the world. She is an engineer, in both profession and personality; for her, what matters are the facts. Life, to her, is what it is—a logical system that can be analyzed, understood and improved. She has an engineer's faith that any properly designed system can be trusted to do the right thing.

It's a straightforward approach that I often envy. I'm more of a poet, a philosopher, a dreamer. I think in broad brushstrokes, trying to reduce every problem to an inner truth, and I've always sensed that in the arc of the world, there is something beyond our grasp.

Of course, we're similar in many ways too. Both of us always put family first. We are both stubborn, sometimes to a fault. We share a private silliness—our inside jokes lovingly ridiculous. And we've always spent our lives searching the world for a special sort of joy—no matter what is in the way.

We always felt that we were *beshert*—a Yiddish word, meaning "fated, meant to be"—brought together by some unseen power to keep each other happy, safe, and whole.

၂၀၀၃

We never seriously discussed ending the pregnancy. Not for religious reasons or because of any risk to the healthy twin—we just wanted to build a family. And perhaps we were both stubborn enough to think that despite all we'd heard—all of the risks—we could make it work. We always felt that with enough knowledge, and a solid plan, we could be prepared for anything.

Tali may once have been happy with two kids; I might have always dreamed of four. But even after hearing the diagnosis, we were in complete agreement.

My great-uncle was quite right. We wanted three.

Chapter 6

APPROACHING STORM

Preparing for the twins was far different than it had been for Tali's first pregnancy. We were now considered "high risk," requiring frequent check-ups and echocardiograms. The celebratory anticipation we'd felt before was now tinged with caution.

Somehow, we had to tell our families. We tried to be as honest as possible, reasoning that—like us—the medical details would give them a sense of reassurance and some cause for optimism. *It's not great, but the doctors have dealt with this before. They have a plan.* And we told Gilad the same thing; he deserved to know the truth as well.

Hardest of all was Tali's grandmother, whose entire family had been murdered in the Holocaust when she was a teenager. I broke the news as gently as possible; waiting until we'd gathered for a family vacation, surrounded by lush gardens in a Hudson Valley resort. But she took it well, patting my hands with calm assurance. I wished I knew where she found the strength.

ഇൻൽ

Tali and I coped by immersing ourselves in the medical details, finding solace in preparation.

Our visits to the neighborhood obstetrician were over. Instead, we started visiting a high-risk prenatal center on the Upper East Side, smartly appointed with the latest high-tech equipment and generically modern decor.

The reassuring, folksy optimism of our first delivery had been replaced with a measured dose of expert seriousness—a team of earnest, white-jacketed doctors who answered our many questions with matter-of-fact poise. They reminded me of experienced airline pilots, entrusted with a safe landing in even the most challenging weather.

ଞୀଓଃ

Unlike other parents, we skipped the normal prenatal routines. No group birthing lessons for Tali, who knew in advance that she'd have a C-section. Instead, we spent our time touring the NICU and meeting the doctors who would help keep Twin B alive.

The most important meeting was with Dr. Nguyen, the cardiothoracic surgeon. His office was in an unfamiliar part of the hospital—pointedly detached from the main pediatric cardiology ward, as if befitting his special role. We'd arranged the appointment with his assistant, a friendly, efficient woman who greeted us with a warm, understanding hug. Having been warned about surgeons' idiosyncrasies, we weren't sure what to expect from her boss.

Dr. Nguyen turned out to be a soft-spoken man who matter-of-factly walked us through what he planned to do, patiently answering our questions without much emotion. He described his plan for the first surgery—the BT shunt—and explained how he'd implant a small GORE-TEX tube to create a new conduit between Twin B's heart and lungs.

We'd gone over this with Shubhi already in the abstract, but talking with the man who'd actually do the procedure made it real. Twin B's life would be, literally, in his hands.

Casting about for other options, we asked Dr. Nguyen if this approach was standard procedure. Did other surgeons do things differently in other hospitals? In other cities? We didn't say it, but the subtext was clear—if the chances were better somewhere else, we'd want to consider it.

This could have been taken the wrong way—*Don't you trust my expertise?*—but he didn't seem insulted at all. "It's pretty standard, even across the world," he said. "Except Australia. For some reason, they do things a little differently in Australia."

For two people who'd spent so much time Down Under, this was a little surprising. (Why Australia, of all places?) But it didn't really matter. Australia was a long way away.

೮೦೧೮

Two other doctors made the time to talk with us, even though there was no patient yet to meet.

The first was a gastroenterologist, who kept us waiting for over half an hour before we were admitted to his office and made no secret of his self-importance when we met. He had a reputation as a "top doctor" and talked down to us as if we were children.

I can't remember much of what he said, but his tone lingers with me still. He was very polite, but underneath his measured manner ran an unmistakable sense of disinterested arrogance and condescension. *You are lucky to have met me*, it said. *I will try to explain the deep secrets I know in terms that you can understand. But rest assured, if needed I will apply all of my expertise to save your child.*

We were meeting him because of Shubhi's hunch that Twin B's other organs had not formed properly either, particularly the digestive tract. If this was true, warned the doctor gravely, the intestines could be at risk of twisting—a "volvulus" that involved massive amounts of "green bile" and could result in death within minutes.

Given this scenario, we had lots of questions: *What exactly does green bile look like? And if we see it, what exactly do we do?* But his answers were terse and perfunctory. And then we were dismissed; our fifteen minutes were up. *Other children need me,* was the unspoken message. *You are taking up their time.*

I did not like this doctor. He treated us like an obligation to be met, a box to be checked, and as a result, I found it hard to fully trust that he truly cared.

But his description of green bile did make a terrifying impression. After that conversation, I resolved to limit my worries strictly to the heart.

ೞೞ

The other doctor we met in the hospital that day was an infectious diseases expert. Shubhi had referred him to us, suspecting that Twin B had no spleen, which was of some concern. The spleen filters the blood; without it, the baby would have a higher propensity for infection.

The doctor answered as soon as we called him after our meeting with the gastroenterologist. "I'll meet you down the hall," he said, and together, we found a quiet spot, crouching on low couches.

He talked to us in earnest, eagerly holding forth on the special wonders of bacteria and viruses, as if we were first-year med students in a special seminar. The conversation kept going off on random tangents—our questions driven by simple curiosity and his explanations reverberating with an enthusiasm that was... well, infectious.

After a while, we finally steered the conversation to our unborn child. I expected another terrifying lecture full of dire warnings about unseen dangers. But the doctor remained relaxed and calm, recommending nothing more than a constant course of antibiotics and increased vigilance during colder months.

Surprised, I asked, "That's it?"

"He has to live his life," said the doctor. "You can't keep him in a bubble."

This, to me, was deep wisdom—that life was more than simply avoiding death. We'd been so immersed in the challenges Twin B would face that it was easy to forget that there were joys to look forward to as well. And I made a quiet promise that no matter what happened in the years to come, we would try to live them to the fullest.

80C8

Gilad's fourth birthday fell right in the middle of Tali's third trimester. Distracted, we abandoned all pretense of creativity and decided to rent a play space for the birthday party. Nothing fancy, just an indoor playground, pizza, and cupcakes. Keep it easy, we said. We already have enough to do.

But even the simplest plan wasn't immune from unexpected problems. As the day approached, we heard that a tropical storm that had formed in the Caribbean was gaining strength as it moved toward the East Coast. To our dismay, it was due to make landfall on the day of the party.

We decided to postpone the celebration, and just as well. Hurricane Irene slammed into New York with brute strength—

the worst storm to hit the city in nearly four decades. We peered out of the windows with Gilad, watching the rain pour down, our car's tires submerged in newly formed torrents, and reassured him that *of course* his party would still happen, *yes* he would still see his friends, and *don't worry!* he would still get his presents.

We endured the disaster, escaping unscathed. The lights stayed on, and the roof didn't leak. And two weeks later, we gathered with his friends to celebrate as originally planned. The kids had a grand time—the candles blown out and the cupcakes devoured—and we returned home to open the presents, one by one.

∽∾

The Wednesday before the scheduled C-section, our family gathered at my parents' house for the first night of Rosh Hashana—the Jewish New Year.

My mother moved our dining table into the living room so we would all fit, carefully setting it with graceful flowers, bright white napkins, and glass bowls of golden honey. It could get hot with so many people in the room, so this year, my parents had installed a gigantic new air conditioner. Tali, thirty-seven weeks pregnant, sat closest to it, with me at her side.

The first course was served: chicken soup, as always, and a bowl of chopped liver for my father. Each of the kids' place settings had a small, wrapped gift next to the plate; inside, as they all knew, my mother had left a special chocolate for dessert.

Just after we'd polished off the soup, the empty bowls whisked away, I felt something strange seeping across the floor. Something wet, flowing down the table from my right. I wondered what it was, and then, glancing at Tali, I put two and two together, and my heart jumped.

"Um, Tali?" I whispered in her ear, as subtly as I could. "I have a weird question. Did your water break?"

"No...," she answered, peering under the table. "I don't think so."

It was a false alarm. The water had come from the air conditioning unit running full blast in the window, its condensation dripping furiously into an overflowing catch basin and spreading across the wooden floor.

෨෬

Two days later—the second day of Rosh Hashana, three days before the twins were due—it happened for real. Tali woke me up well before dawn. "We need to go," she said. "It's time."

Chapter 7

PRECIOUS CARGO

As the first hints of sunrise lightened the sky, we headed to the hospital in our trusty Subaru. The roads were completely empty, except for one impatient driver who tailgated us through an otherwise empty tunnel, flashing his lights because I was unwilling to ignore the speed limit. We must have been the only two cars on the road.

Don't you realize that I'm carrying *precious cargo?* I seethed. *Leave us alone!*

ಬಂಡ

It was clear from the doctors staffing the operating room that this would be no ordinary delivery; it was a high-risk pregnancy, after all. The head of Mount Sinai's NICU was there, as was the hospital's chief pediatric anesthesiologist with two meek medical students in tow. I was glad to have these senior, experienced types at our side, even if their confidence was tempered by obvious caution and concern. Their apprehensiveness was strangely reassuring.

At one point, as they were preparing Tali for the C-section, the chief anesthesiologist snapped at one of the students: a quick, quiet "stop!," its firmness clear.

The student froze, arm outstretched.

"What are you doing?" the anesthesiologist asked.

The student replied that he was reaching for some instrument. (I can't remember what it was; I'd froze too.)

"Never keep anything within arm's reach," the anesthesiologist gently scolded. "Make sure everything is a step away." He explained, "If you have to take a step, it will be deliberate. Otherwise, you run the risk of making a mistake."

It was a teaching moment, not a crisis, and the only tense moment of the whole procedure. It soon became obvious that everything was going well: a few smiles, some bad jokes, and reassuring laughter filled the room. The anesthesiologist, noticing my camera, asked if I wanted him to take some pictures.

Sure, I said, expecting him to take a few shots once the twins were at my side. But he reached over the drawn sheet instead, pointing the camera at Tali's opened belly; the shutter snapping as the OB lifted the twins out, one by one. His first photos are a jumble of bloody body parts emerging straight from the womb— an arm here, a leg there.

It was all a blur, and then they were born—boys! two boys! *we have three boys!*—and suddenly I found myself utterly confused about which twin was which: Twin A (or was it B?) screaming his head off, and the other one (B? Or A?) lying calmly at his side.

We got a proper photo then, but only a quick one. One of our new sons was being rushed to the NICU; his brother heading upstairs to the maternity ward, and Tali lying there in a happy daze. And me: proud, stunned—not sure what to expect, but ready for it all to begin.

৩০০৪

saw Shubhi afterward, making a thoughtless mistake when she referred to Twin A. "Is that the good one?" I said, immediately regretting it. Of course, they were both *good*, even if one of them had an internal anatomy that was completely wrong. "You know what I mean," I said, and she nodded. She'd once made a similar error, her eyes darting downward in embarrassment, just as mine had.

As it turned out, the baby screaming his head off *was* Twin A. His heart and lungs were fine, and he flaunted it; he was so loud that the maternity nurses had to bring him to Tali's room late that night, because he was keeping the other babies awake.

Twin B, on the other hand, was fast asleep in the relative silence of the NICU, where the only sounds were the mumbling of nervous parents and the melodic beeps of baby monitors.

꙳ꙮ꙳

I was relieved that the delivery had been uneventful, but it was only the first step on a precarious path. The NICU doctors had already started Twin B on a course of prostaglandin to keep the connection between his heart and his lungs open, and his nurses kept a close eye on him just in case it closed earlier than expected. In just five days, he'd be wheeled to the operating room for the BT shunt.

We'd planned all we could, but our plan was always based on hope: the hope that the three surgeries would work; the hope that he'd live until his teens; the hope that he'd eventually get a transplant. From here on out, everything had to break just right.

One step at a time.

꙳ꙮ꙳

The only thing left to do that day was to give the twins names.

Our tradition holds that children should be named after a beloved ancestor, in the hopes that the newborn might carry their spirit through to the next generation. So, we named Twin

A "Yaniv," in memory of my grandfather, whose own Hebrew name was similar. The name means "to grow or produce," and we liked how it evoked that cherished garden in Sydney. *A big lift for the family tree*, indeed.

His twin brother—no longer defined solely by his fuzzy, sonogrammed heart—became "Nadav Moshe": *Nadav*, from the Hebrew word meaning "generous," or "giving more than is expected," and *Moshe*, in memory of Tali's grandfather, who spent four years in the forest fighting Nazis during the war. He'd survived into his nineties—long enough to meet three of his great-grandchildren, including Gilad.

When we told Tali's grandmother that we'd chosen her husband as Nadav's namesake, she smiled, remembering how tough he'd been. "He had nine operations," she reminded us, with pride. We'd told her earlier that Nadav would need at least three. The name fit.

I carefully inscribed their long, unusual names on the birth certificate form, fearful that I might spell something wrong.

Chapter 8

SHUNT

Seventy years before Nadav was born, before heart surgeries became commonplace, most children born with heart defects were doomed. They were called "blue babies"—their imperfect, oxygen-depleted circulations paling their skin—and there was little that their doctors could do. One common treatment was to simply raise their legs above their chest, but this did little to help. With no way to properly address the underlying condition, many of them died.

Fortunately, Nadav was born in a much different time. His condition was diagnosed in utero; his doctors knew what surgeries they could do to address his condition, and when he was born, we had a proper plan. But even if successful, these surgeries would still be merely palliative—more effective than the archaic treatments of a century before, but similarly unable to fix the core problem: his malformed heart.

Still, we were lucky to have any options at all—all because of a daring operation undertaken at Johns Hopkins in 1944, the first heart surgery ever performed on an infant. It was borne of a collaboration between three people: the cardiologist Helen Taussig, who suggested it; the surgeon Alfred Blalock, who performed it; and a thirty-four-year-old black man named Vivien Thomas, who—despite his lack of a formal medical degree—guided it.

Nobody at our hospital told us the history of the BT shunt, but when I looked it up, I found it fascinating. Taussig had deduced that a shunt between the carotid and pulmonary arteries might help blue babies, and Blalock, who had been investigating similar procedures while studying the effects of shock, thought that Taussig's idea was worth a try.

Their surgery was controversial from the start; heart surgeries were rarely attempted and unheard of in infants. The first patient was a weak one-year-old girl, weighing just nine pounds. Wary of the risks, the hospital's chief anesthesiologist refused to participate.

But perhaps most controversial was Blalock's insistence that Thomas be at his side during the surgery. Fifteen years before, he'd hired Thomas—a nineteen-year-old carpenter's apprentice—to help run his lab at Vanderbilt. It was a second chance for Thomas, who had hoped to become a doctor until the Great Depression forced him to end his dreams of finishing medical school. Dexterous and smart, Thomas made the most of the opportunity, developing a number of innovative techniques while studying cardiac shock in lab animals. When Blalock was hired at Johns Hopkins, he made sure that Thomas came too.

Some of Blalock's colleagues were dubious that a seemingly unqualified black man belonged in the operating room. But Thomas had already tested the operation on the laboratory's dogs, developing many of the custom surgical instruments Blalock would use. Whispering advice at his mentor's side, Thomas helped Blalock navigate the operation's intricacies, and at the end of the procedure, the girl's bluish skin turned a healthy pink.

The surgery was considered to be a remarkable success, ushering in a new era of pediatric cardiology. Surgical interventions became almost routine, giving parents hope they'd never had.

And nearly seventy years later, a modified BT shunt would be Nadav's first operation, at the tender age of five days old.

ಬಂಞ

The historic operation of 1944—which rightly should be called a "BTT shunt" to credit all of its innovators—inspired a slightly cheesy TV movie adaptation, which Tali and I watched eagerly one night, riveted to the screen. But the film's Hollywood ending—so inspiring to us as new parents of a cardiac kid—masked a more complicated truth.

It failed to mention what happened to Eileen Saxon, the patient who'd undergone that first shunt. Within a few weeks, her skin began to pale again, and after about a month, it was clear to her doctors that something was seriously wrong. The historic shunt had become occluded, clotted by blood. A second operation was unsuccessful, and she died before her second birthday.

We'd drawn strength from the gauzy outcome of the movie's final scene—an optimistic energy that we hoped would carry us through the uncertain road ahead. It barely crossed our minds that the same thing that happened to the Saxon family might happen to us.

Many years after that historic operation, a doctor who attended the first historic surgery shared what he admired most about Blalock—not just his courage in performing the first surgery, but his persistence to continue with other patients after Saxon died.

I'm glad he did. Otherwise, Nadav might never have had a chance.

ಬಂಡ

Nadav's shunt was scheduled for Tuesday morning—the same day that Yaniv was scheduled to go home. We hoped to convince the hospital to allow us to stay in the maternity ward until the surgery, but they insisted that Tali leave her room. They needed the beds.

By early afternoon, we were packed up and ready to go. Giddy from new-baby adrenaline, we waited for an update from the operating room. But when it eventually came, the news was not good. Shubhi found us by the elevators, a frown on her face. "He's not doing well," she said. "Losing a lot of blood."

In that moment, I suppose I should have felt fear, or terror, but I didn't. Perhaps those emotions were masked by the manic excitement that all new parents must feel, perhaps it was simply denial. But I think it was more that at five days old, Nadav remained an abstract concept in my mind, a logic puzzle to be solved on paper. I barely knew him; I hadn't even seen him open his eyes. I wasn't ready to be devastated.

Shubhi wanted to take us downstairs to meet the surgeon. We waited in silence for the elevator for what felt like ages, staring nervously at each other during the ride down. But as soon as the doors opened, we saw Dr. Nguyen, looking unperturbed. "Everything's OK," he said, with a breezy confidence. "No problems. He's fine."

And despite all of the tubes, wires, bandages, and concerned nurses swarming around him, he was.

ಬಂಡ

By that point, our perspective had shifted. What we accepted as "fine" would have terrified anyone else.

Before we left that first night, Nadav's doctors told us that his left lung had collapsed. For us, this was a minor worry; we'd heard that a collapsed lung might be a possibility and were relieved to hear that this was all that had happened. But our parents, who'd been nervously awaiting the results of the surgery, had to be reassured that "he only has a collapsed lung" was actually good news.

It just meant that he'd have to stay in intensive care a little longer, we told them. No, we weren't sure how long. But we knew that we'd have to be patient. Only time could heal it.

৪০০৪

M any of the babies admitted to the NICU were premature; tiny bodies in plastic incubators, spotlit by warm lamps. Compared to them, Nadav looked relatively healthy, except for the various tubes that wound their way around his body and an ever-so-slight blue tinge that shaded his skin. But his monitor told a different story. His oxygen saturation, close to 100 percent in a healthy child, hovered around the low eighties.

It was standard procedure to send preemies to the ward as a routine precaution, even if they weren't sick. We met one family whose twins, born early but otherwise healthy, spent a week there. During that time, one of their newborns contracted meningitis—an unexpected, devastating shock for the parents.

I remember seeing them huddled around a table in a side room, intently discussing the situation with the attending doctor. I didn't know the whole story at that moment, but all three were obviously upset, including the doctor, who was also responsible for Nadav and the other patients in the NICU. (I learned later that the meningitis had caused a brain injury, requiring a transfer to another hospital for surgery.)

Later that day, I approached the doctor with a relatively unimportant question about Nadav, apologetic for bothering him. But he refused to accept my apology. "Your son is the most important thing to you, as he should be," he replied, "and right now, he is the most important thing for me too."

But I could see the weary sadness in his eyes; it was impossible to ignore.

ଛଔ

I once asked an attending doctor how he could handle the emotional stress of leading a pediatric intensive care unit. It's hard enough to care for a single child, I reasoned. Being responsible for two dozen must be impossible. He shook his head. "I get to go home at the end of the day," he said. "You don't."

It made sense, I thought, but I wondered if he was being entirely honest. The best doctors, we found, never stopped caring. And we went home at the end of the day, too, sometimes without our son—entrusting him to strangers who we hoped would take their responsibility as seriously as a parent would.

Chapter 9

HONESTY

From the time he was old enough to listen, we made a deal with Gilad. We would always be honest with him, and in return, he would be honest with us. If he told us the truth, no matter how embarrassing or difficult it was, we wouldn't be angry. But telling a lie would be the worst thing he could do.

We always did our best to hold up our part of the bargain. When Nadav was diagnosed, we told Gilad exactly what was going on. Even though he was four years old, we didn't use euphemisms or gloss over the difficult parts. "Your brother's heart isn't the same as ours," we said. "It doesn't work properly, and he'll need at least three operations to make him better."

We weren't shy about telling him what might happen, even when faced with the terrible truth that one of his brothers might die.

೮೦೦೪

Kids know when you're lying—or not telling the whole truth. They have a remarkable ability to cope with reality—even more so than adults do, sometimes—but they get scared when they don't know what's going on.

They have trouble understanding death. And to be honest, I did too.

Much later, Gilad would ask me, "What happens when you die?" I'd have to answer truthfully. "I don't really know," I'd say. "But I think things just end."

I felt for the many doctors who had to maintain their composure while telling us all of the implications of Nadav's condition. The best of them had just enough emotional intelligence; they cared, deeply, but they didn't let that caring blind them to the truth.

༄༅

Later, Shubhi would share all the things that could go wrong with our plan. All surgeries were risky, of course—so much could happen. He could bleed to death on the table. He could barely survive, needing the assistance of an ECMO unit—a heart-lung machine that we came to fear as a last-ditch effort to avoid the inevitable. But even if all three operations were successful, maintaining a circulation without a proper pump could be tenuous. Pressures could go haywire, blood vessels could leak, there could be neurological issues...

"Stop," said Tali, cutting off Shubhi in mid-sentence; the word *neurological* had stung. "Don't say that. I can handle anything but that."

We were starting to realize our own strengths as parents—a growing comfort with all sorts of medical craziness. But we were also learning to shield ourselves from too much uncertainty, to avoid staring into the blinding glare of possible disaster.

༄༅

To celebrate the twins' arrival, we'd bought Gilad a LEGO set ("from your new brothers!") along with a funny card that played a tinny rendition of "I Like to Move It" when opened.

We asked Gilad if he would like to visit his brother in the NICU, and he said yes. We didn't want his brother's condition to seem scary or unfamiliar, and it was important to us that they spend time together. He'd sit next to Nadav's warm incubator, singing softly, sometimes reaching in to touch his brother's tiny hand.

The NICU was calm, especially at night. Lights low, mothers nursing their children in rocking chairs, both drifting off to sleep; nurses silently hovering, keeping busy, always half-looking at the softly beeping monitors. It reminded me of those nights I'd spent with Gilad four years before, holding him gently as the ward fell asleep.

༄༄

A few days later, I asked Gilad if he'd like to draw some pictures for his brothers: Yaniv's to stick on the wall at home and Nadav's to decorate his tiny bed in the hospital. We cut squares out of card stock and brought a box of crayons down from the shelf. I can't remember what he drew for Yaniv—it was still the scrawling-and-frantic-scribbling phase—but I'll never forget the drawing he did for Nadav.

Reaching for a pink crayon, Gilad traced a shape that was eerily familiar—a three-fingered blob, leaning slightly to the right. It almost exactly mirrored the sketch that Shubhi drew whenever she explained what was going on with Nadav's heart. I was astounded; he'd never seen those sketches, and yet here they were, rendered in a four-year-old's hand.

Even today, the sketch still gives me goosebumps.

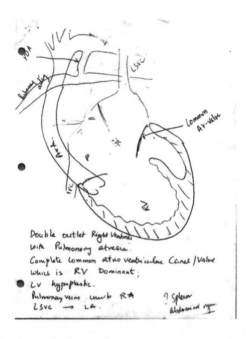

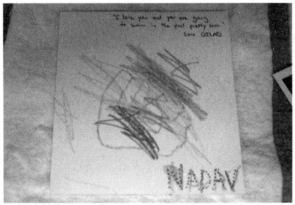

"Should we write anything else?" I asked.

"Yes," said Gilad. "Write: 'I love you and you are going to swim in the pool pretty soon.'"

So, I did.

ଊଓଃ

W e'd taken the first step—a successful shunt. And although it might take Nadav a while to recover (lungs could be stubborn things), we were confident that he would soon be coming home.

The key question facing us now was how to lead a normal life in the face of all of the challenges that lay ahead. We needed to learn how to handle Nadav's medical needs at home, rather than in a hospital. At the same time, we had to give all three brothers a normal childhood—or as close to normal as we could get. In short, I needed to be a father.

Just as it had four years before, the challenges of parenthood filled me with pride. But this time around, that responsibility came with a terrifying reality. Shubhi's tense update during the surgery—*he's not doing well*—lingered uneasily in the back of my mind, an unsettling reminder of how little we knew about what was to come.

Only one obligation of fatherhood ever really worried me. There was a chance that someday I would have to tell Nadav's brothers that he had died, and the thought filled me with a special sort of dread.

Chapter 10

THE REALM OF THE UNKNOWN

n utero, we knew that Nadav's internal anatomy was likely to be unusual. After he was born, an anatomy scan confirmed it. Most of his organs were not quite the right shape, nor in the right place: his left lung had three chambers (like his right) not two (as most people's do); his intestines had a few odd, extra curves; and his stomach was shifted slightly, as was his liver. But his doctors reassured us that everything seemed functional—everything except for his spleen, which (as we'd suspected) was nowhere to be found.

This curious anatomy fascinated the NICU staff. One radiologist, unfamiliar with his condition, stared at his abdominal scan as if it were a rare and valuable Picasso. Another medical student, rotating through the NICU, drew an exquisite sketch of his circulation as part of a class paper, later presenting it to us as a memento of our time there.

When Gilad was born, the thought that we had brought another human being into the world left us spellbound. But I hadn't fully appreciated how truly amazing it was until his brothers were born, four years later. We can't help but take it for granted when things form properly; no need to reckon with those wonders until something goes awry.

Despite its many defects, I started to feel a sort of pride in Nadav's heart. It made him unique—one in a million—and as his parents, it gave us a special sense of purpose.

And, in all of its wrongness, it opened my eyes to the magic of how things ever go right.

ಲೋಡಿ

Later, when I learned what caused Nadav's condition—not from any of his doctors, mind you, but from an article in the *New York Times*—I was astonished by it. Scientists have only just begun to reveal how our organs form, and it turns out to be a process full of magic and wonder.

We are all conceived in perfect symmetry—a bundle of cells surrounded by swirling amniotic fluid, an embryo in which right and left are mirror images, exactly alike. As these embryonic cells divide, again and again, this simplicity soon yields to increasing complexity.

Two and a half weeks into the pregnancy, a small cluster of tiny hairs forms at the embryo's midline. They are called cilia—similar to the minute filaments that propel amoebas and paramecia, a familiar sight to any tenth-grade biology student gazing through a microscope at a wet-mount slide.

These cilia have a specific purpose. Tilted in a single direction, they beat against the amniotic fluid surrounding the embryo, spinning it into curls and eddies. This swirling fluid determines where particular proteins will form—some on the left, and others on the right—mapping an asymmetrical path that organs follow as they grow. This is why, for most of us, certain organs (like the heart, or stomach) are located on the left, and others (like the liver, or appendix) are on the right.

If the cilia are somehow facing the opposite direction, one's organs will follow the opposite path, causing what's known as situs inversus. One in around twenty thousand people have this, their organs arranged in a mirror image—a curious anatomy that remains perfectly functional. Unless something goes wrong, they may never realize it.

But if the cilia sway randomly, or not at all, the path of the proteins becomes unpredictable. The organs meander, forming in their own unique way, not quite following the intended path.

Only the faintest movement is needed to lay out these proteins; some researchers believe that it requires the beats of just two cilia. And the whole process happens in just three or four hours. In enough time for dinner and a movie, one's fate is sealed.

⋈

It suddenly became clear what had happened to Nadav. His embryonic cilia had failed to beat properly, causing his amniotic fluid to swirl haphazardly and scattering the all-important proteins into the wrong arrangement. As he grew from embryo to fetus, his organs dutifully followed the flawed map. The first organ with a visible asymmetry is the heart, forming in concentric loops; confused, his formed with a single ventricle instead of two.

Had he been born two decades earlier, this would all have remained a mystery. But even as researchers reveal the science behind how our organs form, some things remained beyond our understanding. Why had this happened to Nadav? What had caused the problems with his cilia?

Why him?

Why us?

Years ago, in grad school, I took a seminar in essay writing—an inspiring course whose syllabus included a particularly memorable assignment. We were asked to seek out an artwork that "spoke to us," and give it a close reading: to focus on its details; to investigate the artist's decisions; and ultimately, to look inside ourselves and try to understand why we'd selected the piece in the first place.

The artwork I chose was Gerhard Richter's *Townscape Madrid*— a square, monochromatic overview of a densely packed metropolis. Its white blurs gave the impression of a bright sunny glare;

its angular grays and blacks detailed the linear layout of the city's solid structures; all of it intersected by long, diagonal boulevards. From afar, the city's structure was clear, but up close, the image blurred into imperfect, abstract blocks of paint.

I've lost the original essay I wrote in response to the painting. All I can remember is that, somehow, it triggered memories of a funeral I'd attended for a friend's father. Perhaps, in retrospect, I'd subconsciously realized that Richter's impressionistic city was completely empty, devoid of life. Much later, I read that he'd been affected by similar images of Dresden, firebombed by Allied planes during the war and empty with death.

৪୦୯୫

Even though my essay has disappeared, that image remains vivid in my mind. It reappears whenever I attend services in a synagogue, holding a prayerbook filled with dense clusters of Hebrew text, the black letters tracing ancient patterns across the bone-white page, commentary inscribed in agate font at the bottom. My knowledge of the service is often incomplete; I do not read the language fluently, even though I know most of the prayers by heart. But like Richter's *Townscape*, I find myself able to rise beyond the fuzziness of the individual words and somehow find comfort in the patterns of the whole.

I enjoy solving crosswords and acrostics for similar reasons. Their empty grids and white spaces arranged in regular intervals challenge me to find a way to fill the blanks with meaning. If I'm able to reveal enough of the answers (some through knowledge, others by leaps and guesses), the entire solution quickly comes into focus, its ultimate revelation only a matter of time.

Once the entire mystery is revealed, it's impossible to look at the original patterns the same way again. Solving the puzzle grants a special intimacy with the creator, a sense of how their mind worked to cleverly fit it all together just so.

But occasionally, a solution remains elusive; no matter how hard I try, the dominoes refuse to fall. Frustration sets in, the discomforting knowledge that there is some understanding lying just beyond my reach, and I'm forced to admit that it's time to set aside the riddle and make peace with the unknown.

৪০৪

Rabbi Abraham Joshua Heschel, one of the twentieth century's most influential Jewish thinkers, wrote that we must simultaneously inhabit two realms: that of the real—what we can name, explain, and comprehend—and that of the ineffable—what is beyond our understanding.

The practice of medicine straddles these two worlds. By expanding their scientific knowledge, doctors push against the boundaries of the unknown, hoping to counteract the random, unpredictable forces that so often result in disaster and death. But even as we explain the mysteries of how we grow and heal, we still cannot control our fate. The BT shunt helped Eileen Saxon but ultimately could not save her; a world-class NICU routinely keeps premature babies alive but is helpless to prevent the occasional bout of meningitis.

৪০৪

Even though scientists have revealed how misplaced proteins caused Nadav's organs to form the way they had, I still didn't understand what had caused his cilia to malfunction. I wrestled with the inexplicable accident of his strange physiology, my mind searching for anything that might bring meaning to an impossible situation.

And so, as if I was trying to solve a particularly vexing cross-word, I started noticing coincidences and patterns, unexpected parallels and resonances. In whatever context they presented themselves, I couldn't help but grasp at them, as if they were faint signals of a deeper truth.

❧

The Hebrew calendar would come to hold many ironies for us over the next few years. I couldn't help but notice how closely they paralleled our own experience and wonder what inner meanings they might hold.

For instance: the day the twins were born, the Torah reading was the story of the *Akedah*, when Abraham was nearly compelled to sacrifice his son Isaac on Mount Moriah. It ends, of course, with Isaac's life spared, and the previous command suddenly reversed—giving me some hope that we, too, might be spared an unspeakable grief. Another was the story of how Moses spent forty days on Mount Sinai before descending with the Ten Commandments. Likewise, Nadav (whose second name was Moshe, mind you) spent forty-nine days in the NICU of a hospital named…Mount Sinai.

Jewish tradition tells us that on Rosh Hashana, the book of life is opened. Over the next week and a half—as our prayers remind us—one's fate is inscribed: *How many shall pass away and how many shall be born / Who shall live and who shall die / Who in good time, and who by an untimely death.* On Yom Kippur, ten days later, the book is sealed.

Our twins were born on the second of those ten High Holy Days, their lives a blank page: Yaniv's sheet unblemished, Nadav's slightly creased. On the seventh day, Nadav underwent his first surgery to connect his heart to his lungs. On the ninth day,

Yaniv was circumcised, our family and friends gathering in our living room for the traditional *bris* while his brother recovered in the NICU.

That evening, as the Yom Kippur fast began, I stood in our synagogue amongst bearded men swaying in prayer shawls, thankful that Nadav's life had been spared.

෴

ike the stark, monochromatic streets of *Townscape Madrid*, the Hebrew prayers we read seem uninhabited. They remain static on the page, unchanging through the generations with their authors long since departed.

And yet, Jewish prayer—what we call *davening*—brings these words to life. The communal prayers that fill the room become a celebration of our shared existence: the lilting cadence of the congregation; the ancient melodies, full of emotion; a togetherness that connects us to a past we never knew.

A Jewish congregation requires a quorum of ten. Any Jew of age is welcome, no matter how pious or learned—none of us are perfect. But together, we are permitted to approach the sublime. Unlike a properly crafted word puzzle, unable to withstand a single mistake, our lives are built on the sum of our flaws.

Perhaps this is the solution to the inexplicable unknowns we face: each of us holds only a small part of a greater truth, and only through our relationships with others are we permitted to search for deeper meaning.

෴

Others in our situation found solace in faith as well—unfamiliar religions, glimpsed at arm's length, sometimes overlapping with our own.

Early on, we met one little girl who survived a particularly difficult surgery. When she left for home, her joyous cousins celebrated by handing out little embroidered angels to everyone in the cardiac ward.

Even though it wasn't our tradition, we hung ours on Nadav's IV pole. And when he was finally discharged, it came home with him too.

Chapter 11

"OUR PATIENT, YOUR SON"

After nearly six weeks in the NICU, Nadav's lung finally started looking better. With his discharge on the horizon, we started preparing to bring him home.

Shubhi's main worry was making sure that Nadav got enough calories. He needed to be as strong as possible for future surgeries; but given the low oxygen levels in his blood, encouraging his small body to grow would be an ongoing concern.

Luckily, unlike some cardiac kids, Nadav could nurse. Lactation consultants had warned us that he might not latch, or suck vigorously, but Tali patiently insisted on it—as always, stubbornly unwilling to give up. In the NICU, she'd nurse him at the bedside, then head to the parents' room to take care of his twin.

(When Nadav came home, we bought a special pillow that wrapped around Tali's waist like a lifesaver, one boy at each side—an arrangement our lactation consultant called "double footballs.")

But breast milk wasn't enough. Nadav's low weight meant that we had to aggressively supplement his calories. Tali pumped additional milk that we mixed with a calorie-rich powder and a special type of vegetable oil. In the NICU, we fed him this concoction in small bottles—gently tilting his head back, just so, as we softly whispered words of encouragement.

ഇൻൽ

Our crash course in pediatric cardiology was not yet complete. In order to take Nadav home, we'd have to learn how to place an NG tube.

NG stands for "nasal-gastric," a hint as to its intended use—a long, thin yellow tube, placed through a nostril down the esophagus into the stomach. Having an NG in place would allow us to supplement Nadav's daily intake with overnight feeds. An external pump would slowly push our milk-formula-and-oil mixture through the tube, ensuring that he got the calories he'd need.

Since there wouldn't be any nurses to help at home, we'd have to place the tube ourselves, and put it back in if it ever came out.

This, frankly, was the most terrifying thing I'd ever heard.

"There's a wonderful nurse practitioner who'll teach you," a nurse assured us, sensing my hesitation. "It's really not that bad."

ഇൻൽ

The nurse practitioner was great, actually. Like all of the best medical people we met, she combined empathy ("I know it's a little disgusting") with a matter-of-fact directness ("It needs to be done so let's do it").

And then, using a doll, she showed us how to do it, step by step: how to measure the NG to make sure it would be inserted to the right length; how to lubricate it, to help it go down; how to tilt the baby's head back, to give it the right angle; how it should feel going in, and why a cough makes it easier; how to tape the tube to the cheek, so that it stays put; how to use a syringe and a stethoscope to check that it's in the right place.

The last part was especially important, because if it accidentally went into the lung (which can sometimes happen) it would be *very dangerous*.

"So, check," she said. "Put some air in the syringe and attach it to the NG tube. Place the end of the stethoscope on the baby's stomach, and push. You should hear a little 'whoosh.'" And if you did, you were done.

The whole thing sounded impossible, but somehow, I learned how to do it. From then on, I'd associate that "whoosh" of air with a calming sense of achievement: the knowledge that I'd placed the NG tube properly, that I wouldn't accidentally drown my son's lungs in milk, that I'd faced my fears and done something uncomfortable—all so my son could grow, increasing the chances he would survive.

ಬಂಡ

Having satisfied the NICU staff that we had absorbed enough basic nursing skills to care for him ourselves, the big day came. Nadav was ready to go home.

Before we left, I asked his doctors and nurses for any last words of advice. We are the sort of parents who ask a lot of questions—we coped with knowledge—and had already absorbed dozens of useful tips: how to properly measure the amount of medicine in a syringe, without wasting any; other ways to check that an NG tube was placed properly; how to swaddle him tightly, so that he wouldn't tug at the tube and pull it out.

But one wise doctor gave us perhaps the most important advice of all. "Never forget," he said, "that he is *our patient*, and he is *your son*."

With all of the medical obligations that came with Nadav's condition, this was sometimes hard to remember. He had heterotaxy, low oxygen levels, and an NG tube—but when he came home, we had to leave all that behind, as much as we could.

ෳbeඃ

We were discharged on a Friday—home in time to light the Shabbat candles—and for the first time in nearly two months, the twins were reunited. It was a pleasure to see them together, home at last—two swaddled lumps sharing a crib in our bedroom.

We'd decorated the wall above with little photos of famous duos: Ernie and Bert, Waldorf and Statler, the Blues Brothers. On one side of the crib, we'd attached a mobile filled with animals—lion, elephant, giraffe, monkey. On the other side stood an IV pole holding a Kangaroo Joey enteral feeding pump, gently whirring.

And above it all, a tiny angel, embroidered in pink and gray, keeping a silent watch.

ෳbeඃ

During our six weeks at Mount Sinai, the hospital had been a source of comfort. Under the watchful eye of experienced, caring nurses, we'd absorbed the NICU's rhythms and routines; it had become a place of safety and reassurance. But now it was time for us to come home, where none of that existed. We'd have to reinvent that sense of security on our own—as best we could—without it overwhelming our lives.

Tali's birthday was a month after Nadav came home from the hospital, and although we were exhausted and distracted, I wanted to plan something special. The easiest option was to go out for a steak—her favorite meal—with friends a few blocks from our house. We trusted my mother to look after Nadav, but it would be the first time we'd ever left him with someone other than a nurse. The timing would only work if he'd just been fed.

I remember checking my watch anxiously as Tali nursed the boys, double footballs on her huge nursing pillow, finally declaring, as the boys fell asleep in milk-induced bliss, "OK! Let's go!" Grabbing a favorite bottle of Australian wine, we wished my mother a hurried farewell, and raced down the block to the restaurant, ten minutes away.

The place was packed when we arrived, full of laughing twenty-somethings, waiting couples crowded by the bar. I'd tried to arrange a table in advance with the owner the day before—they didn't take reservations—but the maître d' couldn't care less. "We don't take reservations," he reminded me in a haughty tone, although I'd already discussed it with his boss. I held my temper in check; it was Tali's birthday, after all.

Eventually, a table opened up, a steak appeared, and a few hours later we returned home, thankful for the breath of fresh air; my mother, reading on the couch; and our three lovely boys, safe in bed, sound asleep.

FATHERHOOD

Chapter 12

COMING HOME

When we'd brought Gilad home from the hospital as new parents, we'd been completely focused on the tricky logistics of raising a child. We carefully installed a crib and a changing table; stacked closets with tiny, adorable hand-me-downs; and painted the walls of his small bedroom a vivid canary yellow.

Over that first year, we'd learned the ropes of parenthood, figuring it out as we went along. We somehow mastered the rhythms of newborn life—the tactical battles of feeding and soothing; the joyous relief that accompanied each tiny milestone; the tense adrenaline of too little sleep.

By the time Nadav came home, four years later, those hurdles seemed distant and quaint. We knew how to be parents—those dormant skills easily re-emerged from our muscle memory—but now we also had to learn how to think like the doctors and nurses who'd cared for him in the NICU. Nadav's life felt especially fragile, a priceless gift we needed to protect.

Still, as important as it was to focus on Nadav's medical needs, we couldn't let them suffocate us. The doctor was right: we were parents, not nurses. And yet, when I think back on that first year, the medical aspects—the medicines, the NG tube, the doctors' visits—are the most memorable. Everything else, unfortunately, remains blurry and indistinct.

※CS

Unable to sharpen my fuzzy memories, I've come to rely on the thousands of photos and videos I took when the kids were young—the best chronicle of our everyday life together. I took so many that even my parents gently complained. ("Why are there seven shots of everything?" my mother once asked politely.) But I didn't want to miss a moment; every little thing was so precious.

The earliest snapshots, of course, are completely adorable—Gilad, aged four, clutching his tiny brothers on the couch; Yaniv bundled up in a towel, face glowing in a beaming post-bath smile; Nadav's focused stare, gazing serenely from the back of the stroller on a visit to the aquarium, his tiny face lit by the thin blue glow of the jellyfish tank.

The albums make those first months together seem like an idyllic, uninterrupted celebration. Every week another family member pops into view, smiling for the camera. But of course, things were not always so easy. Whenever one of the twins started bawling, suddenly inconsolable in a stranger's embrace, the camera disappeared—the baby rushed back into our arms.

We'd come to learn that tears were usually triggered by physical discomfort—and once we figured out what was wrong, we had a fair idea of what to do. When they were hungry, Tali nursed them; when they needed a new diaper, we soldiered forth to the changing table; and when they were tired, I did my best to soothe them with a mental jukebox of my favorite folk songs.

I'd rock them gently on my shoulder in the darkened bedroom, singing selections from the Paul Simon albums my father had played when I was young, feeling their breaths slow to gentle snores. But as soon as I placed them down, they'd inevitably let loose a complaining cry—and the cycle of songs would begin again. Each time, I vowed I'd double the choruses, hoping that it would be enough.

I have no photos of our exhausted faces, long and drawn from the strains of juggling three children; nor do I have any videos of me and Tali snapping at each other, completely worn out. But those moments were part of our lives too—a jumble of giddy, reactive emotions, emerging here and there, as we tried our best to build a family.

ঙ০ত্ব

As we settled in to our new life together, our home started to fill up with medical equipment: Nadav's NG tubes, with their associated paraphernalia; a pulse oximeter to monitor his blood oxygen levels; and what felt like a million prescriptions for various oddly named medicines.

We didn't want to miss a dose, so I took great care to keep the medicines organized. The bottles stayed next to the sink, each its own shade of translucent orange, and to tell them apart I wrote letters in red sharpie on the top: "S" for spironolactone; "D" for digoxin; "R" for ranitidine, and so on.

Nearby lay up to a dozen syringes, drying slowly after a quick rinse, upside down on paper towels on a white plastic tray. On Hanukkah we stood nine in a row, like candles, and sent a snapshot to our families with season's greetings.

I devised my own system to keep track of it all. Fairly proficient at creating spreadsheets, I couldn't resist making one for the medicines: printed on card stock, prefilled with calculated amounts (which, at every appointment, changed ever so subtly). After each dose was gently pushed into Nadav's mouth, I'd mark it down with a bright red "X."

Whenever a nurse or doctor asked about Nadav's medications, Tali and I were able to recite the list by heart. The complicated routine had become a mantra, a shared cadence of our regular routine: measuring, filling, dosing, washing, over and over again.

౼౷

The spreadsheets and checklists I'd devised gave me some sense of predictability and control. But we quickly learned that few medical things are truly straightforward, and we often found ourselves facing some perplexing wrinkle or ambiguity.

Our system was not perfect. On day trips, we brought along pre-dosed syringes of Nadav's medicines, safely contained in a plastic pencil case. Sometimes we'd forget to refrigerate the medicines, which wasn't so bad; but on rare occasions we'd forget to bring them at all, and that was the worst.

Most of these hiccups, we eventually learned, weren't such a big deal. Once, we lost track of whether Nadav had had a dose of a certain medicine and called Shubhi in a panic. Was it better to give it again, just in case we hadn't? Or not give it at all, just in case we had? "Don't give it," she said. Better none than too much.

౼౷

Since Nadav was born without a spleen, he had been prescribed antibiotics from birth—amoxicillin, the same sticky pink stuff I remembered from my childhood sick days. It was the least complicated medicine we had to deal with, but the arcane rules printed on the label didn't quite make sense. A standard bottle held enough mix for two weeks but had to be discarded after ten days.

Why the discrepancy? I wondered. What horrible things might happen if we used it for four extra days? It was never made clear.

There was also confusion about how the amoxicillin should be stored. One pharmacist insisted that it needed to be refrigerated, right away; another said that it could just as well be left out, at room temperature; another wasn't sure, but felt it didn't really matter. In the end, we kept it in the fridge door, on top of the eggs.

೪ುೞ

The reasoning behind some of Nadav's medicines was similarly opaque. One, called digoxin, served a mysterious purpose, difficult even for Shubhi to explain. At high doses it can stop the heart, but administered in small amounts, it supposedly helps it function. More than anything else, its use seemed to be an artifact of years of anecdotal tradition.

Curious, I looked it up, discovering that digoxin has an ancient history; apparently the Romans ate sea onions for the cardiac glycosides within. Medieval doctors were the first to derive it from the foxglove plant—a method that is still used today. (In this respect, at least, modern medicine still resembles the Middle Ages.) Ever-curious, we took a short trip to see foxglove for ourselves, our pilgrimage ending in a small section of the Brooklyn Botanic Gardens dedicated to medicinal plants. It was midwinter, so most of the plant was hidden in the snow. But we saw the sign ("Digitalis purpurea"), which was enough.

As Nadav grew, we asked Shubhi whether we should adjust the dose, but she shrugged, and seemed fine with it gradually fading away. Like so much of medicine, it was an educated guess, she admitted. "Let's see how it goes."

☙❧

Apart from a misplaced NG, or the mythical "volvulus of green bile" (which we thankfully never saw) the biggest danger to Nadav at home would be a sudden drop in his "sats"—the oxygen saturation of his blood. A normal circulation has a saturation of close to 100 percent; Nadav's hovered between 80 and 85 percent. If the numbers dipped into the 70s or below, Shubhi warned us, it would be cause for immediate concern.

We were told to monitor Nadav's sats constantly, running a line from a pulse oximeter to a tiny sensor taped to his big toe, glowing bright red. But the machine rarely sounded an alarm; and if it did it was almost always a false reading, often in the dead of night. It was always the same story: the tape had come loose; the sensor falling off; the machine beeping furiously, flashing zero.

We tried every type of medical tape imaginable, but none of them could reliably keep the sensor fastened to his toe. Eventually, bleary-eyed from false alarms, we abandoned the constant monitoring. We could tell from his complexion that everything was OK, and we only used the pulse ox every so often to spot-check our instinct.

Still, every hospital visit started with a quick check of Nadav's vitals—including a routine check of his sats. The nurse would wrap a small sensor around a finger or toe, watching the monitor for the magic number. Knowing him as well as we did, we knew these checks were a mere formality. We'd watch the red digital numbers flicker up and down, silently willing it higher and higher—fearing the overreaction that would likely occur if someone less familiar with Nadav accepted the mistakenly low readings as cause for concern.

If the number was too low, Tali would gently ask the nurse to readjust the sensor. It might take a while, but they always climbed back up.

ॐ♋

During our stay in the NICU, I'd come to believe that our medical plan would follow a carefully calibrated path. But now that we were in charge of navigating Nadav's daily care, I saw how much of that plan was based on educated guesswork, informed by no small amount of gut instinct. Doctors relied on their expertise—what they'd seen in their many years of practice—to make decisions about how to proceed, as best they could.

But as Nadav's parents, we quickly realized that we had an expertise that his doctors did not. We gave the medicines; we placed the NG tube; we could recognize what worked and what didn't. In medicine—as in daily life—we knew him best.

That knowledge gave us the confidence to talk with his doctors as partners, not merely as interested bystanders. We'd learned to speak the language of medicine, but it was just as important that we were listened to as well.

To their credit, most of Nadav's doctors realized this too. They answered our questions as best they could, and asked for our perspective as we planned the course ahead. After all, this was just the start of what we hoped would be a long journey together. And the next step—the Glenn—was just around the corner.

Chapter 13

THE GLENN

Nadav's second surgery was scheduled for late February, five months after he and his brother were born.

The "Glenn" was the first of two operations that would force his blue blood to bypass his heart, redirecting it directly into the lungs. The second, the Fontan, wouldn't happen until after he turned three, at the earliest. So, the Glenn was a big milestone. If it went well, we could finally look forward to a long break from major medical procedures.

We met with Dr. Nguyen to review what he would do. This time, he pulled out something to help him demonstrate—a tiny metal stent, intricately designed. Tali and I marveled at its elegance as he described how it worked. It was made of nitinol, a nickel-titanium alloy that remembers its shape, expanding on its own when implanted. You can buy trick spoons made of nitinol, he told us. They're pretty neat.

I found myself transfixed, suddenly wanting one of those nifty spoons. But all Tali wanted to know—detail-oriented as always—was the size of the stent he planned to use.

"I don't know," he said. He'd decide when he went in.

It was his subtle way of drawing boundaries: his patient, our son.

ഽഠയ

On the day of the surgery, we arrived at the hospital at the crack of dawn, greeted by a clipboard full of forms and a few quick questions. We called my mother, who was looking after Nadav's brothers back home—both still asleep, she assured us. And then, as usual, we settled in, waiting for the anesthesiologist to arrive.

There was always lots of waiting before a procedure, usually in some empty room, walls undecorated—as if to grant us a moment of peace before the doctors showed up and the bustling began. We'd do our best to remain calm, masking our nervousness—unwilling to interrupt the room's silence, as if the space held some unspoken sanctity.

This time, the three of us found ourselves in a huge, unused ward—empty except for two adult patients, quietly waiting for their own operations in adjacent stalls. I assumed that they were strangers, brought together by the coincidence of the calendar—but as they looked at each other, chatting quietly, they clasped their hands together, as if in a shared prayer.

ഽഠയ

Soon enough, the anesthesiologist appeared, a nurse in tow; hurried, but not rushed, the medical system swinging into action. I always found something particularly reassuring about this moment—everyone on the team having trained their entire lives for this one instant, just so they could be here, doing their best to save our son's life.

Before they put Nadav to sleep, I put my hands on his forehead, whispering a brief prayer:

May the Lord bless you and keep you
May the Lord shine his countenance upon you,
and be gracious unto you
May the Lord look kindly upon you and give you peace.

It was the same blessing my grandmother had sung softly to us, whenever we were lucky enough to spend a Friday night together—her hands pressing down on our own heads, firm and strong.

And then I kissed him gently on the forehead, and he was off.

༄༅

Whenever Nadav had a procedure, Tali and I would pass the time by taking a walk. It has always been the easiest way for me to relax—the repetition rhythmic and calming, my steps mindless yet focused, each stride filling my lungs with fresh air.

One summer's day, just out of college, I left my apartment to get milk from the corner store, with only my flip-flops on my feet and a five-dollar bill in my pocket. It was such a nice day that I decided to walk to the supermarket instead. And then, not wanting the walk to end, I walked right past the store, along the waterfront, to the slow slope leading onto the Brooklyn Bridge, up the West Side Highway—until I finally stopped at 125th Street, eleven miles from home. It was one of the happiest days I can remember.

But hospitals are for pacing, not walking; there is no calm to be found in their fluorescent hallways. To walk, you need to leave.

Nadav's hospital was on the Upper East Side, just across from Central Park, a lovely spot for a good walk. And so, after bidding him farewell in the operating room—blessing recited, forehead kissed—we'd stroll along its winding paths. Our aimless wandering revealed hidden sanctuaries: a quiet wood, a sudden waterfall, a secret garden.

Despite the lush surroundings, the walk was tinged with anxiety, a subtle fear of what would come next. We kept our phones close, knowing that we'd soon get the call to come back to the cold reality of the hospital.

Thankfully, the Glenn passed without incident; and before we knew it, we were back at Nadav's side in the pediatric cardiology ICU, a nurse gently settling him in, doctors murmuring by the door.

෬෬෬

This time, Nadav's recuperation from surgery would be relatively brief. He returned home ten days later, with no major issues.

That summer, we posed him sitting on the floor, holding a big sign reading "Thank you Dr. Nguyen"—and sent the photo to the surgeon with a small note thanking him for all he'd done for us. His knowing hands had kept us on track, everything was going to plan, and we were deeply grateful. When we next visited his office, we saw the photo pinned behind the desk. I nudged Tali and smiled.

By that point, Nadav's medical team was starting to feel like our extended family. We shared a common language, a mutual trust, and the same goal—to get Nadav to his teens. After the Glenn, it didn't seem so far-fetched: two operations down, just one more to go.

ɞɷɢ

With the Fontan at least three years away, we were anxious to catch up to normal family life. But before that could happen, there was one more important procedure that had to take place: Nadav's bris.

Jewish boys are meant to be circumcised at eight days—the "bris," one of the most significant rituals in Judaism, representing the covenant with the Almighty. But eight days after Nadav was born, a circumcision was out of the question; he was still in intensive care, recovering from his first surgery. It wasn't until five months after the Glenn that his doctors judged him stable enough to undergo the procedure—which by then would require a urologist, not a mohel, and a visit to the operating room, under anesthesia.

Usually, a bris is attended by family and friends, who wish the infant well in his life ahead, the first of many happy moments to come. But it was somehow appropriate that Nadav's was held in a hospital room, with just the three of us—me, Tali, and the urologist. The doctor was Jewish, too, and after the procedure, when Nadav was wheeled into the recovery room, he produced a small bottle of grape juice so we could say the proper prayers.

At Yaniv's bris, the mohel had made a big show of announcing his bar mitzvah date. But we didn't do the same for Nadav. Perhaps it seemed a little presumptuous—thirteen years was still a long way away.

Chapter 14

SEARCHING FOR NORMALCY

Nadav's condition was much less precarious after the successful Glenn. With a more stable circulation, we no longer had to worry as much about his oxygen levels. But the lines between "patient" and "son" were still blurry. Our days remained full of routines, both medical and mundane.

Taking care of these obligations—so intimidating at first—eventually gave me a deep, gratifying sense of achievement. I felt a personal satisfaction in mastering new and unfamiliar skills; doing so gave me a sense of control and agency in helping Nadav survive. Medicine had become an indelible part of our lives, part of the fabric of our family; and—whether I liked it or not—it was now a core part of my identity as a father.

Still, I longed for a time when we could finally be free of Nadav's day-to-day medical burdens, and focus instead on simply living our lives.

శుఖ

The equipment I had most feared was the NG tube, but I actually became quite adept at placing it—so much so that I could probably do it with my eyes closed.

In fact, I'd often have to do it in the dark. Nadav would sometimes cough the thing up in the middle of the night, sounding the pump's alarm, and we'd awake to find the tube thoughtlessly pumping precious milk all over the crib. Once we cleaned up the mess, it would have to go back in. Nadav would scream, of course, but after a while, I learned to do it quickly enough so that he'd barely feel it—my secret talent.

I was once chosen for a silly "get to know you" profile for our company newsletter, and when the questionnaire asked for an "interesting fact" I said something banal about cooking Indian food. But what I really wanted to answer was, "I know how to put an NG tube up a sleeping baby's nose without waking them up."

In all of the time Nadav needed the NG, only once did I ever accidentally hit the lung. It felt wrong going in, like trying to push a straw into foam, and I stopped suddenly, deeply shaken.

𝔰𝔬𝔠𝔰

Even though our mastery of medical responsibilities made me proud, I often yearned for a break from the constant vigilance required by Nadav's condition. Many times, I wished it would all disappear—especially that damned NG tube, which wouldn't come out until he really started to grow.

In Jewish families, home life usually revolves around food—but even more so for us. Nadav was small for his age: when he came home, we were able to weigh him using a kitchen scale. And while his twin predictably chugged up the height and weight charts, Nadav stayed stuck below the lowest percentile. So, the tube persisted.

We got used to the NG tube, jokingly calling it the "nose hose." But we still hated it. Tali always insisted it was temporary, until Nadav could get past the 3 percent height and weight threshold. Whenever someone suggested that we consider putting in a more permanent G-tube, directly into the stomach, she bristled.

Still, everything about the NG was a nuisance—even the tape we used to attach it to Nadav's cheek. The hospital had recommended Tegaderm, a special transparent adhesive film, but it started leaving nasty red rashes on Nadav's face. We spent a lot of time looking for alternatives, but none stuck as well—and no matter what we tried, his skin always suffered.

At first, we were so afraid of placing the NG that we'd get upset whenever it came out. But before long, we'd start pulling it out on purpose, just to give him a break. With the tape removed, his skin could feel fresh air, and try to heal. He was more comfortable without a tube up one of his nostrils. And to look like a normal kid, if only for a few hours, was no small thing.

ℝ

Caring for Nadav was difficult enough, but we found it almost impossible to care for ourselves as well. I looked for any opportunity to escape the stress of daily life, hoping to find some way to recuperate. But the reality of our situation always had a way of catching up to me.

Books had always been a reliable late-night refuge, an easy way to clear my mind as I drifted off to sleep. Trying to avoid anything too heavy or challenging, I devoured pulpy mysteries instead. It wasn't too hard to lose myself in gritty L.A. police stations, chilly Scandinavian lakes and genteel English manors—all haunted by ruthless murderers, cleverly hiding their tracks, until they were inevitably caught by dogged, hard-edged detectives.

But even these mysteries, so detached from reality, contained eerie echoes of what we were going through. In one, the culprit's motive remained baffling until the very end, when it was revealed that he owed a debt to a talented cardiologist who'd saved his infant son. "How can I ever repay you?" the thankful father had said, or something along those lines; to which the vindictive doctor replied that all he really wanted was for the poor guy to kill his wife.

Another who-dun-it, to my dismay, was set in a nursing school. In the opening scene, the trainees (just like us just a few months before) were learning to properly place NG tubes—one of which turned out to be an especially devilish murder weapon. The culprit had poisoned the milk.

Undeterred, I kept reading. Two hundred-odd pages later, after two more poor nurses were dispatched by more conventional means, the killer was finally unmasked; and I could return to real life—back to our own world of NG tubes; utterly safe, unless you accidentally hit the lung.

༄༅

Even after the twins started to eat solid food, we still struggled to help Nadav grow. Once we saw a magazine article about the foods to avoid if you wanted to lose weight and read it avidly, knowing that we'd do exactly the opposite. It taught us little tricks to add calories—like adding chia seeds or dipping everything in olive oil. We tried everything we could.

Inspired by Indian lassis, Tali invented a concoction we called "mango milk"—juice, yogurt and milk swirled together in a sippy cup. To make it easier, I'd prefill a dozen cups at a time, enough to get us through the week; but every so often, one would leak, dribbling yellow-orange ooze into the depths of the fridge.

Whether it was the chia seeds, the extra oil, or the mango milk, something must have worked. By the time the twins reached ten months, Nadav's feeding therapist—satisfied with his progress—finally gave us permission to stop his overnight feeds.

"*Woo hoo!*" Tali replied—relieved, exuberant, victorious.

The NG was finally out, and we could all breathe a little easier.

Chapter 15

LIFE AT HOME

Every year, Mount Sinai Hospital hosted a Valentine's Day party for their cardiac patients—announced by a small postcard in the mailbox, addressed to Nadav.

I only remember going once, a year and a half after the twins were born. The hall was packed with young kids and grinning doctors, red and pink and white balloons straining for the rafters. It was festive, chaotic, and strange. I wasn't used to us being in the hospital for anything other than an appointment; and it was odd seeing Nadav's doctors beaming at other kids. In a way, it made the hospital less of a special place.

We did get a lovely photo of the five of us, all smiles amongst the happy crowd. But by that point, I felt a sudden urge to leave. *We've spent far too much time in hospitals already,* my inner voice insisted. *Enough!*

With the NG tube gone, the pulse ox ignored, and the Glenn complete, the boundaries between medicine and parenting were becoming clear. Hospitals were places for crisis and care; they might even offer comfort and relief. But happiness was reserved for home.

༄༅

We used to keep a small black notebook in our living room, within easy reach of the couch. When the boys were little, Tali and I used it to record funny sayings and special milestones. In it, scrawled near the front, are some of the twins' first words—"Abba!" (Hebrew for father), uttered by Yaniv, thirteen months old; and "Ah dah!" (baby talk for "all done"), spoken by Nadav, just two days later.

Yaniv's milestones always came first—standing, talking, walking. But Nadav kept up, as best he could, catching up quickly enough. What his body lacked in oxygen, it made up for in determination.

༄༅

It was not always obvious to others that Yaniv and Nadav were the same age; they were as different as fraternal twins could be. Yaniv was noticeably bigger, his face rounded with pinchable cheeks, blue eyes twinkling with a wide smile. Nadav's features were more delicate, his gaze watchful and calm, an old soul.

Because of Nadav's lower-than-usual blood oxygen levels, his skin had a slightly pale tinge. And so, Tali resolved that all of the blue cups, plates and cutlery—as well as every blue stuffed animal—would go to Yaniv. In contrast, almost everything Nadav used was some warm shade of red, as if the color would somehow inspire his oxygen levels to stay high; subtle charms to ward off desaturation.

Even their hair grew differently. Yaniv's blond locks sprouted quickly, falling over his ears, while Nadav's brownish wisps stayed straight and fine. After Yaniv's first haircut, leaving him neatly trimmed, this shifted: Tali refused to let the barber cut

Nadav's growing curls, which eventually arranged themselves in an unruly, adorable mess.

⊱⊰

M y favorite memory of those early years was reading to the boys at bedtime. We'd cuddle in bed, heads propped up on pillows, stacks of books at our side. Dr. Seuss was their favorite, especially *Hop on Pop*; *Hairy Maclary from Donaldson's Dairy* too; and of course, Curious George—sometimes replaced, if I was feeling especially goofy, by his evil cousin, Blasé Fred.

Tali especially enjoyed *Curious George Goes to the Hospital*, touched that it had been written for the young patients at Boston Children's. We liked *Peter Pan* for the same reason: as the cover page of our aging edition noted, all of its royalties were donated to the Great Ormond Street Children's Hospital in London, where Nadav's surgeon had trained.

While reading, I couldn't resist some silliness, knowing it would earn me a few laughs before frustration set in. Sometimes I'd smuggle in one of the twins' stuffed animals, peeking its head above the book while I read, and hiding it again as soon as they noticed. Or I'd stray from the text—using silly voices, or reading it backward, or upside-down.

Inevitably, they'd complain, sometimes giggling, sometimes more firmly, urging me to stop. Nadav, in particular, had little patience for silliness. "Read it *properly*," he'd scold, fed up, and sensing the impatience in his voice I'd quickly switch back.

As they grew older, the groans started to outnumber the giggles. I missed the earlier days, when they still had patience for their father and his goofy jokes.

༄༅༃

The boys never spent the night in our bed—"the biggie bed," they called it—but it became a favorite play space in our two-bedroom apartment. When I asked the boys what they most remember about those years, their memories inevitably gravitated to the biggie bed.

On weekends, when Tali made breakfast, we'd sometimes hide under the covers, daring her to come look for us. "You cannot find us!" the boys would yell, giggling. "You do not know where we is!!"

After we started reading the Peter Rabbit stories, Tali became Mr. MacGregor, the boys little rabbits hiding in his garden. "We're eating the *cawwits*!" they'd whoop from beneath the sheets. "We're chopping the *un-yuns*!!" And then they'd wait, quietly listening for footsteps—but she was too crafty, lifting up the covers with a roar; triggering a scramble of shouts and screams.

The biggie bed also served as a mock hospital, the site of many medical adventures perpetrated on Nadav by his brothers. They'd drag our stash of medical supplies out of the closet, putting stethoscopes around their necks, and lie Nadav down so they could give him a checkup. Without access to sophisticated equipment, they relied on more primitive methods—lifting and dropping his arms and legs, peering down his throat, wrapping him in bandages and sheets.

Nadav didn't mind the poking and prodding. He was used to being a patient, and he enjoyed having his brothers as his doctors for a change.

৪৩

Gilad also helped with the real medicine too. Most of Nadav's medicines were taken by mouth, but he was also prescribed an anticoagulant called Lovenox, to prevent blood clots. "You're not going to like it," warned Shubhi. It was to be injected. By us. Twice a day.

Tali, ever unflappable, administered it, rotating each shot from arm to thigh, thigh to arm, left to right, and around again. We used Lidocaine to dull the pain, but it didn't really work. Nadav wouldn't struggle—after all, he was used to far worse—but sometimes he'd let out a rat-a-tat scream: "owieowieowie owie owie!"

Gilad would join us in bed, gently holding his brother's hand, promising him small treats if he could just hold himself to a certain number of owies. "Just two this time," he'd say. "You can do it!" And when it was all over—"yay!"—he'd bring him some small trinket, like a pencil eraser, as a special reward.

Chapter 16

THE WORLD AROUND US

There were times—especially early on—when our apartment may have resembled a hospital. But by the end of the twins' first year, it was starting to feel like home. Most of the major medical responsibilities had faded away, leaving only occasional appointments on the calendar—periodic checkups with Nadav's cardiologists and regularly scheduled visits with our family pediatrician.

Thanks to Nadav's unique physiology and our hard-won medical expertise, I arrived at these visits with the smug superiority of a VIP. In particular, Nadav's lack of a spleen gave me a special sense of priority access. Whenever we arrived, the waiting room inevitably packed with sniffly kids, we'd ask to be admitted early. "He's asplenic," was the whispered code word; and—shielding him from the invisible germs lurking in the lobby—we'd be whisked right in.

Our pediatrician, who'd done her residency in a pediatric cardiology ward, took a particular shine to Nadav. His progress was always the highlight; Yaniv would be quickly dismissed after a brief check-in, about as unexciting as a patient could be. And she'd talk to us candidly, sharing her thoughts as if we were medical peers.

She once went on an extended rant about the meaning of the word "lethargic." "Parents call me up, and tell me that their kid is *lethargic*," she'd complain, thinking back to her days tending to the hospital's sickest kids. "Well, I've seen lethargic, and that ain't it. They bring the kid in, and they're just *sleepy*."

We nodded knowingly. After all of our medical adventures, I couldn't imagine freaking out about something so minor.

ಬೆಂ

We may have finally banished the pulse ox and the NG tube to the bathroom closet, but we still had to keep track of Nadav's many prescriptions—a list that seemed to change with every doctor's appointment.

As Nadav grew, Shubhi prescribed sildenafil—better known by its brand name, Viagra—to avoid pulmonary hypertension. She warned me that for some reason, it would be difficult to fill the prescription. Apparently, insurance companies really do not want to prescribe Viagra to young children, even if they are high-risk cardiac patients.

I asked if perhaps they were afraid that I'd keep the pills for myself, but she laughed. "The dose is much too small for you," she replied—and immediately blushed, before we both laughed it off.

So it was that I spent a lunch hour at work researching the best way to get cheap Viagra, without resorting to any of the breathless come-ons from pill pushers in my spam folder. My colleagues, ever supportive, gave me high-fives when I finally scored.

ಬೆಂ

The most helpful people we met worked right below our apartment. We lived directly above a pharmacy, and so we got to know all of the pharmacists pretty well—particularly one named Gerard, who coincidentally shared the twins' birthday.

The pharmacy was part of a national chain, and Gerard was a persistent master of the baffling rules, policies, and billing procedures set by our insurance and his employers. When there was a problem, he'd loom above his computer, alternately punching in codes and scratching his head. If he eventually figured out the tortured logic, he'd grin, and explain it to me; but if he couldn't, he'd just nod, and tell me not to worry. "Just come back in an hour," he'd say. "I'll figure it out."

Finding medicine in the proper form was a particularly frustrating riddle, especially since Nadav was too young to swallow pills. One critical medicine cost only a few dollars in tablet form but was almost fifty times that price as a liquid. Even worse, it was apparently against policy for pharmacists to work around this by just dissolving the cheaper pills into a solution themselves. (Someone even told me it might be illegal.)

Not to worry, Gerard assured me. "Just bring me the pills," he said, "and we'll make it work." So, every month, I'd slip him a small bottle, and return in an hour—issue solved, no questions asked.

Once, the store's computer insisted that the bubble gum flavor Gerard added to bad-tasting medicines should incur a twenty-dollar surcharge. He ignored that one too.

All of these policies could make filling prescriptions a confusing mess. But Gerard's workarounds helped us realize that not all of the rules, however strict they seemed, had to be followed. It was a lesson that extended far beyond the pharmacy. During those years, we learned to trust our common sense, and do what was best for us—even if some boundaries had to be crossed.

࿔

We could not have made it through those first years without the help of others—friends old and new who came through whenever we needed it most. I never felt that their generosity stemmed from pity; but rather from simple compassion, an intrinsic instinct for kindness that shines brightest in the most difficult circumstances.

We knew only a few other families who were dealing with medical issues. The hospital introduced us to another family with twins, one with a similar heart condition. But they lived far away, and our visits to see them were infrequent. Mostly we interacted with people who—however well-meaning—had no point of reference for what we were going through.

We were lucky to live close to our own families. Our mothers doted on the boys; our fathers shared sage advice (even if we didn't always ask for it); our siblings helped out however they could. Tali's sister, a pharmacist, was a sounding board for tricky questions about prescriptions; my elder sister, a trained counselor, was there whenever I needed a listening ear. But it really didn't matter *what* they did, just that they were there.

My younger sister is a musician; a talented and creative performer with a gift for creating achingly beautiful songs. My favorite is called "You Have My Heart," written long before Nadav was born. For many years she played it to close out her shows, kids starting to squirm in their mothers' laps. "I have my fingers, I have my toes," it goes, listing out all sorts of body parts. "I have my hips, I have my fingertips, I have my lungs…but you have my heart."

A few months after the Glenn, we went to one of her concerts. Seeing us in the crowd, she made a last-minute adjustment to the lyrics: "I have my spleen" became "I have no spleen." Nobody else noticed, but when she sang it, she looked at us with a wry, loving smile; an inside joke, just for us.

∞⟨∞

But at the end of the day, it was up to me and Tali. No matter how much the people around us cared for us, it was hard for them to truly understand what we were going through. Nadav's condition helped us see humanity at its best; but at the same time, it was a chasm that separated us from the rest of the world.

Friends and family could help with logistics—a quick night out for a birthday dinner, taking the boys to the park across the street—but we never quite trusted anyone else with Nadav's medical needs at home. ("*What if they screw up the medicines? What if his oxygen levels plunge and nobody notices?*") Even after the hospital arranged for a visiting nurse service to help, we turned most of them away. The worst were the ones who arrived complaining about how difficult it was to park in our neighborhood. *If you care more about your car than our son*, I thought, *how can we have confidence in you?*

At times, the distance between us and others seemed infinitely vast. Other parents' worries—getting into preschool, dealing with childhood ailments, worrying about developmental milestones—seemed trivial in the face of what we were going through. *How lucky they were*, I'd sometimes tell myself. *How little they knew!*

Even as I allowed myself an occasional dose of soothing self-pity, I hoped never to succumb to the "why me" bitterness that seemed to lie in that abyss, the insidious jealousy of parents whose children would never die. I feared that once that poison seeped into my veins, it would corrode my own sense of who I wanted to be.

Staying strong was already difficult enough.

Chapter 17

STRESS

Even as we learned to cope with Nadav's medical challenges, I found it harder and harder to keep a positive attitude. The stresses of daily life, the pressures of Nadav's care, the uncertainty of what lay ahead—*Another surgery, and who knows what after that?*—weighed me down in subtle ways.

The optimism I'd relied on was starting to take its toll. I'd gotten into the habit of banishing negative thoughts to my subconscious, where I supposed they would do no harm. But once there, they quietly festered—a dull, lingering ache that never quite disappeared.

ഇൽ

I decided that I needed to find some time for myself. And so, a year after the twins were born, I decided to take a short trip to a work conference out west. Nadav was stable, and we'd settled into a comfortable routine, so Tali and I agreed it was fine for me to go. I looked forward to feeling like a human being again; for most of the past year I'd thought of little more than parenting and Nadav's survival.

My trip to the conference that fall would be a treat. I was just happy to be on the flight—a few hours in the air, surrounded by strangers, able to read or watch a movie in peace. I loaded some films onto my phone, packed my carry-on with reading material, and settled in—finally able to relax.

The feeling didn't last. Just after takeoff, I opened a copy of the New York Times Book Review—*ever so civilized!*—only to see a headline that made my heart sink. "A Death In The Family," it read, in bold black letters, followed underneath by this description: "A father describes, and rages at, the loss of his teenage son."

It was—of course—a memoir of another cardiac kid; the story of how another's man son, a teenager, succumbed to a similar heart condition. Somehow, on my first day away, on the first hour of my flight, a fellow father's grief had found me, blindsiding me in an unguarded moment—and I realized, to my dismay, that running away was ultimately futile; my own heavy heart impossible to escape.

∞∞

At some point in those first few years, I started feeling excruciating pain in my lower back. At times, especially in the mornings, the agony was so bad that I could barely stand up.

I suspected this was physical. There seemed to be no end to lifting things—children, strollers, groceries. And I'd put on some weight, thanks to a lack of exercise and occasional bouts of late-night stress eating.

A friend recommended a doctor, so I scheduled an appointment. When the x-rays showed nothing wrong, he recommended a regular course of physical therapy. And so, every week I'd head uptown after work, lying face down as some therapist pummeled me for half an hour.

It wasn't terrible—it felt pretty good, actually—but all that pummeling barely made a difference. The pain persisted, and I began to suspect it wasn't physical at all.

ꕥ

I eventually learned to find solace in music.

While Nadav was recuperating in the hospital after the Glenn, he'd had regular visits from a wonderful music therapist, one of the most tranquil souls I have ever met. He tempered our nervous energy with subtle calm, strumming a few quiet tunes on his guitar whenever he came by, even if Nadav was asleep. We'd stop what we were doing and listen—his music reminding us to breathe.

His gentle playing was more than a distraction. It somehow felt necessary, a reminder that healing required more than just medical intervention; that there were other ways to channel the mysteries of the universe in the service of recuperation.

I'd done this at home too, lulling the babies to sleep with my silly songs. Those melodies helped me find calm amongst chaos, focusing my mind on what mattered—even when the lyrics cut close to the bone.

ꕥ

It isn't until you have a child with a heart condition that you truly realize how many songs are about hearts, especially damaged ones. Take, for example, Al Green's beautiful rendition of the Bee Gees' "How Can You Mend A Broken Heart?"

I'd loved the song before I became a parent, its drifting melody in 6/8 time a soothing balm in times of stress. I never paid much attention to the lyrics, focusing instead on the song's gentle pace. But after Nadav was born, I couldn't ignore its double entendres, ironic words that suddenly echoed a latent sadness buried deep below.

I used to try to escape that melancholy, but I've since learned that it's sometimes better to embrace it. Now, whenever I listen to the song, it's because of those mournful lyrics, not in spite of them—even though whenever that lilting chorus returns, tears inevitably tug at the corners of my eyes.

Music allows me to immerse myself in the hidden pain I so often tried to ignore: to accept it, to allow it to exist, as it insists it must—and then to let it evaporate, gently, into the air.

Chapter 18

GROWING UP

I n retrospect, those years seem to have flown by. As the saying goes: "The days are long, and the years are short." Even Gilad realized this as he watched his brothers grow. "They're not such babies anymore," he declared as they approached their third birthday. "I feel like they're teenagers!"

Realizing that they were, indeed, no longer babies, we moved the twins out of their crib into Gilad's room. I installed a bunk bed to maximize the space and built a small model train that ran around the tops of the walls, chugging in an endless loop.

⁎℃℟

That fall, we also enrolled the twins in a Jewish preschool about a mile from our house. I remember nothing about their first day, but I have a snapshot of them standing outside: Yaniv posing in front of their double stroller, head slightly tilted, and Nadav behind him, hands clasped, laughing at something in the distance.

It was typical of the pair—Yaniv grounded and steady, Nadav off in his own little world. Rewatching the videos I'd taken back then, the pattern repeats itself over and over: Yaniv earnestly singing "Twinkle Twinkle" while Nadav goofs off in the background; Yaniv belting out "Happy Birthday" while Nadav raises his arms, as if conducting an orchestra; Yaniv complaining that his toy fell of the table as Nadav happily pushes his own onto the floor.

We still have the notebook that we sent to school every day, filled with updates to and from their teachers. Reading it back, the pair seemed inseparable. "Yaniv makes sure Nadav has his lunch and snack," the teacher wrote in September. "And they play together in the kitchen a lot. It is very cute!" In November, Yaniv told us that Nadav hit someone with a block; Nadav proudly admitted it.

One of my best friends in college was an identical twin. Although she and her sister went to different schools, they still talked for an hour every night. "We're twins," she explained, even though she knew that I would never understand.

Yaniv and Nadav must have shared a similar bond. In one video, fuzzy and pixelated in our darkened bedroom, they lie together on the biggie bed. Nadav turns the pages of a board book as Yaniv sounds out the animals: *Wion! El-fant! Fwa-min-go!* In another, they hug in the bathroom, giving each other sloppy kisses. "*Not on the lips!*" Tali yells, off-camera.

℠Ↄ

The boys loved to sing, especially after being introduced to the pop songs that had become popular amongst Gilad's elementary school classmates. (In the third grade, he had been scolded for singing the Korean hit "Gangnam Style" because a teacher had objected to the lyrics "sexy ladies." Undeterred, he simply replaced the line with the words "sixty babies.")

"Party Rock Anthem" was the twins' favorite. They'd try to copy their brother's dance moves, shouting mangled lyrics into the air. "*Party Rockets in the house tonight!*" they'd yell, spinning around the room with glee.

Life wasn't always a party, of course. We had our fair share of short tempers, petty bickering, and exhausted arguments. But in the photo albums I've saved, all of that has evaporated away—only the laughter and smiles remain.

The videos we took are a particularly precious gift. In most of them, Gilad takes center stage: lifting his brothers into the bed like sacks of potatoes (all giggles); headlining an impromptu living-room concert (*"Give me the microphone, Yaniv!"*); teaching them how to push their new scooters—a late-summer present for their third birthday. Being an older brother suited him well.

⊱⊰

With three boys in school, we now faced a new challenge: getting them all up in the morning.

Yaniv was an early riser, but Gilad and Nadav (like their parents) were not. Hoping to inspire their inner energy, we turned to music—a progressively chaotic playlist that began with "Oh! What A Beautiful Morning," (from *Oklahoma*) followed by "Good Morning!" (from *Singing in the Rain*). If all else failed, we went nuclear—a series of college football fight songs blasted at full volume.

It rarely worked. Gilad used passive resistance, burying his head under the covers, refusing to stir, as Nadav bellowed in a small voice: *"Two more minutes!"*

⊱⊰

Of course, Nadav preferred to sleep in; he was often the last one to fall asleep at night.

His twin brother, with the normal energy of a toddler, raced through the day like a firecracker—manic bursts of energy that yielded to sudden yawns at bedtime. But Nadav compensated for the low oxygen in his bloodstream by pacing himself throughout the day, conserving his energy.

Later, as his brothers gently snored, Nadav would stay awake in their shared room, singing softly to himself. When the singing ended, we'd peek in, hoping he'd finally fallen asleep, but more often than not we'd see his brown eyes quickly dart toward the door, still wide awake.

೭つಛ

Mealtimes could be difficult too. Nadav's NG was long gone, but mindful that he still had at least one surgery left, we continued to search for calorie-rich foods. The more he weighed, we were told, the better the chances that everything would go well.

One of the best foods for adding weight is ice cream, but Nadav was perhaps the only boy in the city who didn't care for it. We once took the boys out to a local ice cream parlor for the twins' birthday, hoping Nadav's tastes had changed. But after agreeing to taste a single, small spoonful, he spit it out.

The most fattening food he *did* like was duck bacon, sold from a gourmet stand in the Sunday farmer's market near our house. It was expensive but worth it; we'd stop by each week to pick up a new packet. Soon, his brothers—seduced by free samples—developed a taste for the exorbitant gourmet cheeses sold in the next stall. Not willing to play favorites, we grudgingly bought those too.

೭つಛ

remember only one medical crisis in the two and a half years between the Glenn and the Fontan—a near-miss, but an unexpected shock; a jarring end to a moment of delight.

We were horsing around one weekend, having a tickle fight on the biggie bed, and amidst the laughter someone decided it would be a good idea to ask me for a piggy-back to the kids' bedroom. Gilad and Yaniv argued about who'd go first, and for some reason I told them *both* to climb on.

And of course, as I waddled precariously toward the hallway, someone's hand slipped; and I felt both of them tumbling suddenly downward, their heads both connecting with the floor—two mighty cracks, and nothing but silence.

Silence, of course, being the one thing you don't want to hear from an injured child. I knelt down, hoping to hear a sob or a cry—some evidence of pain, rather than unconsciousness—but it never seemed to come.

And just as I was beginning to panic, their pain kicked in; and those welcome sobs, and their copious tears, convinced me that we'd dodged the worst, and they'd pull through.

"Oops," said Nadav. "Glad that wasn't me."

It broke the tension, with perfect timing—and Tali couldn't help but laugh, relieved. An unexpected medical emergency was the last thing we needed.

Chapter 19

ON THE ROAD

As the boys grew into toddlers, we started to travel again. Our Subaru was reliable as ever, allowing us to roam farther and farther away, and we even started to think about flying somewhere new. We couldn't wait to show the boys the world—to encounter new things, discover new places, and look beyond our familiar surroundings.

ಬಂಡ

We started by exploring our own city, seeking out new sights. Zoos were a particular favorite. The Prospect Park Zoo, close to home, was small and convenient. They had a small collection of exotic animals—wallabies, otters and red pandas—but the ordinary ones were the most entertaining. Feeding ducks and domestic animals was always a highlight; two quarters bought a handful of food at the pond and the barn. But Yaniv's enthusiasm was dampened after his finger was snapped by an overzealous turkey. (He's held a grudge ever since.)

The Bronx Zoo, farther away, was large and distant—every attraction an extra charge, with endless, intimidating lines. It could be enjoyable, particularly at feeding time: helpless fish tossed at barking sea lions by sea-sprayed keepers; cabbages and other greens falling from the sky in the gorillas' enclosure, smashing onto the ground. But those long waits to see the most popular animals required a patience we didn't always have.

I'd been to both of those zoos as a child, but I'd never visited the Staten Island Zoo, which turned out to be more elaborate than I'd expected. The entrance was guarded by a majestic, caged bald eagle, and in the central plaza stood a concrete reptile house, home to the zoo's collection of snakes and lizards.

It was in that sweltering room, on the explanatory panel right next to the boa constrictor, that I learned something startling: snakes' hearts have only three chambers. Just like Nadav's, they lack a septum—the thin central wall separating the two ventricles.

The display explained that some congenital heart defects in humans are caused by a mutation in the gene that builds that septum—a genetic trigger that snakes also lack. That gene (Tbx5), and the proteins its builds, are now considered by some scientists to be an evolutionary landmark. They represent the threshold between cold- and warm-blooded animals; the former with a single ventricle, the latter with two.

I found the exhibit mesmerizing, staring at it long after Tali and the boys had moved on to other rooms. Would we ever discover what had caused Nadav's heart defect? Perhaps his condition was some sort of strange evolutionary glitch, an echo of the genetic randomness that had somehow determined that for certain animals, a single ventricle was best.

It was too much of a puzzle, and the kids were waiting outside, impatient to go. And so, I left the snakes—and their mysterious, puzzling hearts—to slowly slither behind the steamy glass.

ೞೞೞ

We'd taken our first big trip outside the city just before the twins turned two, driving down to Philadelphia to see an old friend whose young daughter was about the same age. We decided to meet at the Franklin Institute, which would keep the kids happily engaged while we caught up with our friend. And we could see the famous "Cardiac Adventure" exhibit—a giant human heart big enough to walk through.

Clambering inside, Tali excitedly pointed out the various chambers and vessels, explaining to the boys how Nadav's was different. "He doesn't have this here," she'd say, pounding on a papier-mâché septum, "and this goes here, not here," peering through a narrow vein. Nadav was nonplussed as his brothers raced ahead. But Tali and I took our time, paced by the steady "thump-thump" of a pre-recorded heartbeat.

An entire corner of the museum's second floor was dedicated to the heart. One room displayed the tools of heart surgery—dozens of razor-sharp blades arrayed in rows. After a quick glance, I decided to skip it. Giant hearts were fine, especially if the walls were plaster and the heartbeat was fake. But to see the actual tools used to cut them open was too much for me to handle.

Tali lingered, mesmerized by a video wall of open-heart operations. She'd watched similar videos before each of Nadav's surgeries, gazing at her laptop late into the night, learning all she could about how he might be fixed—studying every last detail.

Completely immersed in the exhibit, we suddenly realized that Yaniv had disappeared. He'd somehow wandered off— nabbed at the exhibit entrance by an alert security guard before he could make it to the exit. When she waved at us, the spell was broken. Suddenly, we were parents again.

After a quick snack in the cafe, we headed downstairs to the planetarium show, lights dimmed as the boys stared upward, our minds spanning the edges of the cosmos.

ഹര

As the twins grew, we felt more comfortable traveling farther away. A month before the twins' third birthday, we packed up the Subaru for a late summer vacation. We'd decided to visit a favorite beach in North Carolina that my family had often visited when we were kids. Now, I'd be able to share the same happy memories with my own children.

I looked forward to the relative calm of the open road. A well-paced walk was good for physical distraction, but long-distance driving, with its mindless, constant focus, was the closest I've ever come to a meditative state. And so, we decided not to rush it. When I was young, we usually did the ten-hour trip in two days. This time, we drove just two or three hours a day, spending each night in a different city.

Tali and I enjoyed showing our sons the sights at each stop—the Baltimore Aquarium, the White House, the Lincoln Memorial. But the boys were just as happy to explore the hotels. Yaniv and Gilad would beg to visit the pool, if there was one. Nadav, more sensitive to cold than his brothers, would quickly tire of the water. Sitting off to the side, bundled in towels, he'd shiver slightly as his brothers splashed around.

Ever-conscious of Nadav's calories, we learned to look for a Denny's whenever we were hungry for breakfast, a hidden benefit of heading South. Their kid's breakfast could be ordered with turkey bacon—thirty calories a strip, and more cost-effective than our gourmet duck back home.

ഹര

When we arrived at our beach house, we discovered that the surf was a little too rough for Nadav's comfort. While Yaniv fearlessly jumped over the little waves, his twin preferred to dig in the dry sand. Gilad had formed an imaginary conglomerate called "The Working Company," subcontracting us and the boys to do most of the heavy lifting. "*Working Com-pan-ee! Working Com-pan-EE!*" they'd sing as we worked; scraping deep trenches, filling our buckets with sand.

Tali would sometimes dig big holes for them, where they'd sit, laughing. She pushed sand around their waist, shaping the piles into boxy cars, hand-drawn circles forming headlamps at the front.

I taught the boys to fish, although Gilad was the only one large enough to handle a rod. We caught two little ones, and then a good-sized flounder, which we grilled out the back, squeezing lemon on top for lunch.

∞⌘

Only once was our peace and quiet interrupted by the outside world.

One evening, my parents called with terrible news. My uncle had died suddenly, unexpectedly, on a trip to Israel. He'd been there with my aunt for their son's wedding the previous week; they'd been looking forward to seeing their daughter get married in Sydney that fall. It was a tragedy that none of us were prepared for—and as I stood on the balcony of our rental house, sun setting over the incoming surf, I struggled to process what it meant.

No location, however idyllic, could shield me from the devastation of death. But being together—the five of us, as a family—offered some solace. We caught two small spots the next evening, which we ate on the balcony, sharing memories of my uncle. Together, we found refuge by remembering the past—threading a line between a life abruptly lost, and the three new lives that we had brought into the world.

༄ཅ

That fall, we decided to take the boys even farther afield. I needed to go to the Southwest for a work trip—twin events a week apart in San Diego and Arizona. We decided to take the whole family and turn it into a mini-vacation.

The boys loved it all—the flight, the fancy hotels, the stops at Legoland and the San Diego Zoo (which they unanimously agreed was better than the Bronx.) But the unexpected highlight was a reception at the work event in Phoenix, a party with a Wild West theme. Some guests found it tacky, but the boys had a ball. They shot toy arrows into wooden targets; pumped pellets at a bad-guy silhouette; and watched, transfixed, as a cowboy brandishing six-shooters looped a fiery lasso around his head.

The flight back was a red-eye, and despite their stubborn refusal to fall asleep ("*we want to watch A MOVIE!!!*"), all three eventually surrendered, dreaming by the time we landed.

Everything about traveling together—the planning, the logistics, the sheer thrill of discovering and exploring new places—made us feel happy and whole. After all of the medical adventures that had worn us out—the doses and shots and tubes and duck bacon, all of it—we finally had a chance to enjoy our lives together.

༄ཅ

Still, Tali and I yearned for some quiet time alone. Over the past three years, we'd barely had time to schedule a weeknight dinner date. Now, we finally decided to take some proper time for ourselves.

Tali had been invited to a cocktail party in Boston that fall to celebrate the successful completion of a museum project she'd worked on. It was only a few hours away—why not fly up and stay overnight?

So, we made arrangements: two plane tickets from LaGuardia to Logan, a night at a nice hotel, dinner reservations at a top-notch restaurant in Cambridge. Even before the plane took off, we switched off our cellphones, having told our families that we'd be out of touch.

We disembarked with a giddiness we hadn't felt in years, off the grid and looking forward to the evening ahead. For once, we had no obligations save for our own happiness—nonmedical conversations with other adults, a luxurious meal without hot dogs or chicken fingers. We ordered freely from the menu, mentally amortizing the cost of the feast to account for three years of social isolation.

Walking back to the hotel—just the two of us in the cool fall air, rediscovering each other, as if we were on our first date—the rest of the world faded away.

୫୦୯ଓ

We slept in the next morning. The flight home wasn't until the afternoon, leaving us time for a long, kid-free brunch in the hotel restaurant—the perfect coda to a much-needed break.

While we waited for the eggs to arrive, Tali switched on her phone—and to her shock suddenly saw dozens of missed calls from her family.

Her grandmother had died the night before.

She had lived a long and inspiring life. During the Holocaust, having seen her whole family murdered by Nazis, she hid in a hole in the ground with only a few gold coins to keep her safe. But she lived long enough to meet her great-grandchildren, including a remarkable boy who showed a similar instinct for survival. She'd always felt a special connection to Nadav.

We didn't regret the trip; we deserved an evening away. But the news threw us for a loop, and we flew back in grief. No matter where we found ourselves, the world around us continued to spin.

Chapter 20

THE FONTAN

I t hadn't been easy, but as we approached Nadav's third surgery, all of our hard work seemed to be paying off. We'd managed to navigate a tricky path, avoiding any major issues, and so far—touch wood—everything was unfolding as we'd hoped.

We'd made it to the Fontan, in which Nadav's venous circulation would finally be completely redirected away from his heart, directly to the lungs—leaving only red blood to circulate through his single ventricle.

Nadav's doctors decided to schedule the operation earlier than we'd expected, three months before his fourth birthday. He was doing well, they reasoned, and as a rule it was best to do big surgeries in warm weather, before the fall flu season began. And if they waited another year—who knows what might happen?

We knew how unpredictable surgeries could be. But we'd also learned that cautious optimism was better than anxious fatalism. As Nadav's doctors admitted, you just had to make the best guess with the information you had—and trust that everything would work out, hoping the odds were in your favor.

৩০০৪

Before the Fontan, Dr. Nguyen ordered a special CT scan—which the radiology department then used to print a small white plastic 3D model of Nadav's heart. He twirled it in his long fingers when we met, pointing out all of its intrinsic strangeness, and explained what he hoped to do. The model was incomplete, but strangely compelling; I asked if we could keep it after the operation, and he agreed—no problem.

He eventually sent it over, and I put it in a little plastic box. It's there on our bookshelf, still, a little souvenir; its hard white plastic reminding me of the incredible toughness of the real thing.

ဆုပ္တ

As always, the day of the surgery started early. We arrived around dawn, stifling our nervousness with a practiced calm. The hospital's familiar routines granted us some comfort. We knew the drill.

Nadav sat on a chair at Tali's side, wearing a gown with little tigers on it, sometimes glancing at the TV mounted high above. It was the usual routine—the visit from the anesthesiologist holding no surprises. We put on scrubs to help bring him inside, and then, in what had become a practiced custom—a whispered blessing to give him strength, a kiss on the forehead as he fell asleep.

And then just us, with nothing to do for the next eight hours.

I can't remember exactly what we did—we probably went for a walk in the park to clear our minds; we may have gone to a diner for breakfast. But I do remember being summoned by Shubhi after just few hours—earlier than we'd expected—and hearing the terrible news:

"He's not doing well."

We'd heard this before, during Nadav's first surgery—when after a few brief moments of panic, everything turned out to be OK.

But now, standing with Shubhi in the hospital's atrium, it seemed much more serious. Nadav's blood pressure was dangerously low, she said, and the doctors didn't know what to do. Except tell us the truth, with a serious look of concern: "He's not doing well."

I was hit by all of the emotions that I'd avoided in his first surgery: fear, terror, devastation. I felt the bottom sink out of my soul—this could be it. And there was nothing we could do.

ഇരു

For the next forty-five minutes, I found myself paralyzed by sheer terror.

We did nothing but pace the halls: back and forth, back and forth, back and forth. Past the cafeteria, past the chapel, past the coffee bar and the piano and the busts of previous hospital administrators, past all of it all again, and back again. Back and forth, back and forth.

What frightened me most was the thought of telling Nadav's brothers that he had died. We'd chosen to be completely honest with them with everything: our gut told us that children were strong enough to handle it, and their constant strength confirmed that we were right. But I couldn't imagine having to tell them this. It was my greatest fear by far.

Tali and I stopped in a large empty space behind the auditorium and held each other's hands. I don't remember what we said.

Staring death in the face and feeling nothing but fear.

ഇരു

At some point in those forty-five minutes, we somehow got word that the doctors had decided to try something they'd never done before—transfer Nadav from the operating room to the diagnostic cath lab, where they might be able to better determine what was happening.

They thought it was a long shot, but felt it was their only chance to find out what was wrong. Faced with an unexpected, inexplicable crisis, they looked for some way to handle the situation—without quite understanding what was going on.

And on the way, before the doctors even had a chance to do anything, Nadav's blood pressure somehow started rising again. Later, they'd admit that they weren't sure exactly why. But his mighty heart had made it through.

ဆေ

I wonder how many of Nadav's surgeries and procedures included moments where something curved this way or that. As parents, we were shielded from the gory details; even the OR reports were hidden from us until formally entered into his medical record.

For Shubhi to tell us, so honestly, what was going on in the moment, must have been heart-wrenching. I wonder if she felt the same fear that I did—if having to break the news of a death was the most terrible part of her job, even worse than losing a patient.

ဆေ

We met Dr. Nguyen in the intensive care unit, comforted somewhat by the usual post-op routine. But something within me had irrevocably changed. Death was no longer a far-away abstraction; it had been present, immediate, for forty-five long minutes. For the first time, I was forced to directly confront my deepest fear—a dress rehearsal for that terrible day that I worried might eventually come.

I'd always assumed that I had two primary duties as a father: to teach our children what I knew about the world and its wonders, and assume responsibility for their care. Over the past eight years, I had done my best to fulfill these obligations: travel agent, party planner, piggy-backer, paramedic.

I realized that if Nadav were to die, I would be faced with a third obligation: to somehow explain the inexplicable mystery of life and death to my two surviving sons. For this task, I was utterly unprepared. If that time came, I had no idea what I would do.

ಬಂಗ

The Fontan had reminded us—in that piercing moment, puncturing the balance we'd sought for nearly four years—how little we could predict what lay ahead. The future remained unknown, a mystery that would always lie just beyond our reach.

The memory of that horrible day would always cause a fearful shudder; but although that brush with death was terribly upsetting, I tried not to dwell on it. As one doctor advised us, sensing that we were struggling to deal with everything that was going on—

"You must always remember that you have no control."

ಬಂಗ

As we neared the twins' fourth birthday, we counted our blessings. Nadav was coping well with his new circulation, and everything appeared to be going smoothly. We didn't want to keep him in a bubble, and so we resolved to focus on the things we *could* control: to live our lives as best we could, seeking joy in all the places we knew to look.

We drove down to our favorite beach again later that summer but made fewer stops on the way down: a waterpark outside Washington, DC; a nature park near Richmond, Virginia; a minor-league baseball game in rural North Carolina. The stadium was small enough for the boys to explore on their own, bugs buzzing around in the warm summer air, all of us entertained by the antics of a silly catfish mascot who tumbled around the field.

That evening lingers in my memory, perhaps because of the short video clip we have of it: Yaniv complaining about the snacks ("This isn't real popcorn; real popcorn is what we make at HOME!")—as Nadav wandered off, holding his new baseball cap, dancing quietly by himself at the section's front rail.

There were fireworks after the game, but Nadav found them upsetting. So, I carried him back to the car, holding him tightly as the stadium cheered, explosions coloring the sky behind us.

ೞೞ

Gilad's eighth birthday was just after we returned from the beach, and at his suggestion, we decided to have a "Robin Hood" party. My mother volunteered to make felt hats for the kids, and I headed to the hardware store to find some materials for handmade bow-and-arrow sets.

I'd thought they would be pretty simple to construct—just some pieces of wood, and some twine—but was seduced by some bendy fiberglass driveway markers I found in aisle ten, on sale for a buck each. When I got home and built a test bow, I realized that I'd unwittingly constructed a lethal weapon. The dowel it shot was surprisingly fast and dangerously inaccurate.

Instead, I eventually retrofitted the bows to shoot rubber bands, which were cheaper and safer. But Gilad saved the test bow and would surreptitiously show it to friends when I wasn't looking, impressed by its forbidden power.

The costumes were adorable. In addition to over a dozen carefully sewn felt hats, my mother had made simple green ponchos to be worn as tunics. But Nadav, ever the contrarian, did not want to wear a felt hat or be one of the Merry Men. Instead, he put on a plastic crown, and proclaimed himself Prince John. "I want to be the bad guy," he explained—and lifted a bow, shooting my sister in the chest with a rubber band.

∞

The park we chose for the party was large and rambling, with dirt tracks winding through densely wooded sections. Dressed as Merry Men, we followed the path through our own Sherwood Forest. (I'd mapped out the route the night before, shielding a GPS tracker from a misty drizzle.) Along the trail, whenever the kids weren't looking, I'd toss a bag of fake coins for them to discover.

It actually felt pretty realistic, until we spotted a charity walk in the distance; the marchers dressed in bright purple shirts, intersecting our path ahead. We paused a moment, unsure what to do—the hypnotic spell of our imaginations almost broken—and then, one of the kids cried out, as if on cue: "The King's Men! The King's Men!"

"Run away, run away!" we shouted—the magic recaptured, the illusion restored, all of us immersed again in our imaginary world.

It was nice to linger there for a while, experiencing life from the dreamlike perspective of a child at play: where the future is infinite and reality can be transformed with a simple thought.

Chapter 21

DECISION TO GO

For all our traveling, we'd never taken the twins overseas. We hadn't been invited to any faraway weddings, and even if we had, we'd been too busy to go. But I was soon presented with an opportunity I found hard to resist. It came out of a chance conversation with my friend Tom, who told me a story one day about how he was invited to take a free trip to Australia—and turned it down.

Tom was a professional contact I'd known for years. We had similar jobs at similar media companies; me in New York, him in London. Along the way, our relationship shifted from acquaintance to friend, and whenever we found ourselves in each other's cities, we made a point to catch up over a drink. We'd trade gossip, share some stories, tell a joke or two.

And so Tom and I found ourselves chatting over a late afternoon beer, the trendy, wood-paneled bar empty before the evening rush.

"Hey, you won't believe what happened," Tom said. "I turned down an all-expenses trip to Australia."

Apparently, some conference had invited Tom as their keynote speaker—but at the last minute he couldn't make it, so a junior member of his team went instead.

"Hey, next time—tell me!" I said, half-joking.

As soon as the words left my lips, I realized that I wasn't joking at all. There was something about travel that helped us feel alive. We hadn't been to Australia since my grandfather died. And as I told Tom, there was something about the country that pulled at my heart.

"Well, they have the conference every year," Tom said, off-handedly. "I'll put in a good word for you, if you're interested."

ༀ

I found myself on the phone with the conference organizer the following spring. Tom had dropped my name; they'd reached out. "Let's chat," I'd said.

Australia was a long way away, but it was hard not to be tempted. It was a great gig in the lush Hunter Valley a few hours north of Sydney, deep in the heart of wine country. The conference organizers were springing for the hotel, as well as round-trip airfare in business class. And I'd been raised never to pass up an opportunity.

"Would you be able to make it two economy tickets instead?" I asked the conference organizer. Perhaps Tali could join me. Or perhaps we could all go together.

I thought back to all the times I'd been, and how special it had been to introduce Gilad to the country I loved. I also thought back to how much the twins had enjoyed our trip out West. My grandparents were no longer around, and we wouldn't see any cowboys. But it would still be an amazing experience.

Sure, they said. We'd love to have you. Hope you can make it work.

ॐ

"Is it crazy?" I'd asked Tali later. "It's crazy, right?"

With our accumulated frequent-flier miles added to the conference's offer, the five of us could fly to Australia for a little more than a single fare. The twins could meet their cousins; we could have a weekend to ourselves, enjoying wine country. It was pretty tempting.

"Is it crazy?" we asked Shubhi a few days later. "It's crazy, right?"

Nadav had already had three heart surgeries, after all—but all the evidence showed that he was doing well. "It might be possible," she said, and after conferring with her colleagues, she reported back. He could go, they'd agreed, provided that we took some precautions on the flight—and identified an Australian cardiologist in advance, in case of emergency.

Tali and I discussed it again and again, thorough as always—balancing our common-sense awareness of the risks against the inexorable pull of a country we loved.

Eventually, we decided to go.

ॐ

In retrospect, our decision seems pretty crazy. Some might say dumb.

Tali uses stronger words than "dumb." She'll never forgive herself for that decision.

I can't say I blame her. In retrospect, I can see her point.

After all, we knew that there was a risk. We'd even prepared for it, bringing along a thin green binder filled with important information—Nadav's diagnosis, a summary of his medical history, contact information for his doctors back home, and a recommendation for a cardiologist in Sydney, just in case.

But I still insist it doesn't mean we shouldn't have gone.

&OCB

I wasn't in the room when Nadav's doctors discussed our plans. But I imagine that in their conversation, they allowed us a certain deference; that knowing us well, they sensed our enthusiasm and trusted our judgment—not just about the course of his medical care, but about what his life should be.

He was their patient, but he was our son.

And no matter how involved we were in his care, we knew that life was not merely maintaining a heartbeat—it was much more than that. And to ignore that—I reasoned—would be doing him a disservice, denying him the full life he deserved.

There was a reason we decided to go and a reason that our doctors allowed us. It wasn't the free plane tickets—we'd flown to the West Coast a year before with no issues. It wasn't a spur-of-the-moment carelessness—we never made a hasty decision. We did what we always did: we gathered the best information we could, carefully weighed the risks against the benefits, and made our choice. Everything we did was always a conscious step away.

Most importantly, we never wanted to keep Nadav in a bubble. Like all of our children, we wanted him to experience the breadth of wonder that the world offers. We wanted him to live. And we were never very good at sitting still.

AUSTRALIA

Chapter 22

ARRIVAL

We left for Sydney in mid-November, on my fortieth birthday.

The flight was terrible—two flights, actually, nearly twenty-four hours door-to-door—and nobody was happy, least of all Nadav. But when we arrived, exhausted, we immediately fell into the soothing arms of my extended family.

We were staying with my second cousin, whose huge, comfortable house felt like a mansion. It was a maze of lushly furnished rooms on the first floor, surrounding a gigantic central staircase that led to the bedrooms upstairs. My cousin had been a familiar face when I'd visited Australia as a child. Slightly older and infinitely cooler, she'd once given me a CD of her favorite Aussie band. Now, we found ourselves at similar stages of life. She had three kids—twins and a sibling, just like us—and a dog who loved the extra company. They all got on famously, rollicking up the stairs and around the yard.

Their youngest, a daughter slightly older than Gilad, was a plotter. She pulled Gilad aside, detailing the plan for that night— what she referred to as a "midnight feast." Once the parents fell asleep, she explained, they'd sneak down, and raid the cupboard, full of Australian treats, stuffing their mouths full of assorted biscuits and chocolate frogs.

෮෨෪

We rented a car for our trip to the Hunter Valley and met the nanny who'd help look after the kids while we were gone. My aunt would be there for a few days too. We explained rules for bedtimes and the boys' favorite meals—high calories for Nadav, don't forget!—and wrote out his various medicines on a whiteboard in the kitchen. It was the first time we'd be away from the twins for more than one night, but we felt comfortable that they were in good hands.

Tali and I hit the road, heading toward the Hunter. We took our time: stopping for fish and chips on the way up the coast, spotting a bunch of wild kangaroos out the window once we turned inland. It was great to have a few days of freedom after four years of stress. We felt we'd earned it.

The hotel was lovely; the talk, easy; the pool, warm.

One night, we were treated to a wine tasting session at a local vineyard called Hope Estate. It felt like a tourist trap; they seemed just as interested in luring visitors as making wine. But we played along, giddily mixing blends together like mad scientists, drunkenly designing slightly rude labels with a table of temporary friends. Tali, who is much smarter about these things than I am, thought the wine was "plonk." But we drank it anyway.

On the way back to Sydney, we stopped into some nicer vineyards. Since I was the driver, Tali happily accepted the role of taster. "Now *that's* lovely," she said, sampling a particularly nice Cabernet—and we splurged on some bottles for my relatives, who also knew the difference.

༄༅

We spent the next few days with the boys, seeing family and exploring Sydney. Normal vacation stuff enjoyed together: swimming in a protected pool at Bondi Beach, an impromptu game of cricket in a favorite park, a small playground at sunset in the shadow of the Harbour Bridge.

We went to the zoo, where the boys saw their first koalas, asleep in the gumtrees. A few steps away, we found ourselves surrounded by a troop of wallabies, one with a joey asleep in her pouch. Brightly colored lorikeets visited us at lunch, chirping for a stray morsel. But of all the animals we saw, the boys' favorites were the rabbits in the children's area. We didn't travel over ten thousand miles to see rabbits, but you could hold them and feed them lettuce, and for our boys that was enough.

Thanksgiving was just around the corner, a good excuse for one of my American-born cousins to host a potluck in a large, sprawling park. It was a good chance to see the extended family in one go, everyone happy to greet the boys—especially the cardiac kid. Someone had brought a bocce set, and the next generation busied themselves chasing the balls around. I lay on my side, taking off-angle videos, happy that they all had the chance to meet.

I will never forget those carefree days, the last we'd experience for a long while, and I still wonder whether the happiness we felt then was an illusion or reality. They are the sort of impossibly perfect moments that you see in ads or movies—the reason we decided to make the trip in the first place. Family, freedom, fun.

A welcome reward for all of the anxiety and fear we'd felt since we first heard Nadav's diagnosis. The sort of joy we insisted he'd still be able to experience, despite his condition.

&oc&

O n Friday night—our last Shabbat in Sydney—we gathered at another relative's house. It was the sort of chaotic, loving evening I remembered from my childhood; kids spilling into the yard, racing around, as I'd done myself decades before. My cousin had bought a giant salmon on the way to work, storing it in a cooler under his desk. Now, it steamed slowly on the grill, large enough to feed the assembled crowd.

I presented one of our Hunter Valley wines to our host, who nodded approvingly. "We shall cellar this for the next time you visit," he announced, retiring to stow it somewhere under the house; he returned with an older half bottle from the same vineyard, so we could enjoy it in all its glory.

&oc&

After dinner, we came inside. Tali and I wanted to stay and talk, so we sent the kids to bed. Despite the usual protests, they eventually relented, and as the house fell quiet, we moved to the living room.

Tea was poured, chocolates passed—but just as we began to stretch out and chat we heard a small whimpering from down the hall.

It was Nadav. He couldn't sleep.

It wasn't unusual for Nadav to be the last to fall asleep, singing quietly to himself as his brothers snored. But this night, he wasn't singing. He was crying.

I must have made a dozen trips back and forth that night. Each time I managed to calm him down, tiptoeing back to the living room; but by the time I was ready to sit down he'd start crying again. Nadav was behaving more like a newborn than a four-year-old—and there was nothing I could do to keep him quiet. Each trip made me more and more frustrated, and eventually I lost my temper.

"Nadav, this is ridiculous," I said, or something like it. "You need to sleep. Enough."

But he wouldn't stop. So, we bundled him up with his brothers, and reluctantly said our goodbyes, hoping that a more familiar bed might help him fall asleep. Eventually, he did.

☙ଓ

For our last weekend in Australia, we'd arranged a quick overnight visit to Katoomba and the Blue Mountains—a scenic spot a few hours west of Sydney. On the way, we'd planned to visit a wildlife park. The boys would hold koalas, we'd get some fresh air, and then we'd head home, back to our everyday lives after two fantastic weeks away.

But before we left, we headed downtown one last time to bid Sydney adieu.

We sat on the train, passing all of the North Shore stops so familiar from my own childhood: St. Leonards, Wollstonecraft, Waverton. But as we began to curve toward the Harbour Bridge, I started to notice that Nadav was much quieter than usual.

Tali looked over at me: "Does he look right to you?"

He didn't look well, truth be told. His face was puffy, and he looked exhausted.

"I'm going to take a picture and send it to Shubhi," Tali said. "He doesn't look right to me."

Once she sent the photo, Shubhi's response came quickly.

"You should get him checked out."

Chapter 23

SOMETHING'S NOT RIGHT

That evening, we consulted the green folder we'd packed with Nadav's medical details. The cardiologist Shubhi had recommended worked at a hospital near Parramatta, west of Sydney—an area I'd never visited before. The only thing we knew about the place was its name: The Children's Hospital at Westmead. But at least we knew where to go.

It's on the way to the Blue Mountains, we reasoned. We'll stop by on the way and make sure nothing's wrong.

But soon as we arrived, it was clear something *was* wrong. After a brief wait in the emergency room, Nadav was admitted, the doctor was paged, and we sat around, unsure of what to do.

Well-acquainted with the slow pace of medicine, we had become pretty good at waiting around. In New York, it had been just part of the routine. We knew why we were there, what forms we had to sign, what doctors we would meet. But this wait—so far from home, with no idea what was going on—was disconcerting, to say the least.

I tried to bury my anxiety beneath a veneer of calm.

ॐ

Eventually, some overly enthusiastic clerk, all happiness and light, came over with a clipboard full of forms. "Routine procedure!" he chirped, obviously expecting me to fill them out.

But I refused to sign—a lawyer's son—having noticed a sentence that would have made me personally responsible for the entire cost of Nadav's stay.

"You have to sign," he said, growing impatient.

"I'm not signing anything," I said. "Especially if I don't know how much it will cost."

"*Everybody* signs," he insisted.

"Tell me how much it will cost," I said, increasingly irritated myself, "and then we can talk."

"It depends on what the doctors order," he said.

"Then I'm not signing," I answered, with finality. He stomped off.

ଚ୦ଓଃ

He returned a few minutes later, with his boss—obviously put out.

"You have to sign," she said, firmly.

"I'm not signing anything," I said. "Right now, all I care about is finding out what's wrong with my son."

"But you must," she said, getting angry. "Our procedures require it."

"Are you really going to refuse care to my son if I don't sign this form?" I said, my voice rising. My New York bluntness was taking over, forcing a stalemate, and—eventually—surrender. I held my ground, and they left us alone.

ଚ୦ଓଃ

The cardiologist eventually arrived, prim and tart—all raised-eyebrows and sideways frowns. She ordered some tests and told us that Nadav would be admitted to the cardiac ward. The boys were returned to our cousins' care in Sydney, and our hotel in Katoomba was canceled. And a troubling thought entered my mind: I started to wonder if we might have to delay our return flight as well.

I remember almost nothing about that first night on the cardiac ward, except for the giant, heavy fire doors that guarded the entrance—every ward in the hospital had them—and the low, dimmed lights when we first moved in, long after the evening shift change. The nurse at the front desk gently welcomed us with an air of apologetic understanding, as her colleagues settled Nadav into a proper bed. We must have seemed a little dazed.

When Nadav's brothers returned to visit the following day, we introduced them to the nurse on duty, perhaps hoping that a friendly face might make the situation easier. Sure enough, it was a role she knew well. "Do you know about the heart beads?" she asked, emerging from behind her desk. "Come here, I'll show you." And she led them across the hall to a long steel cabinet, each drawer filled with a selection of colorful glass beads.

Each symbolized a different milestone, she explained. Small red orbs were blood tests, patterned blue cylinders were cardiac catheterizations, and dark striped cubes were surgeries. Some of the drawers were packed with little painted animals: a ladybug represented a scan; red-eared mice, echocardiograms; pastel fish, other procedures. Yellow smiley faces stood for good days, black crystals for bad ones.

The nurse helped the boys pick out some beads for Nadav—a bunch of assorted letters that spelled out "N-A-D-A-V-4-Y-R-S"—along with a length of string and a small pewter heart. She gently dropped them all into a small cotton bag decorated with boats, along with a folded leaflet explaining the program, and handed them to the brothers for safekeeping.

༺༗༻

I studied the leaflet later, amazed at how detailed and exquisite each bead was. Some were beautiful but ominous: a jade ECMO turtle, various emerald "complication" shapes, and an opal "Heart Angel"—a dreaded euphemism used by the cardiac parent community for a child who didn't make it. (A "warrior," on the other hand, is a child who is still fighting.)

These terms may have consoled others, but for us they caused an instinctive shudder. Tali and I didn't believe in angels—or euphemisms.

But some of the other beads seemed hopeful and happy: iridescent charms for birthdays, transparent crystals for transplants, paisley hearts for discharges. My favorite, I decided, was the small blue and white willow-patterned cat, which meant a Super Brave Day.

I was fascinated by the beads, but I hoped that we wouldn't have to collect too many. Let's just get a paisley heart, I thought, bid our farewells, and get back home.

༺༗༻

But the news the next day was not good.

"It's a clot," we were finally told. There was something partially blocking Nadav's new circulation, right in the middle of the Fontan.

Any plumber will tell you what happens when a pipe is blocked: the fluid flowing through builds up pressure, and it starts to leak. And that was exactly what was happening with Nadav's circulation. The puffiness we'd noticed was a clear sign that his pressures were out of whack, causing fluid to leak out of his blood vessels, swelling his abdomen.

His appearance was the only indication that something was wrong. Even a simple blood pressure cuff wouldn't have revealed the problem: the key measurement—central venous pressure—could only be determined by an interventional procedure. When Nadav's CVP was finally measured, it was unusually high—likely causing him unbearable pain.

He must have had some pretty bad headaches, the cardiologist said. Had he been complaining?

I thought back to that night at our cousins' house when Nadav had been so inconsolable, unable to sleep, and my heart sank in guilt—that I'd been so thoughtlessly upset at him when he must have been in such pain.

I am still haunted by the way I lost my temper that night—to not have the empathy to detect that something was seriously wrong, to not have realized how much our son was suffering right in front of our eyes.

෫෬

But that moment had long passed. Now we were here, and the cardiologists were getting nervous. The leakage was a manageable problem; three tubes were inserted into Nadav's chest and abdomen to drain the fluid. But what really worried them was the cause: the obstructed Fontan.

They'd tried giving Nadav anticoagulants to dissolve the clot, but they didn't seem to be working. And even if the clot broke apart, they worried that its remnants might travel to the brain, causing an aneurysm or stroke. "You might want to push your flight back," we were told, confirming my worst fears.

We fired off a bunch of texts to Shubhi, trying to translate what we were hearing. But it was hard to communicate from so far away, and things got garbled—wires crossed, terms confused.

We asked if she could reach out to the cardiologist in Sydney directly to coordinate care. She said she'd try.

It didn't work. The cardiologist on call returned a few hours later, fuming. "I understand that this is a difficult situation for you," she began, in a patronizing tone, "and I will keep Shubhi informed of the decisions we make. But she is not his doctor at the moment. I am."

"I would appreciate it," she concluded, bluntly, "if you could show me the appropriate respect."

She didn't know us well enough to know that this was entirely the wrong approach. Unquestioning deference wasn't our style. Our respect for doctors was built on mutual trust.

৪০৫৪

And so, on the day we were supposed to return home, we found ourselves stuck in a foreign hospital halfway around the world. We had no idea what to do for Nadav. And Nadav's new doctors had no idea what to do with us: our strange accents, our unexpected stubbornness, our aggressive, direct insistence on a particular course of care.

If I had been able to open those drawers full of beads, I would have chosen a black crystal. It was a very bad day.

Chapter 24

SURGERY

The consensus emerged suddenly, clear and grim, from some hidden conference room, in a meeting we were not invited to attend. Nadav's intractable clot required surgery as quickly as possible.

But while the cardiologists agreed that an operation was necessary, it wasn't clear exactly what they intended to do. And—worst for us, who drew resilience from knowledge and planning and close relationships with medical professionals—we still didn't know his new doctors at all.

The irony was that many of my Australian family members had gone into medicine, following in the footsteps of my grandfather and his older brother, although none of them were cardiologists or worked in pediatrics. One of my cousin's classmates from medical school apparently worked as an attending doctor in Westmead's pediatric intensive care ward. But he was off duty, nowhere to be found.

I held out hope that perhaps someone had known my grandfather, somehow crossing paths in the city's relatively small medical community. Perhaps I felt that the connection would bring us some luck; part of me wished he was here to share his calming wisdom. But the doctors we'd met were all too young. He was from a different generation, and his name meant nothing to them.

৪০৪

We were most concerned about who'd operate on Nadav, mindful of Dr. Nguyen's warning about Australia from long ago: *They do things a little differently there.*

Some comfort came from another parent we'd met in the ward, who had only good things to say about Westmead's lead cardiac surgeon. "You'll be in good hands with Dr. Winlaw," she assured us. "Dr. Winlaw is a legend."

Unfortunately, when we asked to meet with Dr. Winlaw, the cardiologist on call shook his head apologetically. "Dr. Winlaw has just left for a six-month sabbatical," he explained—adding, with an exquisite sense of irony: "in America."

Instead, he told us, Nadav's operation would be performed by a talented surgeon whom he simply called "Yishay."

"What kind of name is Yishay?" I wondered. "It might be Hebrew," said Tali, uncertain. "A man's name?"

৪০৪

Given the graying surgeons we'd met in the past, we were taken aback when Yishay turned out to be a young, thin woman with close-cropped brown hair. "I'm Yishay," she said, shaking my hand, an earnest look on her face. "Nice to meet you."

"Well, I'd prefer we didn't have to meet," I said. My go-to joke with doctors.

Yishay smiled briefly, but it soon became clear that she was all business, laying out the various options for the surgery.

There was no question that Nadav was in a tight spot, she admitted. She could try to repair his Fontan circulation, or, depending on what she saw, might even try to revert it back to how it had been after the Glenn. That was a safer option, perhaps, but unsustainable. At times, she'd drift off into thought, musing about possible options, as if we weren't even there.

It was clear that Yishay's first priority was simply to keep Nadav alive. She warned us that this might even mean a stint on ECMO after she'd finished—the horrible heart-lung machine that we'd always thought of as a last resort. "It's a possibility," she said with a shrug.

"We're off the map," Yishay said. "Uncharted territory. I won't really know what to do until I get inside."

୫୦୯୪

Our previous surgeon had drawn a bright line between our world and his, but with Yishay, that line was blurred. She spoke to us with respect—as partners, not as spectators. It was the sort of relationship we always tried to build with cardiologists, but never expected from surgeons. Who was this remarkable woman?

While we were talking, I noticed that she wore a small green *tiki* around her neck—a carved figure native to New Zealand. It triggered happy memories: whenever my father returned from a trip to Auckland, he'd present us each with a plastic *tiki*, strung with a simple length of twine.

I saw it as a good omen, a point of connection, however small—a signal from the universe that we were in good hands.

୫୦୯୪

Nadav's surgery was scheduled for that Wednesday, at eight in the morning. Aside from some slight changes in terminology, the routine was similar to what we were used to in the States. We walked him into the vestibule just outside the operating room (or, as they call it in Australia, the "operating theatre"), and waited for his surgical team to arrive—Tali and I chatting away, as if to ward away our nervousness.

As usual, the anesthesiologist ("anesthetist" in the local lingo, a word I never could pronounce) was the first person to arrive. He seemed older than most of the doctors we'd met, so after he introduced himself, I figured it wouldn't hurt to ask if he knew my grandfather.

"The name rings a bell," he said, thinking for a minute or two—and then it came to him. "Actually, my father shared offices with him," he remembered. "He was a kind man."

"But how do you know him?" he asked me, puzzled by my American accent.

"He was my grandfather," I said. "And this is his great-grandson."

The anesthetist gave me a look of amazement—that of all the children in the world, this one had landed on his list—and I'm sure that same look was on my face too, both of us unable to look away, astonished.

"Take good care of him," I said.

"Oh, we will," he said, patting Nadav's head, but still looking straight into my eyes. "We will."

⁊ಳ

It was time for our pre-surgery routine: the blessing, the kiss, my hand running through Nadav's curls—a ritual as much for us, I realized, as for him.

And then, suddenly, our son was gone—wheeled away by a medical team we didn't really know, led by doctors we had not yet learned to trust. But I'd finally found a link to the Australia I knew. And like the *tiki* that hung around Yishay's neck, that thread somehow gave me the strength to believe that things just might work out.

༄༅

We'd been told that the surgery would last around six to eight hours—which would mean that Nadav would emerge by midafternoon, at the latest. Unlike other hospitals, the nurse at the desk told us that they wouldn't call us with updates. Instead, she handed us a small pager, and said they'd beep when he was done.

"Don't call," she stressed firmly. "Wait for the beep."

So, we tried to keep ourselves busy. We went for a walk, had some lunch, met some visiting cousins for coffee—all the while checking the little beeper, which didn't budge.

༄༅

I wasn't worried about the surgery running long. Ever since the Fontan, I'd always felt an operation ending early was a bad sign—so when the clock struck four, I felt a small sense of reassurance. But as the day drifted from late afternoon to dinnertime, we started getting a little anxious. Tali decided to call the cardiac ward, but there was no update. "We'll page you when he's out," they reminded us. "Wait for the beep."

By 9 p.m., we were seriously freaked out. The hospital had slowly shut down—gift shop shuttered, lights turned down, back doors locked. We saw one of the other parents sitting at an empty cafe table—the one who'd told us about Dr. Winlaw—and Tali sat with her for a while. At least there was someone else for her to talk with.

I just paced.

And then, at 10:15, the beeper finally buzzed, and we rushed upstairs.

☙℀

Once we reached the desk, exhausted and breathless, I asked:

"Is he alive?"

"Yes," the attending nurse assured us, "he's in recovery now."

It took a minute for that *yes* to register, its single syllable rattling around my brain before it finally made sense. And just like that, fourteen agonizing hours of tension suddenly slipped from my shoulders—*yes yes yes*—my body overwhelmed by a deep and grateful relief.

☙℀

We waited to talk with Yishay in the "family room." It was equipped for tragedy, decorated with somber maroon couches, soothing oil paintings (painted by one of the doctors, we'd later find out), and a large box of tissues prominently placed on the center table. But Yishay, excited and exhausted, seemed to think that the worst had been averted. For now.

Yishay explained in detail what she'd done. She'd tried to rework his circulation to something more stable: not quite the Glenn, but hopefully better than the failing Fontan. To do so, she'd kept Nadav on bypass—his heart stopped—for over seven and a half hours. (Someone told us later that she'd had a bite to eat in the morning, said, "Let's get to work," and didn't stop until the sun had set.)

What was most remarkable about Yishay was her patience. It was long past 10 p.m., and Tali and I peppered her with questions for almost an hour. They emerged in a jumble—repeated, rephrased, restated—but Yishay never took a dismissive tone. She walked us through her reasoning, and what she'd done; discussed its implications, and what to watch for; and what to make of the ECMO machine that now kept Nadav alive.

Because, as she'd warned, he had indeed come out on ECMO. Yishay assured us that we shouldn't read too much into it—her patients often needed ECMO. It just gave his heart a chance to recover, she said. It didn't necessarily mean the end was near.

The plan was pretty simple. First, we had to get Nadav off ECMO. Then we'd worry about what came next.

৪৩

It was getting pretty late, but I still had two last questions before we called it a night.

"What do you think of him?" I asked.

"He's tough," Yishay told us. "You can tell when you look at him, inside. His scars are something else. He's one tough kid."

Would he pull through?

"Too early to tell," she said. "But I hope so."

Chapter 25

"I TRUST HIM"

O ver the years, I'd managed to maintain a sense of cautious optimism; a hunch that no matter how dire things
were, they would eventually work out. It would be a
lie to say that it never wavered—during the Fontan, when it
seemed like Nadav wouldn't make it, I stared into the abyss for
forty-five minutes. But we'd somehow gotten past that, and after
he emerged from his fourteen-hour surgery alive I felt confident
that he could survive this too.

୫୦୯୫

After surgery, Nadav was moved to the hospital's pediatric intensive care unit, or "PICU." Security was tighter than it had been
on the cardiac ward: the thick fire door blocking the entrance,
decorated with colorful superheroes, was always locked. We'd
have to push a button and identify ourselves each time we wanted
to be let in.

Inside were the hospital's most critical cases ("SUPERHEROES
FIGHTING BIG BATTLES," the door read) cared for by a new
cast of doctors and nurses. They moved with a practiced intensity
we hadn't seen in the cardiac ward, reminding me of the anesthesiologist we'd met when the twins were born—each action
motivated by a concentrated, deliberate intent.

Nadav's bed had been wheeled to the corner of a large, shared room, parked next to its only window. A polite but focused nurse got him settled, expertly rolling blankets to keep him snug. She glanced at us, smiling, gently placing each origami fold around Nadav's body, deftly avoiding the tubes, wires and lines that lay around his still-open chest.

I suspect that hospitals choose the most experienced nurses to admit a new arrival. The ones we met always had the perfect mix of compassion and expertise—settling both us and our son into an unfamiliar environment, welcoming us into a place where no one wanted to stay.

ॐ

I drove back to our apartment late that night, exhausted, and the next day, I told Gilad and Yaniv what had happened. "Your brother had the operation. He's still not well. But he has great people looking after him."

Life seemed especially vivid that morning. We decided to go for a swim, and as I splashed in the pool with the two boys, every hue seemed saturated with extra color. I hugged them tight, feeling alive in a way I never had before—thankful for our lives, our beating hearts, and the glorious sunshine.

But before long, it was back to the hospital. Their brother was still in critical condition, and I needed to be with him.

ॐ

The corner of the PICU, we learned, was reserved for ECMO patients; it had the most room for the bulky equipment that kept his blood flowing.

Both us and the doctors wanted to get Nadav off ECMO as soon as possible. It kept him alive but was a delicate and fragile system. Two specially trained nurses monitored the circuit constantly, checking the thin plastic lines for clots, as a perfusionist hovered nearby, checking the readings and making small adjustments.

So much could go wrong on ECMO. The doctors hoped he would only need it for four days, max; any longer and his odds would plummet. They tried to disconnect it on the third night—a tricky procedure—but it wasn't right; his heart wasn't ready, and removing the cannulas was deemed to be too risky. They decided to wait until the next day to try again.

୫୦୪

That night, we called Shubhi. We could hear her eyes moisten over the phone—she'd heard he was on ECMO, and she knew its dangers. As her voice cracked, I could tell that her hope had yielded to bleak despair; she was too far away, unable to help. "I'm praying every day," she said.

"To which God?" I asked, knowing that she was a devout Hindu.

"All of them," she replied.

For some reason, I pressed her further. "If we could pick just one," I asked, "who would it be?" We had our own traditions, of course, but I felt it was important to have her faith there with us too.

"Hanuman," she said, definitively—not knowing whether to laugh or cry.

I Googled "Hanuman"—the monkey god—and discovered that in almost every picture he was depicted holding his chest open, blood dripping out, revealing the two deities (Rama and Sita) he was sworn to protect.

I could not think of a better guardian for our son, whose bloody chest was also open, needing protection. So, I printed out the picture and taped it above his bed—the only way I could think of to bring Shubhi closer to his bedside, and perhaps conjure up any hidden power the cosmos might have left.

∞CB

Perhaps it worked. The next day, trying again to remove the ECMO machine, his doctors found themselves in the same situation as the day before. But this time, they judged doing nothing to be riskier than trying to take him off. Out of options, they took a leap of faith—and pulled the cannulas, hoping it would work.

And somehow, his heart kicked in—and started beating again. He was off ECMO.

Yishay was right: *He's one tough kid.*

∞CB

Overcoming the dreaded ECMO machine had lifted my spirits. The day after it had been removed, I planned to leave the hospital early—making it back in time for dinner with his brothers and perhaps even a cold beer.

But that afternoon, as I was preparing to leave, a nurse came by. "We'd like to have a family meeting in the conference room at six," she said.

Family meetings are never good. Good news is delivered at the bedside, as soon as possible. But bad news needs planning and a full cast.

&OCR;

We all gathered in the conference room—Tali and I sitting on a couch, surrounded by Nadav's entire medical team. Sitting directly across from us was the doctor in charge of the intensive care unit, a serious man named Nick. All eyes were on him; it was clear he'd be leading the conversation.

Nick looked around at his colleagues, then at us; paused briefly, and said, "I'm going to be honest with you. Nadav is not doing well."

I felt as if I'd been punched in the stomach. The relief I'd felt earlier was replaced by anxious dread.

"Nadav has a fever, and his white blood cells have spiked," he explained. I could feel Tali at my side, sitting bolt upright.

"There are three possibilities for tonight," Nick continued. "One, he could improve. We don't expect that to happen."

Pause.

"Two, he could stay stable. That's what we're hoping for."

Pause.

"Three, he could get worse. He's already getting all the help we can give him, so if that happens, there's nothing more we can do."

I was shattered, broken into a million pieces—as if Nick's words had been a two-by-four aimed at my gut.

&OCR;

The room was quiet, still; the doctors looked at us, gravely; I said nothing, stunned.

But Tali stayed calm.

"So, what you're saying," she said, "is that it's up to him?"

"I suppose that's right," Nick replied.

"I can live with that," she said. "I trust him."

⁎⁗⁏

Tali was right to trust him. Nadav made it through that night, and many more.

But from that moment onward, I found it hard to be particularly optimistic. It's not that I expected the worst, but after that night, I hoped to avoid any unexpected disappointment. Instead, I tried to keep my emotions level—not too high, not too low—protecting myself from feeling that sort of pain again.

I was grateful for Tali's strength, and I came to rely on it.

⁎⁗⁏

Nadav's final days on ECMO had overlapped with the first nights of Hanukkah—the festival of lights, when we celebrate the miracle of a glorious victory in the face of likely defeat—and a small bottle of oil lasting far longer than anyone could imagine.

It was a calming coincidence for us, parents of a boy whose time seemed to be running short but whose name, after all, echoed the spirit of the holiday—to give beyond expectations.

By tradition, we light a menorah on each of Hanukkah's eight nights—but as flames were banned in the hospital, I contented myself by drawing little candles on a paper calendar I had started using as a journal. I pinned it above his bed, next to the small picture of Hanuman, watchful and vigilant. We needed all the help we could get.

But after that night my perspective began to shift. If I was to have faith, it would be in Nadav—in his small, resilient body, battered by countless procedures and an increasingly unnatural circulation—and in his remarkable ability to adapt, heal, and survive.

Chapter 26

SETTLING IN

U nder the close watch of the PICU staff, Nadav remained intubated and heavily sedated—stable enough for us to settle into a predictable rhythm, a welcome change from the chaos of the previous weeks.

Knowing we were Jewish, one young resident was surprised to see the picture of Hanuman taped to the wall above Nadav's bed. After explaining the story to him, I jokingly asked if there were any other deities he might recommend. "You should put up a picture of David Pocock," he said with a smile.

"Who?" I asked.

"He's a rugby player," said a nurse, laughing.

I explained that I was thinking more along the lines of religious figures.

"Oh, you don't understand," said the resident. "Rugby is my religion. And I *worship* David Pocock."

So, David Pocock went up on the wall, next to Hanuman and the Hanukkah lights. I made sure I picked an especially tough-looking picture—his nose bloodied, body bruised, ready for whatever came next.

ॐॐ

N o longer on emergency footing, I started venturing outside in search of fresh air.

The hospital was nestled next to the mouth of the Parramatta River—at that point a mere trickle, bounded by dense bush, with a thin path running alongside. I discovered a lovely hike, rarely traveled—wildflowers grasping at my heels, goannas sunning themselves on wide rocks. After a while, the path opened into a wide clearing, the gum trees filled with sleeping bats, white long-necked cranes wading quietly in the marsh.

The stream flowed into Parramatta Park, much larger and well maintained, where it became a proper river. A paved road looped alongside, used mostly by cyclists and the occasional slow car. But all around were lush green fields, clutches of swaying trees, and blissful quiet.

৪০৪৪

On Tali's birthday, I arranged a surprise picnic in that park, closer to the hospital. Most of her friends were there, and my family too. They gathered in the bright sun, trying to strike the right tone—not too festive, not too somber. My cousin brought a juicer and a crate of oranges. Someone brought a few bottles of sparkling wine.

Luckily Nadav fell asleep for a nap at exactly the right time, and I was able to coax Tali out of the room, walking down the familiar path to the park. She was astounded to see everyone there, a genuine smile, even a laugh. Small cups of pulpy juice and champagne were passed around; for a few hours at least, caution could be set aside.

In the coming weeks, the park would become our refuge. Tali and I found a small cafe at the bottom of the hill that we would visit whenever we had time—trying to make small talk, distracted by our thoughts.

ঙেওন্স

The boys had moved in with another set of cousins, who had a large house and a pool, but for the time being, anticipating odd hours, I decided to stay in a small apartment my aunt owned on the North Shore. It was close to the boys and not far from where my grandparents had lived.

I drove down their old street one morning, a small detour from my usual route to the hospital—the first time I'd been there since we last visited my grandfather with Gilad. But their house had been sold to strangers long ago, and all I could see from the car was the once-lovely garden, banana tree ripped out, replaced with strange and unknown plants.

ঙেওন্স

As days turned into weeks, we started wandering further afield. The neighborhoods around Parramatta were the heart of Sydney's South Asian community, and one night we stumbled upon a small street full of Indian restaurants. Pungent smells wafted in the warm air; grocery stands piled with colorful vegetables and sacks of basmati rice; windows full of golden statues—including Hanuman, the monkey god, destroyer of evil and protector of the devoted.

We chose a relatively fancy spot for dinner, its sizzling lamb chops slightly too spicy for Tali's taste. We'd arranged to meet an old friend there, downing beers as we told him everything that had happened. Aside from our picnic in the park, it was the first time we'd talked with someone who wasn't a doctor, a nurse, or a relative—and it was hugely cathartic, our pent-up memories pouring out, finally able to relax for the first time in weeks.

A few friends started visiting us in the hospital. A couple whose company we especially cherished brought an odd gift: a kitschy birdcage, complete with a little plastic songbird that every so often would emit a realistic chirp. "It will keep you company," our friend said, knowing that Tali had started spending her nights in a drab room in the hospital's parent hostel.

We were starting to accept the reality of our new situation. We were stuck, not knowing what lay ahead—but although we were far from home, we were not alone.

ଚଞ୍ଚ

With the future unsettled, we needed to start finding moments of normalcy—not just with our friends, but with our sons too. Tali and I had spent every day since the marathon surgery looking after Nadav in the hospital, and we hadn't paid nearly enough attention to Gilad or Yaniv.

Dealing with Nadav's medical issues had always been a challenge for us. But for his brothers, it must have been so much harder—out of the spotlight, battered by second-hand stress, and just as uncertain about what was to come. When we were home, we'd tried to compensate by spending quality time with them as well, whenever we had the time and the energy—and sometimes when we didn't.

For Gilad, that quality time often took the form of spectator sports. The five of us had an annual tradition of seeing a basketball game at a local university: the tickets were cheap, the atmosphere fun, and the level of play relatively high. No matter what sport, a game was always a welcome diversion.

So, I was pleased to discover that the largest stadium in Sydney's western suburbs was not far from the hospital, a half-hour's walk across Parramatta Park. It was midsummer, too early for rugby, but during my morning walk I noticed that the local soccer team, the Western Sydney Wanderers, were playing that night. On a whim, I bought two tickets—and when Gilad came to visit the hospital that afternoon I decided to surprise him. "We're going out tonight," I said. "Let's go have some fun."

☙☙

Parramatta could seem pretty sleepy, at least compared to New York's hustle and bustle, but on game night, it was electric. We ate dinner at a small burger place, surrounded by exuberant fans in red jerseys—and as game time approached, hearing drums and cheers, we all drifted out onto the street. I'd brought Gilad a scarlet t-shirt of his own as a surprise, and he put it on, joining the sea of red, heading toward the match.

The two seats I'd bought—the last available—were the worst in the stadium, right next to the visiting fans' section. Clad in dark blue, scarves swirling, they were from Melbourne; having traveled this far, they were even more boisterous than the home fans, cheering on their side with some brutally colorful language. The only thing separating our red from their blue was a thin aisle lined by nervous-looking security guards.

We felt safe enough, but I worried that the foul language might somehow corrupt Gilad's innocent eight-year-old ears, and after a particularly nasty barrage of f-bombs, I felt I had to say something fatherly. "These are some pretty bad words," I whispered. "So please don't use them at home."

"I *know*, Abba," he said, rolling his eyes. "I've heard it all before. I'm in public school!"

The Wanderers scored the game's first goal, sending our section into a frenzy and the Melbourne fans into despair. One visiting fan, particularly upset, flung his plastic cup directly into the air. Upon its return to earth, it landed on Gilad, hitting him squarely on his shoulder and spilling warm beer into the aisle. Gilad, unhurt, giggled hysterically. We don't remember any of the other goals, but the airborne pint was a highlight I'll never forget.

⁀○‿

The Wanderers eventually took an insurmountable lead; but the Melbourne fans, unbowed, broke out a new chant: "You have to live here, but we get to go home!" they sang, taunting, into the Western Sydney night. "You have to live here…we get to go hoooooome!"

And we headed out too, giddy with the minor transgressions we'd shared, the bad language and spilled beer, forgetting for a few hours that we didn't live here, not really; that our own home—our own teams, our own chants, our own lives—were all so very far away.

Chapter 27

PICU

The Westmead PICU accommodated around twenty-six beds, give or take, reserved for Sydney's most critically ill patients. One of the attending doctors told us that the average length of a stay was just three days, which made me shudder; given the urgency with which new patients were admitted, I could only imagine how many of those stays ended in tragedy. But I was heartened to hear that one patient had remained in the ward for over six months. If Nadav was going to make it, I now realized, it would only be after a long recovery.

Other patients occupied our peripheral vision. We couldn't ignore them, but whether due to respect or our own preoccupations we rarely looked their way. Sometimes nurses would cover multiple patients, loading their vital signs onto Nadav's monitor; Tali and I would try to guess their condition from what we saw. Cardiac kids were easy to spot, with oxygen saturations dipping into the 70s and 80s. We were jealous of those patients with sats at 100 percent, but wary of what else had landed them here.

Every morning, before heading to the hospital, I'd grab the newspaper at my cousin's house, hoping to distract myself with the news of the day. All too often, I'd come across some terrible tale of childhood trauma that concluded with the phrase, "…the child was rushed to Children's Hospital at Westmead." When

I arrived in the PICU, I'd sometimes recognize the new arrival amongst Nadav's neighbors.

Their stories were horrible. A woman had jumped into the path of a train, clutching her daughter; a teen, skydiving for the first time with an instructor, wore a parachute that didn't open; an otherwise healthy toddler suddenly went into cardiac arrest while playing with his father, an EMT who kept him alive for six minutes until his colleagues arrived.

Tali was with Nadav the night after that boy was admitted, quickly bundled into the bed next to ours. All was calm until it wasn't; doctors and nurses suddenly crowding his bedside. His heart had stopped again, and the standard treatment wasn't working—it turned out he was allergic to the epinephrine they used to revive him. But he somehow pulled through.

ഇരുൻ

We spent about a week lobbying for a spot in a solitary room, hoping for some privacy and quiet. But when the opportunity came, it wasn't because of our charm, but rather as a result of suspected infection—solitary rooms were reserved for possible contagions. One positive culture and the patient was quickly isolated, their visitors forced to don bulky yellow robes and uncomfortable paper masks. Luckily, our emergency proved to be a false alarm, and we were allowed to stay in the room for a few more days.

One night, a new patient arrived in the room next door. The parents followed soon after; the father clutching a Koran, the mother sobbing behind the curtains. The next day, a procession of concerned-looking family members streamed in and out, until they suddenly disappeared midafternoon. A nurse poked her head into Nadav's room. "I'm taking the patient downstairs," she said to her colleague—a thinly veiled euphemism whose meaning, to me, was crystal-clear.

Our curtains were hastily drawn for a few minutes. When I was allowed to leave, the room next door was empty, orderlies readying it for the next patient.

∞∞

Nick—the doctor who had led that first family meeting—was in charge of the entire PICU. But even though he bore ultimate responsibility for all of the hospital's most difficult cases, he was always willing to chat.

We quickly came to trust Nick's judgment. He always told us the truth, no matter how brutal. He obviously cared deeply about keeping our son alive. And beneath his stern demeanor was a wry sense of humor, a twinkle in his eyes that emerged when things were calm, giving me permission to exhale.

Underneath the earnest seriousness of the ward, we soon discovered a healthy dose of levity, perhaps a uniquely Australian trait. The doctors' job was to keep desperately ill kids alive, but unless a dire crisis arose, their manner was rarely grim. They never wore white coats, and only very rarely did we ever see anyone wear a tie.

∞∞

Needing a stiff drink after one particularly stressful day, I jokingly asked the doctor on call if they had any "medication" available for parents. "Oh," he replied, "you mean like the kind of medicine that we'd keep in a bottle in a bottom drawer for stressed-out dads?"

"Yes," I said, my hopes raised. He knew exactly what I was talking about.

"Um, no," he replied with a laugh. "None of that around."

৪০৫

Instead, Westmead found other ways to take the edge off—most memorably, a team of clown doctors who roamed the wards in pairs, visiting patients and making mischief.

Ironically, they were the only "doctors" who wore white coats—but for comic effect more than anything else. They eased the hospital's tension with goofy songs and well-worn jokes, occasionally pulling unexpected items out of their pockets: slide whistles, little guitars, stuffed animals—every surprise a well-timed distraction.

But they, too, took their job seriously. Once, at a particularly tense moment, I saw one of them poke his head around the door—I think it was Dr. Silly Billy, a regular we'd come to know well. Rather than burst in, he quickly read the situation; the heaviness of the moment, the look of concern on our faces. He glanced at me, as if to say, "bad time?"—and when I signaled "yes," he nodded in understanding, and moved on.

৪০৫

The PICU doctors changed shifts every few days, overlapping for a day-long hand-over, and so we found ourselves having to adjust to new personalities once or twice a week.

I have fond memories of many of the attending doctors responsible for the day-to-day decision-making in the PICU: a gray-haired veteran who'd hum thoughtfully whenever we asked a tricky question; a well-built, balding doctor with a quick laugh and a gentle demeanor; a tall, glamorous woman, whose light-hearted manner might, in another context, be considered flirty.

They were patient, thoughtful, open—except for one attending doctor, who we instantly disliked. His answers were vague and unfocused, as if talking to us was a chore.

ഇൗൽ

I once asked Nick what it was like to be responsible for dealing with parents, especially when he had to deliver bad news. It wasn't easy, he said, but it was part of his job. And by that point in his career, it was something he was used to.

When training less experienced doctors, he taught them to be mindful of three things. The first two seemed obvious to me: "Be honest and direct. Don't give false hope." But the third was unexpected. "Make sure you get the sex of the child right," Nick would urge his staff. Too frequently, they got it wrong.

We knew firsthand why all three were so important, why honesty is useless without empathy. Only once did a doctor call Nadav a "she"—confused, perhaps by his long, curly hair—and it stung, a careless slip of the tongue that opened an uncrossable chasm between us.

ഇൗൽ

The other avoidable source of tension was whenever someone called us "Mom" or "Dad," as if our real names were irrelevant. Our own children didn't even call us "Mom" or "Dad"—they'd always used the Hebrew terms "Ima" and "Abba" instead.

But I felt some empathy for those medical professionals who had to remember so many faces. I myself have a terrible memory for names and would often forget them, even those of people we saw often. It could be very embarrassing, especially if Tali wasn't there to remind me who was who.

Too often, hospital IDs were unreadable, dangling uselessly in the folds of a shirt or beneath a jacket. I'd have to wait until their body angled just the right way, ever so briefly, and crane my neck to read the tiny type.

I often wished that hospitals issued everyone special IDs—staff and parents alike—with names written in huge block letters. It would certainly have made things a lot less awkward.

ଔଓ

Whenever a new PICU doctor rotated in, Tali and I would bombard them with questions about what they planned to do. We wanted to get up to speed quickly; it was important to us that we were on the same page. But most doctors would plead for patience, politely asking us to wait.

As one told me, pointedly:

"We have to get to know him."

This could have easily been misinterpreted as a deflection, a ploy to keep us at arm's length—but I came to appreciate it as one of the wisest things we ever heard a doctor say.

Not only did it demonstrate a great deal of humility, it also revealed a critical insight. The best doctors realized that their role was not to heal—only Nadav could do that—but to give Nadav the best opportunity to heal himself.

And to do that properly, they had to get to know him.

ଔଓ

Nadav was monitored constantly and his blood was drawn almost daily, but much about his condition remained a mystery.

A few weeks after his stint on ECMO, the doctors decided it was safe to reduce his sedation—but as he gradually started stirring, however slightly, I noticed that his movements seemed to only happen on his right side. I mentioned something about it to the doctor on call—was I imagining things?—and he agreed it was worth a test. So, he scheduled a CT scan, and we waited for the results.

Although the fourteen-hour surgery had brought some stability to Nadav's circulation, it also left many wounds, inside and out: a small contact burn on his forehead, perhaps caused by the oxygen sensor left too long in the same place, and an inexplicably deep three-inch gash on his leg, which the doctors called a perfusion injury. To my untrained eyes, it looked bad—the raw, red flesh cutting almost to the bone.

A plastic surgeon was brought in to consult on the leg, but after considering a skin graft, his doctors decided against it. It was just too risky, they said. Let's see how it heals.

སོୠ

We had also been told of another troubling diagnosis: a particularly nasty fungal infection called aspergillus had taken root inside Nadav's chest, threatening his lungs. So, the doctors left his chest open, worrying that closing things up would allow it to fester.

"Aspergillus isn't great news in a patient this sick," one doctor told us. "It's all around us, normally, and a healthy body can deal with it. But an infection in people with compromised lung function can be bad. Really bad."

And so, they started a course of an antifungal medicine called voriconazole—deeming it necessary, despite everything else that battered his weak and debilitated body.

It was just one of the many medicines and infusions that the doctors had prescribed, hoping to keep our son alive. A precipitous balancing act—and every day we feared its toppling.

৪৩

N adav was in no shape to leave the hospital, much less board an airplane. His cardiologists had quickly shot down any talk of medical evacuation, unwilling to give us false hope. We were stuck indefinitely, our return tickets refunded as airline credit.

But when we spoke with Nick, we were surprised to hear him insist that in his opinion, Nadav needed to be home. "He should not be here," he told us matter-of-factly, as if his presence was evidence of a cosmic imbalance. "His home is in New York, not Australia."

This sounded more philosophical than practical. It was clear that any sort of air travel was impossible, and in any case, there was no medical reason to fly him anywhere. The immediate goal now was merely to keep him alive, and in his condition, it was unlikely that he would survive another procedure. But in retrospect, I wonder if Nick had quietly asked around. I imagined him asking his friends over a pint: "If you had to, how might you get this boy home?"

৪৩

Australia is a large country, sparsely populated; and as a major trauma center, Westmead's staff were well-acquainted with the tricky logistics of moving sick kids around. There was a helipad on the roof, not far from the outdoor patio attached to the parents' room. Sometimes, while taking a break, we'd hear a whir and a whoosh of air, signaling a new arrival.

One of the helicopter services was headquartered along a street where we sometimes parked. Whenever we picked up our car, we'd spend a few minutes wondering whether someone there could help us figure out how to get back.

Of course, a helicopter wouldn't be enough. Getting Nadav home would require an aircraft capable of crossing the Pacific and solving some tricky logistics. For instance: Could it be a commercial flight, or would he need a chartered jet? How could oxygen be reliably administered for a day-long trip, much less all of the other things needed to keep him alive? Who would arrange it? Who would pay for it? And, most terrifying—what if he didn't make it?

The challenges were complicated and countless. And without a medical reason to bring him home, the whole thing was moot. An interesting thought exercise for Nick, and a nice dream for us, to be sure. But nothing more.

Chapter 28

TALKING

O f all the months to be stuck in Australia, I suppose that we were lucky to have been stranded in December. As our friends back home slogged through a New York winter, Australians were still enjoying their summer vacation.

To keep Nadav's brothers entertained and take advantage of the fine weather, we signed them up for a local sports camp. They spent their days roaming cricket pitches and rugby fields—charging into both with a New Yorker's typical aggressiveness—and even made a few friends.

It wasn't the boys' first experience with Australian sports. I'd taught them what I knew about cricket early on, and when they were young, we'd occasionally play in the park across the street. The old cricket bat we owned was a little heavy for the twins, so they preferred to bowl instead—sprinting frantically across the concrete playground, flinging a plastic practice ball wildly in Gilad's direction. Other kids would stop and stare, baffled by the strange sport. Only their Caribbean nannies really understood what was going on.

And so, buoyed by our successful soccer outing, I decided to take Gilad to his first-ever cricket match.

∞ဢ

My cousins had managed to rustle up some tickets to the Sydney Cricket Ground, excited to give us a proper introduction to their native sport. Unlike the slow-moving, traditional form of cricket—each match lasting five days!—we were going to a much shorter three-hour version designed for families. The teams wore bright purple and neon green rather than the traditional white; fans cheered loudly, waving miniature cricket bats; and big blasts of flame shot upward after each big hit.

The first half was great fun—a clear blue, gorgeous day; my cousins' good company; Gilad eagerly soaking it all in. By the time the teams took a break halfway through, I'd finally started to unwind. And then, as we stood up to stretch our legs, my phone rang.

It was Tali. The hospital had called.

Leaving Gilad with his cousins, I wandered around the empty mezzanine, trying to hear what she had to say. I could tell that it wasn't good news, but it was hard to understand her clearly, my second-hand phone crackling with intermittent static. I paced frantically looking for a better signal, hanging up and redialing every few minutes. All I can really remember about that call today was the terrible reception.

But eventually, the message got through. The results of the CT scan were in, and they weren't good. Nadav had had a small stroke during his surgery, most likely due to oxygen deprivation. We'd be meeting a new doctor—a neurologist—the next day.

∞ဢ

In shock, I returned to my seat, my body tense, my mind reeling.

I asked what I'd missed, obviously distracted. The home crowd was going bonkers; my cousin's team (the visitors, in purple) were in the midst of an epic collapse. But my cousin just shrugged, resigned to their incompetence. He seemed more concerned about me.

It was clear to them, and probably Gilad too, that something had happened. But not knowing the details, I didn't want to talk about it. I felt detached, as if I wasn't really there.

හිටස

T he next day, we finally faced Tali's greatest fear—*neurology*, the word she would never let Shubhi utter.

Most parents I know think of their children as smart, and we were no exception. But Nadav *was* smart—a quiet, gentle thoughtfulness that had charmed his teachers in preschool. I suppose we came to take it for granted: despite everything going on in his body, there was never anything wrong with his brain.

Standing next to a computer screen, the neurologist gently tried to explain what seemed to have happened—how the limited oxygen during seven and a half hours on bypass had most likely caused a minor stroke.

It was too much for me to absorb at once. The doctor was considerate and patient, but he was speaking a foreign language. What was an *infarction* again? What did it mean that it was *ischemic*? We'd spent the past four years becoming experts on hearts; we knew nothing about the brain.

I felt helpless, like an unprepared sixth-grader staring at an unexpected pop quiz. We'd become so used to speaking with doctors as peers. Now, we were remedial students at the first page of the textbook.

Our distress must have been obvious to the doctor, who offered a note of reassurance after patiently fielding our many questions. "You know, kids are pretty resilient," he said. "And brain plasticity is a real thing."

What he really meant was that a seminar in neurology wasn't necessary. That ship had sailed; the damage already done. Instead, we needed to get smart about rehab—to challenge Nadav to retrain his mind, and his body, to reconnect whatever connections had been lost.

೮೮೦೮೪

After Nadav's stroke was diagnosed, a steady stream of therapists started to appear at his bedside. There were physical therapists, who helped him sit awkwardly in an oversized, specially constructed wooden chair; occupational therapists, who used toys and games to encourage him to use his weakened hands; and music therapists, who sang gentle songs that filled the room.

But even the smallest tasks were a challenge. It was nearly a month after we'd first arrived in the PICU, and Nadav was still in terrible shape. Long rubber drains draped over the side of his bed, slowly draining fluid from his abdomen. And he remained intubated, his breathing supported by a large ventilator whirring at his bedside.

"When can we extubate?" we'd ask persistently. His doctors wanted the tube out too. But there was nothing they could do. Nadav's lungs, surrounded by excess fluid, were unable to support independent breathing. The question nevertheless became part of our everyday routine: a fleeting hope, a daily disappointment.

Since intubation was an unfortunate reality, we had to work around it. But it wasn't easy. There was a higher risk of something accidentally blocking Nadav's airways, so he wasn't allowed to drink. And since the tube pressed against his vocal cords, he couldn't make a sound.

So, we were surprised to meet a new face at the bedside one day—a bubbly, enthusiastic woman who introduced herself as Gloria, one of the hospital's speech therapists.

"But he's intubated," we said, confused. "He can't speak."

"He can still communicate," she said, brightly.

੪ଠଓ

G loria began by focusing on Nadav's eyes. In the first session, she asked us to choose two of the many books that had piled up around his bed.

Reading had become a way to bring some normalcy to our time together, helping us ignore the ever-beeping monitors and the sterile sameness of the room. The hospital had a small library that we eagerly raided, stacking precarious towers of blocky picture books all over. Soon enough we ran out of flat surfaces to put them on.

Stretching her arms wide, Gloria held two books far apart—one to his left, the other to his right—and then asked, "which one would you like to hear?" It took a bit of practice, but eventually Nadav learned to look at the book he wanted. And we read it to him, a happy reward.

With Nadav intubated, unable to talk, there was none of the goofy back-and-forth we'd enjoyed in the biggie bed back home. The best I could hope for was to see his bright eyes patiently focused on the page. Even if he was asleep, I'd read to him anyway, the nurses listening as they cared for other patients. And once he was able to choose the book he wanted, it became even better. We could finally read together.

੪ଠଓ

One day, making small talk with Gloria, we discovered that her family came from Kythera—that Greek island we'd visited long ago with Gilad and loved. We had a great time sharing happy memories of the place with her—the beautiful beaches, rugged hills, and the hotel manager who'd excitedly asked my mother's name. Like every coincidence we'd ever encountered, it gave us strength and hope.

One day, Gloria brought along a small blue vase, packed with dried yellow flowers. Look, she said, pointing to the words "Kythera" inscribed on the side. "I keep this in my office, to remember where I'm from."

ಬಂಡ

Gloria's strategy was to engage Nadav in what she called "fun and familiar activities"—books, songs, puppets—reasoning that these familiar movements might make it easier for him to recover his skills. She started bringing small bottles of bubble liquid to our sessions, holding a small wand in front of Nadav's lips, encouraging him to blow. Sometimes she'd blow some herself to show him how it was done—small iridescent globes floating around the bed, eventually landing gently on his crisp white sheets.

Nadav did his best to blow too. Even if he was only able to round his lips, he made the effort. And after a while, he was able to do it—just barely. A small bubble bulged past the wand, and we all cheered.

ಬಂಡ

Strange as it might seem, I struggle to remember our boys' first words—despite the excitement I felt when they were first uttered.

Overshadowed by the millions of words they've uttered since—whispered complaints, angry yells, funny stories, "PLEASE CAN I HAVE THIS, PLEASE, PLEASE, PLEASE"—the simple act of talking has become less magical. I suppose that words, like so many other things, are just another marvel that we come to take for granted as our children grow older.

But as Gloria tried to help Nadav regain his speech, I once again felt that same sense of amazement. A month of bubbles finally inspired a word. Gloria had asked him if he wanted the lights on or off, and he answered, moving his lips ever so slightly…

"Off."

Silent, yes, croaked past a tube—but a word nonetheless!

My heart leaped, overjoyed; the pride I felt was the same I'd experienced when each of our boys first spoke. Even if he couldn't make a sound, he could "talk" again. "Nadav just answered a question by mouthing a word!" I reported to my family later that evening, full of excitement. "It's wonderful to be able to 'hear' him."

The "word" was the first of many. In her notes, Gloria wrote that aside from the noisy ventilator, the main limitation to Nadav's communication was "our inability to lip read his long responses." At times, the scene was comical, as if we were all playing a strange game of charades—Nadav persistently mouthing a word we didn't understand, each of us guessing frantically what it might be.

And eventually, he talked, for real. Small, raspy sounds, somehow wrestling their way past the infernal breathing tube, one at a time. It was amazing to see, and to hear; his rediscovered voice a miraculous triumph—our first glimpse of hope amidst weeks of despair.

Chapter 29

OUTSIDE

As time wore on, our excitement about Nadav's words faded, tempered by the reality of his deteriorating condition. Despite the surgery, the amount of fluid leaking from his blood vessels showed no signs of decreasing. He'd had three drains placed before the operation, and he emerged from surgery with another. The thin clear tubes flowed from his abdomen into squarish containers beside his bed, graduated lines marking the total amounts on the side. In the weeks to come, these drains were our only regular indication of his internal pressures. As long as fluid kept flowing through, things were still not right.

All of that fluid, of course, had to be replaced. An IV ran into Nadav's arm, delivering a constant infusion of new blood products to balance out those losses and fortify his blood—mainly consisting of "fresh frozen plasma" (FFP), albumin, or both. Nadav was a first-class customer of the blood bank, and we silently thanked all the unknown donors who'd given the blood that kept him alive.

Tali would arrive at his bedside each morning, lifting up each container to peer at the pale red mixture within, asking the nurses for the totals from the night before. I started a spreadsheet— one of my trusted coping mechanisms—and duly recorded each amount, hoping the colored lines on the chart would fall to zero, and disappear.

Unfortunately, they didn't. Six weeks after the surgery, the total fluid collected by his two drains had spiked to one and a half liters a day. A passing doctor called him "the sickest boy in the ward"—no small achievement in a PICU that handled Sydney's most critical cases.

❧

It was no surprise when Nick called a second family meeting. And as before, characteristically direct, he told us the bad news. "We don't know how long Nadav has left," he told us, "but it's our opinion that your son is going to die. He's not a candidate for surgery, here or in the States, and if anyone told you he was, I'd be really suspicious of their motives."

This news was not as devastating as what we'd heard in the first family meeting. It was clear Nadav was in bad shape; we'd feared for a while that we'd have to bury him in Sydney. The only cemetery we knew was the one where my grandparents were buried, fifteen miles to the east.

Medical details calmed us, so we discussed the specifics of what was going on, and what scenarios we might expect—and then, at some point, a cardiologist off to the side chimed in. "You shouldn't give up hope," she said.

It was a comment that made no sense to me, and I told her so. "We were just told he was going to die, right?" I snapped. "What hope is there left?"

❧

The next day, to our great surprise, Nick suddenly announced that he wanted to take Nadav outside.

Unlike the urban hospitals we were used to in the States, Westmead had spacious grounds. In the garden was a vast playground anchored by a big pirate ship, large sun-blocking sails overhead, surrounded by fragrant flowers. Another shadier courtyard outside the staff cafeteria featured a thin stream that flowed down from a small pagoda and a cluster of rocks on either side that our boys liked to climb. And it was warm—January, the height of the Sydney summer.

Despite Nadav's condition, Nick reasoned, there was no reason for him to stay inside. He apparently thought the fresh air would be therapeutic—for us, if not for Nadav—and he was in charge. So, he assembled a team (another doctor and two nurses) and planned an outing.

It wasn't a great distance—maybe twenty yards to the elevator, down three floors, and then another couple of hundred feet—but since Nadav was in such bad shape, there was a lot to plan. He needed a smaller ventilator, something that could attach to his bed. All of his drains had to be carefully aligned, so that they wouldn't catch on anything while we walked. And since it was so sunny, he needed a hat.

The nurses fussed about, making sure that everything was in the right place, until one slung a bright red emergency backpack over her shoulder—ready to go. And fifteen minutes later (because everything in hospitals takes just a little bit longer than you'd like), the procession began.

It took us a while to get outside—someone forgot the elevator key, I think—but it was well worth the effort. It was a beautiful day, sun blazing overhead, and we were giddy with excitement. Nadav calmly feeling the fresh air, someone holding an umbrella over his head to protect him from the sun, his brothers racing around the pirate ship, us adults chatting happily in the shade. One of his nurses pulled together a collection of fresh green leaves, nestling them gently in his hand.

Nick seemed proud that we'd made it out, allowing himself a smile every so often. But mostly, he watched—an eye on Nadav's breathing, an eye on his ventilator, seeing how he responded to his new surroundings.

∞∞

We went outside again and again, each time a special treat. Tali and I would lobby Nick almost every day, disappointed when something—staffing, weather, crises—didn't allow it. The nurses liked it too, free from the monotony of the ward, feeding off our smiles. We started taking different routes through the hospital, not always the most direct ones, to make it a little more interesting. Once, we even ventured outside at night to look at the stars.

It was clear that Nadav liked being outside, although he was so weak it was sometimes hard to tell. My father had sent him a New Zealand All-Blacks cap, which he'd wear under the umbrella if it was especially sunny. He'd watch his brothers playing, head tilted to one side; they'd leap across the rocks along the stream, careful not to get their feet wet, or climb to the top of the pile, nimbly negotiating crevices and cracks. Every so often, we'd call out, reminding them to stay where he could see them.

But Nadav was the center of attention. We'd watch his expressions, making sure he was comfortable, hoping for a hint of a smile. Nick, ever vigilant, watched the monitor.

∞∞

The trips became almost routine, and we found ourselves starting to ignore the medical equipment that came with us—the rectangular drainage boxes below; the IV pole, reliably dosing his many medicines through dozens of spaghetti-like lines; the portable ventilator that gently helped him breathe, purring a constant, low hum. Fading into the background, it was white noise we rarely noticed.

Until one of our sunny afternoons outside, when—without warning—Nick suddenly switched off the ventilator. The hum stopped, leaving an empty silence. No sound at all, aside from the thin sound of the breeze quietly rustling the trees, and an occasional chirp from a passing bird.

Finger pressed to his upper lip, Nick stood, deep in thought. As the seconds ticked by, he watched Nadav intently, like a chess player feeling his way through the puzzle of the board. And then, just as suddenly, he switched it back on.

Later, when we asked, he answered simply: "I just wanted to see how he'd react."

⁖⁗

The decision to take Nadav outside was one of the most remarkable choices we'd ever seen a doctor make. It served no obvious medical purpose—and yet we knew it was not merely a palliative favor for a hopeless cause. It was clear that Nick considered it to be an essential part of Nadav's care, a critical opportunity to help him heal, and at heart, a deeply human thing to do.

Chapter 30

DNR

Nick's outings made our time at Westmead bearable, but they did nothing to address Nadav's fundamental issues. The drainage from his abdomen continued to increase. By mid-January, it had soared to almost two and a half liters—as much as it been just after his marathon surgery a month before.

The amount of fluid wasn't the only thing that concerned his doctors, who also ordered regular tests to make sure that proteins weren't starting to leak out as well. If they appeared in the fluid, it would be an ominous sign of the "wasting" disease that many Fontan patients experience in their teenage years. The tests were maddeningly inconclusive, but we sensed that he had managed to avoid the worst.

Still, as we watched the numbers grow, we felt more and more helpless. There wasn't much we could do.

৪৩৫৪

As the drains increased, it became harder to keep Nadav stable. His blood pressure started to dip at night, causing the monitor to erupt in all sorts of frightening beeps. Immediately, a concerned resident would appear at the bedside—staring intently at the screen, hand reaching for his pager.

In turn, Tali would stare at the doctor, making sure that he'd avoid any rash decisions, ready to push back against a knee-jerk instinct to do this or that. We'd consented to a course of inotropes to help his circulation, but worried that if we relied too much on drugs, things could spiral out of control. "Don't you dare increase the dose," her stare would say, knowing that a short-term solution could cause a long-term setback.

If they would just give him more fluid, she reasoned, and trust his body to find the right balance—Nadav would make it through the night.

♜♖

Someone suggested that we consider a lymphatic embolization—an intentional blockage of the lymphatic passages that, as rumor had it, had helped similar patients elsewhere. The truth was, nobody really knew how the lymphatic system worked. One specialist on staff had trained briefly with a famous doctor in the States and was willing to try it. The risks were minimal, and who knew? It just might work.

So, we agreed. What else could we do?

The procedure didn't work. In fact, it made it worse. After the intervention, his drainage went haywire. Back in December, we'd come to expect around a half liter a day, but by the end of January, he was losing an average of five—sometimes as much as six or seven. On one day in early February, he topped out at over nine liters of fluid loss—one of his three drains accounting for four liters alone.

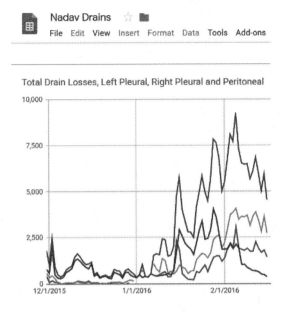

Whatever was going on, it was clearly unsustainable. And—aside from doing our best to keep him alive—we didn't have a plan.

𝔰𝔬𝔠𝔤

The one thing that we could rely on was the generosity of Westmead's extraordinary nurses, who day in and day out did their best to care for Nadav, no matter the prognosis. I was always impressed by their unflappable calm, their quiet confidence, and their clear-eyed ability to handle any crisis—all while dealing with us parents: questioning, opinionated, exhausted.

A nurse once surprised me by telling me that she preferred working in the pediatric ICU to the adult ICU. I couldn't imagine the tragedy of having to watch even a single child die before their time, I'd told her, rather than a patient who'd been lucky to live a full life.

"In the PICU, most of them make it," she countered. "In the ICU, most of them don't."

৪০৫৪

The lead cardiothoracic nurse practitioner, who set the tone for much of his care, was named Glenda. I'd never met a Glenda before, and I kept misremembering her name as Glinda, the good witch from *The Wizard of Oz*. We soon realized that she shared many traits with her almost-namesake. But there was no magic to it. Like the best nurses we'd come to know, she understood the simple power of basic kindness.

One of Nadav's medications caused a frustratingly persistent itch. Even when sedated, he'd involuntarily lift his right arm, and scratch himself, blindly. It was terribly frustrating, and nobody really knew what to do. Doctors were reluctant to stop the medication; and so, unable to stop the scratching, his nurses would bind his hand in a blanket, sometimes even tying it down to the side of his bed.

One overnight nurse, however, had a different solution. She spent her entire shift gently holding his arm, caressing it with her hands, and singing lullabies deep into the night as he slept. Had we not asked in the morning whether his arms had been tied down, we wouldn't have known about this simple act of tenderness—her solving of the problem, if only for one night, with a simple, generous touch.

৪০৫৪

Two months into our stay at Westmead, it was becoming harder and harder for me to cope with what seemed like an increasingly hopeless situation. Dealing with stress had become second nature for us, but every so often, my emotions would get the better of me. Cracks started to show.

I admit that there is nothing more liberating than storming out of a hospital when it all becomes too much. I'd do it every so often at Westmead, especially whenever something upset the delicate balance we'd formed around his bedside—probably a few times too often, in retrospect. But it was great to just leave and disappear, left alone to shake your fist at the world, and let out all of the unspoken rage we rarely acknowledged.

At one especially frustrating moment in Sydney—too many people visiting, too much going on—I walked out, started the car, and drove for half an hour back to the small apartment we'd borrowed, blasting dance music at full volume along the desolate highway.

Back in my empty bedroom, I stood in the silence, just breathing—happy that I was alone, here, and that (for a few minutes at least) everything else was far away, back there.

෨෬

Westmead was the only hospital we visited that had a psychologist as part of the cardiac team. Our sons made it clear they didn't want to talk to a stranger, too caught up in the trauma of the moment, but Tali and I saw her weekly.

The best thing about the sessions was having an hour to talk about how we were feeling and coping, without the minute-by-minute distractions and crises that we dealt with constantly. We needed that space to step back and just let everything out.

The psychologist would always start the session by asking how we were doing. Once, in a sudden fit of honesty, I answered that I was dealing with the pressure by overeating.

"Well," she said, in a friendly tone. "You do burn a lot of calories when you're stressed."

It was kind of her to say so. But anyone who noticed my extra pounds could tell it wasn't true.

ଚୈଓଷ

One afternoon, Nick sat us down in the side room, a somber look on his face. It wasn't a family meeting; just the three of us. But it was as serious as meetings get. Given Nadav's condition, he said, we should consider putting a "DNR" order on his chart. "Do not resuscitate"—meaning that if Nadav was to go into cardiac arrest, the nurses wouldn't attempt to revive him.

After discussing it for a few minutes, there was no question about what to do. Nick warned us that CPR wouldn't work anyway; it would be painful for him and for us, at least twenty minutes of ineffective assault—and ultimately futile. We listened as he spoke, his words tinged with the experience of someone who's seen things he'd rather forget, and signed onto the DNR, hoping it would never be needed.

It's strange, but I don't remember being particularly upset by that conversation. Perhaps we'd become so used to facing the possibility of Nadav's death that it no longer shocked us. Or perhaps we simply refused to believe that it would ever happen.

ଚୈଓଷ

A few days after the DNR went on Nadav's chart, Tali asked our social worker for the packet given to parents when their child died. We knew it existed; I'd long suspected that helping the parents at the end was a social worker's main task, even if was never openly discussed.

The social worker was taken aback, a little surprised by the question. "Um," she mumbled, "I don't think so."

"Why not?" asked Tali. "What secrets are in there? Don't you think we can face it?"

"We just don't like parents to deal with it until they need to," she answered.

But after a few days, she relented, giving us the packet. It was unassuming: a large, rectangular envelope composed of rough, laid paper with blue lettering.

It sat in a makeshift pile of books by Nadav's bedside. Tali never opened it.

Chapter 31

NO END IN SIGHT

By the beginning of February, ten weeks after our arrival in Westmead, hoping for improvement seemed increasingly unrealistic. Nadav's drains continued their inexorable flow, keeping us stuck in a maddening stasis.

We had endured so much. My small paper calendar, still pinned to the wall, now consisted of four well-worn pages, inscribed with nurses' names and daily milestones. And Nadav now had enough heart beads to fill a small cotton bag—including a dozen little porcelain "Brave Day" cats.

He was never well enough to play with the beads, but his brothers had great fun with them, carefully choosing out intricate patterns as they threaded them onto a thin nylon string. The line was long enough to span the room; but one day, trying to attach it to the wall, the boys pulled too tight—and it snapped in two, beads suddenly clattering to the floor.

We scooped them back into the bag, searching every inch around Nadav's bed, and placed it carefully on an upper shelf— fearful that if it happened again, some of them might be lost.

The beads had become as precious as gemstones. They perfectly captured the emotions of hospital life, not just the events. And they were beautifully, thoughtfully made—glowing with a subtle emotional energy that reminded us of all we'd achieved.

We cherished them like battlefield medals. They made us feel like heroes.

೫෮ೞ

We still had no idea how long we might have to stay in Sydney. This was difficult enough for us to accept, to be sure; but even more so for Nadav's brothers. Our family did their best to keep Gilad and Yaniv entertained, but it was a terrible situation for them—a brother in hospital, critically ill; their parents distracted and exhausted, far away from the familiar comforts of home.

Someone suggested that one of us bring the boys back to the States for the spring semester, arguing that they needed "normalcy." But we never seriously considered it. I always felt it was important for us to stay together, and Tali agreed. Instead, we emailed their schoolteachers with frequent updates, receiving scanned homework packets in return, their absences officially recorded as "Extenuating Family Circumstances."

The Australian summer vacation was coming to an end, time for everyone to go back to school—and for our sons, we decided, to do the same. We enrolled Gilad in his cousin's primary school—where at least he'd have a relationship with one of the other kids. And we found a kindergarten for Yaniv, run by a lovely, understanding South African woman, who quickly took to him, warmly introducing him to the group. It was the first time they'd ever worn school uniforms, and they looked adorable. We went with them on the first day and found the teachers to be sympathetic and kind.

School made things a little more normal: new kids to meet, some sense of structure, a daily routine. The boys weren't thrilled to have homework, of course, but it gave them something to do, distracting them from the hospital's suffocating stress. And I suppose going to school in a foreign country was a unique life experience.

For all we knew, we'd be there for months longer. So, they sat for school photos, like everyone else. Gilad even tried out for the cricket team.

∞✿∞

One morning, I came across a story in the *Sydney Morning Herald* that eerily mirrored our own situation. A teenage Australian girl, born with a heart defect similar to Nadav's, was stranded in Columbus, Ohio. Her family had brought her to the States for a treatment that proved unsuccessful, and there was nothing more her doctors could do. There was no medical reason to bring her back; she was coming home to die.

Someone had started an online campaign to cover their costs, which had raised over $250,000—more than enough to pay for her flight.

Tali and I wouldn't have been comfortable asking for help so publicly. We didn't want to be a heartbreaking story, or a worthy cause. Luckily, we had enough money to get by. My cousins had provided housing for me and the boys, other relatives had lent us a minivan, and a strong American dollar and other Australian savings were enough to cover our other expenses.

Still, it wasn't clear who would pay for Nadav's stay at Westmead. The hospital's billing department had spent the past three months trying to navigate the tricky logistics of our American insurer to no avail. Every so often, I'd head up to their offices on the third floor, calmly explaining what I knew about the claims system. They'd nod to each other with vague understanding, not really getting it, and then spend the next week or so sending faxes into the ether or being bounced around American phone trees—until frustration set in and they summoned me again.

The insurance policies were truly baffling. One helpful representative assured us that aside from a $150 deductible, the costs of Nadav's stay would be covered completely. This reassured me, until he realized that he was wrong: Australia was in fact out-of-network—about as out-of-network as one could get, really—leaving us responsible for up to 40 percent of the final bill.

This terrified me, until I discovered that this was wrong too. We would only have to pay an out-of-pocket maximum of $2,500, news that helped me sleep a little easier. But only a little: nobody was ever completely sure what the rules were until the claims were processed and the bills paid out.

In the meantime, the hospital still hadn't seen a dime. Although our conversations were polite and respectful, their sideways glances whenever we talked made it clear that they were still a little nervous.

⚭

In early February, we had a visit from the friends who'd given us the birdcage when we first arrived at Westmead ten weeks before. This time, they brought another unique gift—this one for Nadav. It was a dangling Chinese charm, a red pendant with inscribed calligraphy, golden peanuts hanging below.

"I have no idea what it is," our friend said, "but I just loved it, and I know it will take care of him."

One of Nadav's nurses the following week spoke Chinese, and we asked her what the calligraphy meant. She held her glasses to her eyes, squinting—and read:

"SAFE TRAVELS."

The message seemed a little ridiculous at the time. We had nowhere to go, and no reason to go anywhere.

But soon enough, the charm would come through. And when it did—proving to us, not for the last time, that miracles do indeed happen—those little golden peanuts would hang from his bed, dangling in the wind.

Chapter 32

A PATH HOME

The miracle wasn't a miracle, not really. It was just doctors doing what doctors do: searching for new ways to help those who need it. And it was also Tali just doing what Tali did best—persistently searching for an answer to a medical puzzle, confident that knowing as much as possible would eventually reveal a solution.

Ever since Nadav was first diagnosed, Tali spent hours at Westmead immersing herself in the details of pediatric cardiology, searching medical journals for anything that might help—squinting at PDFs on a tiny smartphone screen late at night.

Those late nights paid off when she came across an article in the medical journal *Catheterization and Cardiovascular Interventions*. It was published in November, around the same time Nadav had been admitted to Westmead. Three doctors at the Children's Hospital of Philadelphia (CHOP) had successfully completed what they called a "Transcatheter Fontan takedown"—a way to revert Fontan circulations to the more stable Glenn without surgery.

They'd tried it on three patients, two of whom survived.

Tali discovered the paper late at night, in her little hostel room at Westmead, and quickly realized that the procedure might theoretically be used to help Nadav. Excitedly, she wrote to Shubhi, asking if Nadav might be a candidate for the procedure.

"I'll ask," Shubhi wrote back.

A few days later, a response came from Dr. Jonathan Rome—one of the doctors who'd performed the procedure. He had reviewed Nadav's medical records and replied with three magic words:

"I'll evaluate him."

꙳

Those three words were the medical justification for an impossible trip. They gave our insurance a reason to pay for it, and CHOP's medical transport team a reason to consider it.

We'd finally found a path home...or close to home, at least. Even if we could somehow make the trip, Nadav would have to stay in Philadelphia while his brothers returned to their everyday lives in New York. We'd have to find some way to make it work.

But all that would be a moot point unless we could solve two immediate problems. Nadav was in bad shape, still draining liters of fluid a day; and CHOP—a hospital that regularly flew high-risk patients across continents—had never before transported a patient this sick, this far. They had no clue how on earth they'd do it.

꙳

Nick spent the rest of the week talking to his counterparts in Philadelphia, trying to figure out the complicated logistics that would make our flight a reality. By Sunday, he told us that they'd finally figured out a way to get Nadav home. The medical team in Philadelphia was ready to go, he said. "We've devised a plan. And—" he said, his words full of exhausted satisfaction, "we've found a plane: a Gulfstream III, fully equipped for a medical evacuation."

"There's just one problem," he added. "It is currently undergoing routine maintenance in Atlanta, Georgia. And it won't be ready for another two weeks."

"Does that concern you?" we asked.

He laughed—a weary, tired laugh—"Yes," he said. "Very much so."

Nadav's fluid losses were taking their toll. In Nick's opinion, he was likely on the brink of renal failure. There was a fair chance he'd be in even worse shape when the plane arrived.

There was nothing we could do—except have faith in our son.

⁎

Having asked for the Gulfstream's tail number, I did some research online. Built in the 1970s, it was originally used by the Royal Danish Air Force, mimicking Soviet fighter jets in NATO war games. Now it was pressed into service whenever some critical emergency called for a reliable workhorse. Someone whispered to me that after 9/11, it had been used to whisk away captured terrorists for interrogation. During the 2013 Ebola crisis, it had evacuated infected doctors from Africa back to the United States.

We arranged a long-distance call with Mark, the man who was coordinating the logistics of the flight. Based in Georgia, his Americanisms reminded us of home. I suddenly realized how much we'd grown used to Australian accents over the past few months.

Mark stressed to us how risky the plan was. The planned route would be in four hops (Sydney to Fiji, Fiji to Hawaii, Hawaii to Oakland, Oakland to Philadelphia), and they had no idea how Nadav's compromised circulation would react to all of the takeoffs and landings. They'd fly low to keep the pressures down, but there were no guarantees he'd make it.

They'd get a good sense of things after the first takeoff, from Sydney. The first hour would be critical. If anything went wrong, they'd turn back.

And after?

"I want to make sure you understand," Mark said. "If Nadav dies in flight, we land at the nearest airport."

We understood.

Toward the end of the call, Mark paused for a minute. "You know," he said thoughtfully, "Y'all are very lucky."

Yes, we were.

∞

I think the most expensive thing ever used for Nadav's care was that Gulfstream jet, which, on the second-hand market, would cost about the same as a large house in a nice suburb. Outfitted with medical equipment and appropriate crew, the total cost of the flight home would be hundreds of thousands of dollars.

Thankfully, Mark confirmed that our insurance would cover it. All we'd be responsible for was a co-pay of $2,500.

I happily wrote the check. I would have paid anything to get Nadav home.

∞

Mark had warned us that the Gulfstream would be packed. In addition to Tali and Nadav, it would hold three pilots, an attending cardiologist, two nurses, a respiratory therapist—as well as two backup nurses, a security officer, and a flight attendant, not to mention all sorts of medical gear. There was barely space for Tali to bring a small backpack; there was certainly no room for me and his brothers.

Making arrangements for our own flight had its own complications. Finding seats on short notice would be tricky—our return tickets had been refunded months ago—and we needed to be able to change our plans if necessary. If something went wrong on the Gulfstream, we'd have to bail.

Fortunately, the golden peanuts worked their magic: I discovered that one of my cousins knew someone on Qantas' board of directors.

He quickly introduced us, explaining our situation; she passed along a note with a number to call; and whomever I spoke to made the arrangements. We'd be on a flight to New York through Dallas, an hour after Nadav took off; no worries if we needed to change at the last minute. "And by the way," she added, "here are some passes for the Qantas lounge."

"I wish you and your family my very best wishes," she wrote. "You are all in my prayers."

80C3

Everything seemed to be coming together, somehow, but I still didn't quite let myself believe that it would actually happen. Tali thought I was being pessimistic, but I wasn't. I didn't expect that everything would fall through. I just didn't want to feel crushing disappointment if it did.

It wasn't until a few days before we were scheduled to leave that I allowed myself to feel a little flutter of excitement. A small blue dot had appeared in my flight tracker app, heading west from Philadelphia. The medical team was finally airborne.

Nadav had done his part. The fluid losses still danced above five liters a day—but his kidneys were somehow holding up. And the magic carpet was on its way.

Chapter 33

MAGIC CARPET

We met Nadav's transport team the day after they landed, four new faces in the suddenly hectic hubbub around Nadav's hospital bed. Having flown from Philadelphia—with stops in Oakland, Hawaii, and American Samoa—they had the dazed look and heroic grins of returning astronauts. They wore matching dark blue jumpsuits, American flags on their shoulders, and "CHOP TRANSPORT TEAM" in big yellow letters on the back.

The mood was friendly and festive. Some doctors had even planned a barbecue on the patio. And we handed out little clip-on koalas that I'd bought from a souvenir shop the day before.

They'd finally made it, all this way. America had come to bring our boy home.

৪৩৪৪

The team was led by Stacie, a no-nonsense intensivist whose usual post was at CHOP's Cardiac Intensive Care Unit. For some reason I remember her chewing gum, but perhaps her personality just had a snap to it. She smiled frequently, chuckling whenever someone made a joke, but it was clear the only thing she cared about was getting Nadav home safely—not a sure thing.

Stacie had assembled a team of people she'd trusted: a tough-looking nurse named John, a kindly respiratory therapist named Alan, and another nurse named Libby who'd actually left CHOP for a job in Texas months before. Stacie had called her up and convinced her to come back for the flight.

Those four would be responsible for Nadav, assisted by a larger flight team. The plane's six pilots worked in two shifts of three, changing over in Hawaii, and there were two crew members aboard. But the extra nurses were strictly perfunctory. They'd been quickly relegated to seats in the back of the plane and spent most of the flight down eating chips.

∞

A stocky man with a close crew cut, John introduced himself by telling us how he'd lost all of his Australian money in Parramatta the night before. "I was just walking around, looking for a place to find a decent steak," he said, "and I looked down, and somehow my cash was all gone." But it wasn't that bad, really; this wouldn't be a long stay. In the morning, if all went well, they'd be heading home—back to the land of greenbacks, Nadav in tow.

John had a calm, confident demeanor, but we sensed a tough, realistic seriousness underneath. He was from North Carolina, he said, and over the years had been a part of some pretty complicated missions. ("I've rescued kids with just a flashlight," he said matter-of-factly.) And then he stepped back, unzipping his jumpsuit. "Check this out," he said, revealing a teal blue shirt underneath.

As soon as I saw the number "88" in big black numerals, I knew what it was—a replica of the jersey worn by Greg Olsen, a tight end for the Carolina Panthers, whose own son had been born with a congenital heart defect similar to Nadav's.

"Don't worry, we'll get your boy home," John assured us. "We'd go around the world four times if we needed to."

৪০৪

Many of our friends at Westmead stopped by to bid us farewell, including Yishay, who—as we talked—bounced nervously on the balls of her feet. She seemed to be wrestling with conflicting emotions. On one hand, she was obviously proud that her patient was headed home. But she was realistic enough to know that his life would always be a longshot.

Tali promised her that if we made it back safely, we'd send her a photo of Rocky, Philadelphia's favorite son—another underdog who'd beaten the odds.

Some of the faces who appeared were unfamiliar. One awkward group turned out to be the surgical team who'd been responsible for placing and adjusting Nadav's drains; they'd come to know him well, but we'd never met. We introduced ourselves and thanked them profusely.

Most of his therapists showed up, including Gloria, carefully holding the blue vase she'd shown us when we first met. "I'd like you to have it," she said, "as a memory of our time together." When we protested, knowing how valuable it was to her, she insisted. "Keep up the great work," she'd written in permanent marker on the side, just under the word "Kythera." "I've enjoyed chatting with you!"

It still sits in our home, its fragile yellow flowers reminding us of all the places we'd been—and all of the people we were lucky to have met along the way.

৪০৪

Both teams huddled closely at Nadav's bedside, speaking the shared language of medicine, quietly rehearsing plans; while Nick carefully checked the list he'd prepared the night before.

He had spent a lot of time thinking about how to replace fluid on the flight. It was a puzzle: the FFP (well over five liters, just in case) had to be kept frozen until it was used, on a twenty-four-hour flight that didn't have the proper refrigeration. To solve the riddle, he'd devised an ingenious system using white foam cooler bins, scrawling specific instructions in blue marker on the lids.

Sitting on top was a portable travel respirator, which the transport team had nicknamed "Hammy" after its manufacturer: Hamilton Medical. It looked just like the respirator that we'd taken on our walks outside—the one that Nick had switched off, deep in thought. And suddenly I realized why he'd done it. Even then, long before we found a path home, he'd been preparing for this moment.

ॐ

When the time came, we all lifted Nadav from the hospital bed into the wheeled travel gurney, carefully minding his drains—almost ready to go.

And then, Nick—always conscious of protocol—turned to Stacie and announced firmly: "He is now your patient."

"I was wondering," Stacie said, "should we sedate him?"

"I would recommend you don't, and see how it goes," Nick said. "We've gotten to know Nadav pretty well. He is likely to surprise you."

ॐ

I said goodbye to Tali and Nadav outside the hospital—the ambulance bathed in blinding sun, us shaded by a concrete overhang. Nadav was bundled up on his trolley, about to be wheeled onto the ambulance, tubes and lines running this way and that. His team milled about: the Americans ready to leave, the Australians wishing them well.

And then, it was time to go.

Glenda, the cardiothoracic nurse practitioner who'd quietly overseen much of Nadav's care, asked if she could say a few words to him before he left. Like the good witch of *The Wizard of Oz*, who taught Dorothy how to get home, she wanted to make sure that Nadav knew the way too.

She leaned over, and asked him, "Do you know where you're going?"

He looked at her, eyes wide, and whispered faintly (past his breathing tube, as he'd learned to do)—

"Home."

Glenda smiled and gave him a kiss on the forehead.

"Get home PROPER," she said.

Not just to the States, she meant. Not just to Philadelphia. To New York. To his own bed, in our own apartment, surrounded by friends, stuffed and otherwise.

Home...PROPER.

A command, as much as a request; more than a wish, because she knew he could do it.

PHILADELPHIA

Chapter 34

SYDNEY TO PHILLY

O n February 18th, eighty-six days after we arrived at Westmead, we were finally free to go.

There was a strange sadness in saying goodbye, a wistfulness at odds with our eagerness to depart. We'd adjusted to life here, with all of its twists and turns, learning to navigate a once-unfamiliar territory so well that it had come to feel like our own.

Tali climbed into the front seat of the ambulance, Nadav safely ensconced with the medical team in the back. On went the flashing lights, and off they went. We waved goodbye and watched them go.

I headed back to the PICU, hoping to capture for the last time the magic we'd felt over the last few months. But it was odd being there without Nadav. I got a few smiles as his nurses and doctors bustled around, but they were already busy with other patients. Sentiment only lasted so long; there was too much to do.

I gave a hug to a doctor who'd helped arrange the trip, but there wasn't much to say except "thank you." I quickly sensed it was time to say good-bye and left him to the others on the ward: the next crisis, the next tragedy, the next miracle.

৪৩

All that was left was for me to pack up a few odds and ends from Tali's room in the parents' hostel. I walked down the hall for the last time, overwhelmed by emotion, when my phone rang.

"Hello?" said a young voice. It was our case manager from the billing department.

My heart sank, fearing a last meeting; some bill still unpaid, some drastic lien levied—and decided to pull at their heartstrings. "I'm on the way to the airport," I said, bracing myself for another frustrating impasse. "Nadav's being discharged today, and we're flying him home."

But her voice was chipper and chirpy—much different from the dour tone I was used to from our tense meetings on the third floor. "That's great to hear!" she replied. "We just wanted to let you know that your insurance company has agreed to remit payment for all of our charges."

"All of it?" I asked, dumbfounded.

"That's right," she said. "One hundred percent."

The timing was suspicious, and I wondered if the hospital had somehow forgiven the charges out of compassion. But when I asked Nick later, he insisted they hadn't. The twenty-five-hundred-dollar check I'd written for the medical transport company had fulfilled our out-of-pocket maximum, and the rest had been paid in full.

We were in the clear.

৪৩

Tali and Nadav departed first, their Gulfstream a tiny, pixelated icon on a Google map.

Sitting at a rickety round table in the Qantas airport terminal, I watched it head over the Pacific, fearing a sudden change in direction, some unseen emergency, another devastating setback. But as the dot kept a steady pace on its northeast course, slowly inching across a flat expanse of blue, I finally allowed myself to surrender to the boredom of the boarding lounge.

As it turned out, the crisis I'd feared missed us by just two days. Forty-eight hours after Nadav's flight left Sydney, a gigantic hurricane struck Fiji. The storm knocked out the power grid in Nadi, closing the airport—the first stop on Nadav's miracle flight home.

ঙ০িয়

Our own flight was not packed. We'd found some empty seats at the back of the plane, so the boys could stretch out as they watched movies. I tried to strike up a conversation with the flight attendant, but he didn't seem terribly interested. Our special status had evaporated: I'd become an ordinary passenger, another name on the manifest, a face with a seat number. He brought me a beer and left us alone.

I tried not to think about what was happening on the Gulfstream. Thankfully, there was no Wi-Fi on our flight, so I couldn't track its progress. When we touched down in Dallas, I opened the flight-tracking app, and was relieved to see it had just taken off from Oakland, still on its way.

Dragging our bags behind us, we cleared customs, interrupted only by a sleep-deprived tantrum and a bag search prompted by an uneaten cheese sandwich. And then it was back on the plane. When we landed at JFK in the early evening, just after sunset, I checked my messages.

Tali was pleased: the magic carpet had made it. Nadav had arrived at CHOP, safe and sound.

ເ℧Ƈຽ

Tali's parents met us at the airport terminal. The plan was for them to take care of the boys while I headed to Philadelphia.

They'd brought along warm winter coats, and our aging but beloved Subaru, which had spent three months parked outside their house in the suburbs. Assuming that I'd be too tired to drive to Philadelphia, my brother had come along to take the wheel.

"There's just one problem," he admitted, as we lingered in the parking lot after the boys had left. The car's "check engine" light had come on, he told me, and whenever the Subaru hit forty miles an hour it started making horrible sounds.

So, the Subaru stayed in New York. I took the last train down instead, arriving in Philadelphia's 30th Street Station at one in the morning—over twenty-four hours after we'd left Sydney.

ເ℧Ƈຽ

The hospital was only a mile away, and after all those hours in transit, I was glad for a chance to walk, the night chill a refreshing change from Sydney's summer heat. The streets were empty except for a road construction crew, steam rising from the blacktop past flashing yellow lights.

I got a visitor's badge from a bleary-eyed security guard in the hospital's lobby and headed up to see Tali on the sixth floor. Giddy but exhausted, she pointed to Nadav, comfortably ensconced in a freshly sheeted hospital bed. His new nurse was double-checking his lines in the half-lit private room, a tiny koala already pinned to her scrubs.

༈

Buoyed by the adrenaline of our journey—*we'd actually made it!*—Tali and I were more hungry than sleepy. We headed downstairs to the near-empty cafeteria (open for the overnight shift, but just as welcoming to weary world travelers) and she told me about the flight.

The nurses had barely slept. They monitored Nadav's drain losses hourly, adjusting the replacement fluid as needed. He'd needed a slight sedative when things got a little iffy landing in Hawaii, but otherwise he was fine.

The small army of souvenir koalas that we'd handed out to the medical crew had been put to good use. They clung tightly to nametags, sleeves, and various parts of the plane, including a makeshift toilet paper holder that one of the nurses rigged out of medical tubing.

Tali's phone was filled with random snapshots from the flight: Nadav loaded on the plane on a conveyor belt; "Hammy" the ventilator chugging away, nestled in a bulkhead; the backup nurses eating Pringles. But my mind was already on our son, upstairs, and how remarkable it was that he'd made it back.

༈

When we returned to the room, we heard some unexpected news. They'd be taking Nadav in for the Fontan takedown *that morning*. No, not the next day, *this* one. Just hours after we arrived on our magic carpet ride.

"So soon?" we asked. "We've only just landed."

"Why not?" was the reply. "He did well on the flight. We're ready for him. And there's no reason to wait for something to go wrong."

Just after the sun rose, he went in. We'd been told it would take an hour for Dr. Rome to determine whether the procedure was even possible. And then, if he determined it was—fingers crossed—they'd go ahead and do it.

Thankfully, they didn't use beepers here. They took our phone number instead, promising to call us after an hour to let us know what was going on.

Chapter 35

FONTAN TAKEDOWN

The innovation of Dr. Rome's procedure was that it mimicked a surgical intervention, without the huge risks that came with surgery. It relied on a familiar procedure called cardiac catheterization—in which an interventional cardiologist inserts a small catheter into a blood vessel, snaking it through the body to the heart.

Nobody actually used the word "catheterization." In a busy hospital, six syllables was five too many. Like everyone else, we just called it a "cath."

Nadav underwent countless caths—sometimes to merely read pressures or see what was going on, other times, to widen a blood vessel or insert a stent. But this one would be different. If successful, it would revert Nadav's circulation to an approximation of what it had been before the Fontan—ending the runaway pressures and massive leaks that had caused such problems for us in Australia.

Or so we hoped. There was nothing routine about this procedure. By the time we arrived in Philadelphia, Dr. Rome's technique had only been tried on fewer than a dozen children, and not all of them had survived.

ঙ০෬

While Tali scoured medical journals in search of new innovations, I'd sought out histories of cardiac surgery, intrigued by the doctors who had pioneered the procedures that kept Nadav alive. I wondered what prompted them to try something new, how they balanced the risks of death against the possibility of success, and how many unnamed surgeons tried things that didn't work and remain forgotten.

The invention of cardiac catheterization was particularly fascinating. The first person to try it was a German doctor named Werner Forssmann—a man so convinced that a catheter could be inserted into the heart that in 1929 he decided to try it on himself.

He needed some help, of course—if only to take an x-ray as proof that it worked. He approached a nurse, asking if she would agree to undergo the procedure. She was apparently unaware that it had never been done before, thinking that he was merely trying out some new equipment. After being prepped, she waited patiently, feeling nothing. Wondering why Forssmann hadn't started, she turned around—and was startled to see that he had inserted the catheter into his own arm instead.

Forssmann urged her to take an x-ray—*quickly*. But the room he'd chosen didn't have an x-ray machine, so they stumbled down the hall to the radiology department, catheter still in his arm. When they finally reached the machine, he gently pushed the tip into his heart's right atrium and took a picture.

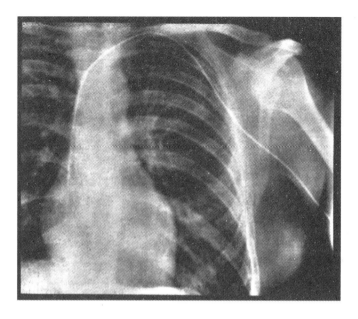

The questionable ethics of Forssmann's experiment left his colleagues wary. He eventually left cardiology for urology, and after the war, he worked as a lumberjack and country doctor in the Black Forest. In 1956, he was unexpectedly awarded the Nobel Prize in Medicine, sharing the prize with two other physicians who'd been inspired by his work. By the time Nadav was born, the procedure had become almost routine.

Nadav's doctors were hesitant to schedule unnecessary caths, wary of putting too much stress on his system; they would read us the obligatory warnings ("risk of death," etc., etc.) before each procedure. But we never really worried too much about what might go wrong—not nearly as much as when he went in for a surgery.

This cath was no different. We were more excited than nervous. Perhaps, after all that happened over the past twenty-four hours, we were too numb to really worry.

৪০৫১

The hospital called us an hour later. Dr. Rome had decided to go ahead.

Tali and I looked at each other. It was actually happening—*wow*.

Soon after, we got another call: it was done. He was coming out; meet us in intensive care. And as Dr. Rome told us, exhausted, "We did it. Now let's see what happens."

What he'd done wasn't a cure—in fact, reverting Nadav's circulation to what it had been before the Fontan was in some ways a step backward. But after spending nearly three months in Westmead just hoping that Nadav would stay alive, we finally had some reason to hope for improvement. Enough improvement, maybe, to actually get him home.

৪০৫১

That night, Tali and I headed to a local Irish pub, celebrating the whirlwind wonders of the past few days with shepherd's pie and tall, cold beers. The familiar atmosphere was comforting—the bar packed with college seniors on a night out, a small table in the middle just for us.

As we sat down, we spotted a familiar movie poster across the bar: *Rocky*, starring Sylvester Stallone. It was as if the universe had remembered our promise to Yishay—*we'll send you a picture of Rocky when Nadav makes it to Philadelphia*. And so, we did: Stallone's arms raised in triumph—the underdog hero, exceeding all expectations—embraced, victorious, by the city of Brotherly Love.

෨෦ഝ

Adjusting to Philadelphia was not as jarring as our chaotic arrival at Westmead had been three months before. Nadav was in stable condition—we were told it would take some time for him to convalesce—and the city was not exactly foreign territory.

CHOP was located right next to the University of Pennsylvania, where Tali had gone to college. It had been a while since she last spent time there, and she couldn't believe how much it had changed—dangerous corners replaced by health-food stores, empty blocks suddenly packed with lively bars.

Unlike Westmead, CHOP had no parent hostel—and we had no family in the area who could lend us a bed. But we still had somewhere to stay. Tali had found a Jewish charity that owned a building a short walk from CHOP and lent rooms to families needing accommodation.

The apartments were located above a decidedly unkosher seafood restaurant, "Fresh oysters!" written brightly on the windowpane—as if it were a front, concealing the building's true purpose.

Charity ("tzedakah" in Hebrew) was always a big part of the boys' Jewish education. They'd been taught a catchy song in pre-school to remind them of its importance:

"Tzedakah, tzedakah, tzedakah,
That is what we give
To the poor people
To help them live…"

Now it was our turn to benefit from others' generosity.

For those first few weeks, we stayed on the top floor, all by ourselves. It was comfortable, if a little eclectic—the kitchen missing some utensils, the sheets slightly mildewed—but it was a life-saver, and we were hugely grateful.

𝕊𝕆ℂ𝔹

Unlike Westmead, whose modest entrance was nestled at the far end of a suburban road, CHOP was situated in the middle of a vast urban medical complex, its lobby a bustling hub of foot traffic.

Right past the entrance was a magnificent machine built by the artist George Rhoads, a kinetic sculpture in which dozens of colorful balls navigated through a maze of rails and spinners, gently filling the atrium with clinks and chimes.

Children loved watching the balls fall, mesmerized. It was much more engaging than the goldfish tanks so common in hospital waiting rooms, shiny tetras warily circling around, waiting patiently for their next sprinkle of food.

It was a neat trick. The balls whirred around and around, full of energy, giving the illusion of freedom and movement. It was easy to forget that they were encased in glass, going nowhere fast.

Chapter 36

PERSISTENCE

Within a week, Nadav was deemed stable enough to move from the PICU to the pediatric cardiology ICU, and Tali and I found ourselves meeting yet another new medical team.

We quickly realized how much we'd adapted to the Westmead PICU. Now that we'd returned to the States, we had to adjust to a new set of routines, a new cast of personalities, and an altogether different approach.

Dealing with these unfamiliar doctors could feel like a tug of war. Our role was to advocate for Nadav; their job was to protect him from the unexpected. We gently pushed and prodded on all sorts of things—our polite persistence usually paying off with some small compromise. And then, after a brief truce, we'd start pushing again.

৪৩৫৪

Even something as simple as water could be a hard-fought battle.

When we arrived in Philadelphia, Nadav was constantly thirsty. He had been intubated for months—his throat must have been parched—and his doctors in Australia had come to allow small drinks, or at least ice chips, to soothe him. So, we asked the same question every day, for weeks: "Can Nadav start drinking water?"

"But he's intubated," the attending doctors said, quoting the conventional wisdom: "Drinking puts him at high risk of aspirating."

We knew the risks, but Nadav was thirsty. In our minds, not letting him drink was cruel, or at least unfair.

He took small sips while intubated in Australia, we'd reason, never choking once. Explaining this to the doctor, patiently but firmly, usually resulted in an "what-type-of-barbaric-medicine-do-they-practice-down-there" eyeroll.

Until, one day, a doctor relented. "He can have a sip," she said. "A *small* sip."

So, he did. And it was fine.

But he was still thirsty.

ॐ

Here were the rules, they said. Nadav could have a small sip of water every twenty minutes. And it needed to be thickened, using a tasteless, gelatinous additive. (Apparently this made it safer.) Tali and I called it "Philadelphia water."

But Nadav could tell the difference and complained. "I want *real* water," he croaked.

One nurse came up with a clever solution. She found a monkey sticker, and put in on the clock, near one of the numbers. "When the big hand hits the monkey, you can drink," she said.

And we'd sit, staring; watching the big hand moving, ever so slightly, toward the monkey—twelve hundred agonizing seconds until another sip.

Nadav was impatient too. After each sip, he made it clear he wanted more. But the nurse was firm. Doctor's orders: he needed to wait.

ಬಂಜ

Our conflicts with Nadav's caregivers were subtle and professional, and we always tried to stay polite. It was the only way to get things done; nothing came of open war.

Usually, we eventually made progress. But the woman who'd ordered "Philadelphia water," for some reason, was especially stubborn:

"It tastes terrible," we said.
"I know," she replied.
(He's parched, we grumbled.)

"When can he have real water?" we asked.
"When he passes a swallow test," she said.
(He doesn't need a swallow test, we grumbled.)

"Can we do a swallow test?" we asked.
"It needs to be in a controlled environment,"
she said.
(Just give him the water and see what happens, we grumbled.)

Nadav eventually took a swallow test and passed. *(Of course he did, we grumbled.)* But by that time, unbeknownst to everyone but us, the Philadelphia water was long gone, the packets quietly disposed of in a far-off trash can.

So, we were skilled at guerrilla warfare too. But we kept it quiet.

ಬಂಜ

We knew that it would take a while for Nadav to be able to go home, but we weren't sure how long. His circulation had to readjust; his drainage had to stop; his body had to recover. At the same time, we had to somehow find a balance with our "normal" life back home.

Nadav's brothers had returned to school soon after we returned to the States—their classmates excitedly welcoming them back with hand-lettered signs—and so Tali and I had begun to split our time between New York and Philadelphia.

It was almost as if the kids were divorced and sharing custody of us. I'd drive down during the week in our red Subaru, spending a few hours with Tali and Nadav; then she'd head back on the afternoon train, arriving in time to take care of the boys. Our parents helped fill in the gaps.

Those few hours of overlap were precious. We spent most of our time together discussing Nadav's condition and the logistics of caretaking: insurance, procedures, errands, plans.

Sometimes we'd grab a bite in the cafeteria downstairs. Or we'd pick at one of the lunches generously donated by the local Jewish community; shrink-wrapped meals with a wide plastic band reading "KOSHER" in red lettering. I confess that we didn't always eat what we were given. The occasional pastrami sandwiches were a treat, but we sometimes left uneaten meals for others in the shared family room.

Eventually we discovered favorite restaurants that would become sources of comfort in a stressful time—a jerk chicken truck on Spruce and 38th, a Pakistani place that delivered spicy kebabs with piles of steaming rice, an overpriced ramen place closer to the train station. All within walking distance, just in case we needed to hurry back.

Once, meeting an old friend for dinner, we decided to venture across the Schuylkill River to visit an Egyptian restaurant that someone had recommended. The food was great, and it was all very civilized: three types of hummus, white cloth napkins, hushed conversations.

But it didn't feel quite right, as if our distance from Nadav was a form of betrayal, the comfortable surroundings insensitive to the difficult circumstances we'd left behind. We rarely ate that far away from the hospital again.

80C8

Even back in New York, I found it difficult to reconnect with old friends.

To be honest, those friends hadn't always understood what we were going through, even before we got stuck in Australia. When you're in such a challenging situation, a gulf opens up between you and the rest of the world. Even our close friends found it difficult to know what to say or even listen to the details of what we were going through.

We often didn't share photos, because the things we had become used to—respirators, masks, tubes, and wires—might be too difficult for others to see, or too private for us to share.

Once, after one of Nadav's surgeries, a close friend had reached out in sympathy. "It's not the same thing, but I know a little bit of what you must be going through," she said, proceeding to tell us about a minor procedure her child had a few weeks earlier.

It was nothing like what we were going through, actually. But I didn't blame her for saying it. However clumsy it came out, she said it because she cared. And that's a tricky thing to enunciate properly; most people have trouble finding the words. They might not even realize that words can be unnecessary or insufficient.

୫୦୯ଽ

As a parent in that situation, you tend to cherish the people you meet who have been through—or are going through—something similar.

I quickly learned how to recognize others who knew what it was like. Instead of asking, "How is he doing?" they'd ask, "How are *you* doing?"

There was real comfort in being with people like that. You didn't have to explain. You didn't feel that distance. They cared, but there was something more; they *knew*. The sort of relationship that didn't require any communication at all.

Shortly after we returned, I unexpectedly bumped into an old friend on a busy street. He'd known the broad outlines of what had happened, but we hadn't talked about it in any detail. And so, I stood there, unsure how to explain it all.

He didn't say anything, either. He just opened his arms and gave me a hug—what felt like the longest, warmest hug I'd ever had. He clung to me tightly, not letting go; his silent empathy washing over me like warmth in the cool winter air.

It was exactly what I needed, at that moment; and that memory still lingers, filling me with warmth—even now.

୫୦୯ଽ

On one of my first trips back to New York, I went to see Shubhi at Mount Sinai. She welcomed me with a big smile; but as we hugged tightly, I could sense her eyes filling with tears.

They were tears of joy, that we'd made it back; but it seemed to me that they were also tears of sadness, that the whole thing had happened at all. I suspected that she felt some responsibility for what had happened, for Nadav's suffering—that we'd entrusted our precious son to her care, and by allowing us to travel, she'd somehow let us down.

ଛୀଓଷ

Tali, too, couldn't help but feel similar emotions—not directed at Shubhi, but at ourselves. Why did we decide to bring him halfway around the world? How could we have listened to the doctors, even after they agreed to it? What on earth were we all thinking? "We should have known better," she said. "We shouldn't have gone."

Tali and I would argue this point over and over again, our back-and-forths often lasting late into the night. She was insistent, but I always felt differently. Regret is irrelevant, I argued. We're human, not all-knowing. And at the time we made them, the decisions we made were the right ones. Otherwise, we wouldn't have made them.

Yes, we got unlucky in Australia. And Tali's right: it might have been a mistake to go.

But there's nothing to say that Nadav would have done any better if we had stayed at home. Perhaps other complications would have emerged. Perhaps another extraordinary event would have blindsided us, spiraling us into a crisis. Perhaps the intensive-care team in Sydney did a better job of keeping him alive than our home hospital in New York could have.

Much later, I read *Why Religion?*, a memoir by Elaine Pagels, whose son was also born with a congenital heart defect. Fearful of the risks of high altitudes, they decided to forgo a trip to Colorado in favor of the relative safety of the California coast. But even at sea level, the child nevertheless developed the condition his doctors had warned her about.

I always felt that hypotheticals missed the point: the indisputable fact that we will never know—we *can* never know—what might have happened.

We are, after all, only human.

∞

We'd come to learn how doctors draw on their experience and knowledge while making decisions—keeping in mind that the choices they make are not infallible. Information isn't perfect, and nobody can predict the future. The best we can do is imagine outcomes, weigh them against each other, and then decide, hoping for the best.

We made countless decisions, large and small, in Nadav's life. In every decision, there was uncertainty—a quiet worry that the choice may not have been the right one. For big decisions, that sliver of fear chills your bones if you stare at it long enough.

I always found solace by resolving not to look back, that nothing good could come of it. The decisions of the past were unchangeable and ultimately irrelevant; with each choice, life's alternate paths were erased, as unknowable as the future. To wonder what might have been, I felt, could only result in bitterness, and grief—a sadness as corrosive as a pillar of salt.

Chapter 37

TOUCH

A co-worker once told me about a friend who'd also had a son born with a congenital heart defect. Their experience had been much different from ours: the condition was undiagnosed at birth, the baby sent home as if he was healthy. When the parents noticed at home that their child was having difficulty breathing, the doctor told them that it was probably just a cold, nothing to worry about.

So, their first surgery was an unplanned emergency. It did not end well.

Hearing this story made me realize how privileged we were to have had found such extraordinary doctors. In New York, we had Shubhi; at Westmead, we had Nick. At CHOP, we found two more—each special in their own way, both destined to tell us painful truths.

∞⋅∞

Chitra, Nadav's cardiologist, was a close friend of Shubhi's, and handled everything with a quiet wisdom. She chose her words carefully, often deflecting particularly tricky questions with a small laugh that we came to interpret as her way of saying: *be patient, we'll see, not yet.* "Chitra knows *everything*," someone once told us, and even though she never quite shared everything she knew, it soon became clear to us that they were right.

When Nadav first arrived, she tended to defer to the doctors on call, whose decision-making was more conservative. But as time went on, her influence gradually increased; and with it, our comfort with Nadav's care. Perhaps it just took a while for her to get to know him.

୫୦୦୫

Her counterpart was Dr. Rome, the interventional cardiologist who had performed that first procedure. I did not know quite what to make of him when we first met; his explanations were dense and specific, based on a complicated understanding of fluid dynamics that I did not quite grasp. But for Tali, it was familiar ground. She had found a fellow engineer.

My first introduction to Dr. Rome had been the paper that had brought us to Philadelphia, which—typical for a medical paper—was dry and dispassionate. There was virtually no discussion of why Dr. Rome and his colleagues had decided to try the procedure, beyond that they "thought it might be advantageous to avoid heart surgery." And when discussing outcomes, it stated merely that "two of three patients remain alive at latest follow-up."

Reading the phrase "two of three patients remain alive" made me wonder to what extent doctors think about their patients as outcomes. It's an odd phrasing, evocative of the difference between doctors and parents. As a father, I might have chosen a more direct way of saying it: "One of the three patients died."

There was definitely something in Dr. Rome's approach that made it clear he saw Nadav's condition as a challenge—a puzzle to be solved, a particularly tricky crossword that he could somehow force to yield. But it eventually became obvious how much he cared for our son—not just as an outcome or a learning opportunity, but as a human being.

He just had a different way of showing it.

☙◊ℂ

One day, Tali mentioned something about Chitra that I hadn't noticed before. "Do you know why I like her?" she said. "Every time she sees him, she touches him."

It became something I started looking for, and it was true. It wasn't a purposeful touch, like prodding below his stomach to measure the size of his liver or feeling his forehead for a fever. It was contact for its own sake, a means of saying hello and making a connection.

Helen Taussig, considered by many to be the founder of pediatric cardiology, suffered from partial deafness—an impairment that forced her to find a way to use her fingertips, instead of her ears, to listen to those tiny heartbeats. She must have passed it down somehow, because the healers we trusted most knew to use their fingers to listen too.

☙◊ℂ

While a doctor's touch was usually gentle and inquisitive, Nadav's many therapists were more direct. They used their hands to push, to motivate, to inspire. The best therapists didn't just use physical contact—they insisted on it.

Just days after we arrived at CHOP, I walked into Nadav's room to find his physical therapist up on his bed, straddling him. She was utterly unfazed by the fact that he was recovering from a cath, still woozy from sedation, and had barely stirred in over three months. "Let's get moving!" she cried out, holding his arms, ready to go.

Therapy could sometimes feel like a chore. But the best therapists made it fun. Nadav's first occupational therapy session also took place that first week, even before he got out of bed for the first time. His therapist had lined up a row of rainbow-colored pins and helped him take aim with a bright-orange Nerf gun. With a little help, Nadav managed to weakly pull the trigger—the foam bullet making contact with a satisfying clink, the pin spinning slightly away.

When his brothers came to visit, they immediately found the Nerf gun—bombarding the room with a hail of bullets before we pleaded with them to PLEASE stop.

∞

I never quite knew how to describe occupational therapy. Eventually, I figured it out: physical therapy (PT) was about gross motor skills, like walking, while occupational therapy (OT) focused on fine motor skills, like writing.

Our most beloved therapist at CHOP was his primary OT, a bundle of steely energy who wouldn't take no for an answer. She'd waltz into his room each morning, singing "get out of bed" songs, frowning that I'd helped him put on his socks without making him do it himself.

Looking back, I suspect that the critical part of occupational therapy is that sense of touch—the subtle art of clenching and manipulation, the nuanced ability to rebuild subconscious connections. Nadav's natural left-handedness had been compromised since the stroke, so his therapist helped him learn to draw with his right. He sometimes had trouble with a fork, so she taught him to use special wooden tongs instead. When those activities got monotonous, she brought out games that encouraged delicate movement, like "Crocodile Dentist" (push a tooth, hoping it doesn't bite!) and "Don't Break the Ice" (hammer small plastic cubes without collapsing the whole structure).

Throughout it all, my focus was not on Nadav's hands, but on the therapist's—her long, strong fingers, resting on his elbow or gently guiding his arm, teaching him that despite his weakness, he could do it himself.

My grandmother's hands had been that way too—strong and gentle, worn by years of shaping and kneading, carrying the power of a whispered blessing.

∞∞

Nurses inspired us with their hands too. Whether changing dressings, lifting legs, or cleaning wounds, the best nurses never shied away from a necessary touch.

At playtime, Nadav and I rarely pretended to be doctors—diagnosis and analysis was impossibly dull. It was more fun to actually *do* things, imitating the meticulous persistence of a diligent nurse. On one particularly boring day, I borrowed medical equipment from the room's cabinet—gauze, tubes, straws, tape—which we used to gleefully bandage Nadav's many stuffed animals. Inserting things here, taping things there, the foot of his bed soon became its own little ward.

The nurses we loved most approached their tasks as opportunities to care, not merely as chores. Bathing was a perfect example. Nadav had long curly hair, which in long hospital stretches could become matted and clumpy; because of his drains, the doctors at CHOP were hesitant to allow him to use a bathtub. One nurse, deciding that his daily sponge bath wasn't enough, took the initiative to shampoo his hair as well, filling a bucket with soapy water and vigorously massaging his head until it was clean. Afterward, she rubbed in masses of Johnson & Johnson's detangler, painstakingly combing it out strand by strand.

When she was done, Nadav sat in his bed, beaming—damp towels scattered everywhere, his freshly washed hair in an angelic halo above his head.

୫୦୯ଓ

Most of the nurses we met inspired us with their caring, patience, and dedication. We knew how lucky we were to have them around. On the rare occasions when we were assigned an indifferent nurse, or found ourselves in a poorly staffed ward, we got anxious, knowing that it put Nadav at risk—and we appreciated the great ones even more.

In all of our time at CHOP, I can only think of a handful of times that we were upset at his nurses. One, in particular, stands out in my mind: a nurse who accidentally inserted his NG into the lung—the one thing we were warned not to do. Even worse, she pushed down a dose of medicine before realizing her mistake.

What upset me most was how vigorously she denied it. We usually tried to defer to others' expertise, but I knew a thing or two about NG tubes and knew exactly what had happened. It was one of the few times we'd asked for a nurse to be re-assigned to another patient.

Afterward, whenever we'd see her in the halls, I'd avert my eyes.

Chapter 38

NOURISHMENT

When Nadav was finally extubated, ten days after we arrived in Philadelphia, we had three reasons to celebrate. Not only could he breathe properly—and drink water without restrictions—but he now also had permission to try solid food. While intubated, all of Nadav's nourishment had come through an NG tube. He hadn't eaten in over three months.

His nurses asked him what he wanted for his first meal.

"Sushi," he croaked in a small voice.

Surprised, the nurses consulted with the attending doctor. Nobody had ever asked for sushi before. Could he eat sushi?

"Why not?" was the reply.

So, I went downstairs to the cafeteria—much nicer than the one at Westmead, with a bigger selection—and fetched a small box of salmon *nigiri*. He nibbled at the pieces, happy to be eating again.

It was the talk of the hallway. "Sushi!" the nurses muttered—of all things!—and from then on, it became part of Nadav's story: the boy who asked for sushi.

෨෬

Nadav was never a big eater, picking at his food as his brothers wolfed it down. At CHOP, getting him to eat was as important as ever—he had to gain weight and rebuild muscle—but it wasn't any easier. Sushi aside, Nadav had little interest in eating.

Chitra shared Shubhi's concern about nutrition, insisting that he have a minimum number of calories each day. We could feed him by mouth as much as we could, but the balance would have to come through supplements like Ensure, fed through the ever-present NG tube.

We wanted the supplements weaned down and the tube gone. So, each day became a quest for calories. We bought a tiny scale from Amazon, the type typically used for diamonds, and weighed everything we served him—before and after, to see how many calories he'd taken. Every day, we tallied it up in a spreadsheet, announcing to the evening nurse how much he'd need overnight, quietly rejoicing every time we managed to lower the daily feed.

Sun 1/8 872 calories (146 ensure), 34g protein, 1276ml fluids (778 PO)						_Previous 7-day average_	
Mon 1/9 496 calories (226 ensure), 24g protein, 793ml fluids (711 PO)							
Date	Meal	Food		er 100 cal / p	Grams eaten	Net calories	Net protein
Sun 1/1	Drink	Water		0 0	43	0	0
Sun 1/1	Breakfast	Smoked salmon		179 20	11	20	2
Sun 1/1	Breakfast	French toast		229 8	5	11	0
Sun 1/1	Breakfast	Sharp cheddar		404 23	4	16	1
Sun 1/1	Drink	Ensure		100 4	33	33	1
Sun 1/1	Drink	Water		0 0	131	0	0
Sun 1/1	Breakfast	Cheerios		371 12	4	15	0
Sun 1/1	Drink	Water		0 0	27	0	0
Sun 1/1	Drink	Ensure		100 4	20	20	1
Sun 1/1	Drink	Water		0 0	150	0	0
Sun 1/1	Lunch	Pasta with parmesan		136 5	9	12	0
Sun 1/1	Lunch	Olive oil		884 0	0.5	4	0
Sun 1/1	Supper	Pasta (plain)		131 5	5	7	0
Sun 1/1	Supper	Matzo balls		137 5	30	41	2

Anything oily was a calorie bonanza. At the age of three, Nadav had developed a taste for *sproti*, small smoked sprats packed in oil, imported directly from Latvia. I'd discovered them during my year living in Russia—they're especially tasty on dark *Borodinsky* bread—and brought some home one day. Tali was overjoyed to find that Nadav liked them, and soon our cupboard was filled with small dark cans of "little fishies." The cans were pungent when opened—a smell we all came to savor.

At CHOP, we realized that Nadav had developed an even deeper affinity for strong flavors, the smellier the better. Something in the past year seemed to have affected his sense of taste.

໕໖

Now that Nadav was extubated, we had permission to move about. Since his legs were still too weak to walk, Chitra arranged for a wheelchair to be brought to his room. We hooked his cannula to a green oxygen tank that I could pull behind us like an old-fashioned golf cart, and once his remote travel monitor was linked to the nurses' station, we were allowed to wander beyond the cardiac ward.

Glad to escape the room, we started going to the cafeteria together for lunch—drains hanging off the back of the chair, IV pole dragging awkwardly behind. Sometimes we splurged on sushi; other times, I'd get him a hot dog or chicken cutlet, chopped into little bites. Often, Nadav would ask for pizza, always topped with dried oregano.

Eventually, I figured out that he ordered pizza just for the oregano topping; he'd start asking for oregano no mattered what we ordered. So, we asked the pizza guy for little plastic containers of dried oregano, even if we weren't having pizza, and we'd sprinkle it on everything he ate.

ℬℭ

Nadav's wheelchair allowed us to explore every inch of the campus—ranging as far as a brand-new outpatient building, accessible only by a complicated path of elevators, corridors, and a covered footbridge over the main road. The building's top floors were still being finished, but I'd smile at the guard on duty, and ask if we could walk around. They always said yes.

Security guards are great friends to have in a hospital. Unlike the other familiar faces you encounter, they'll never blind-side you with life-or-death news. Once you get to know them, they are always ready with a happy "Hello!" And they can literally open doors for you.

In *Kitchen Confidential*, Anthony Bourdain warned diners to be suspicious of restaurants with dirty bathrooms. If they couldn't make an effort to keep the toilets clean, he reasoned, you'd have to worry about what they did in the kitchen.

I came to apply this thinking—that an organization's culture pervades all of its spaces—to hospitals as well. And the best way to get a sense of a hospital's culture is at its front desk. The manner in which security guards do their job invariably reflects a hospital's "tone"—how it treats its patients and their parents, no matter the context.

Mount Sinai's guards had been quiet and unobtrusive, the lobby as busy as a public plaza. The guards at Westmead were almost invisible, with sensitive areas protected by locked fire doors instead. The guards at CHOP were cautious but caring. They were fastidious about things like proper identification and visitor's passes. But in the grey areas, they'd usually give us the benefit of the doubt.

I'm glad that they let us explore so freely; it was nice having an empty building to ourselves. The high floors offered sweeping views of South Philly, and every so often I'd catch a view of a freight train in the distance. But Nadav was much less enthusiastic. Resting his chin on his hand, he'd call the view "boring," and ask if we could head somewhere else.

℘ℭ℥

Truth be told, the hospital *could* be a little boring. Every so often, someone famous would visit, making the rounds and taking photos with the kids. We'd seen this at every hospital we'd been at, and although the visitors doubtlessly had the best intentions, it always felt a little forced to me.

One morning I saw a tall, poised woman enter the lobby and take a glittering tiara out of a wooden box. She adjusted it on her head, and then looked around for someone to meet. Curious, I asked a security guard who she was.

"Miss Delaware," he said. "I think."

As we headed upstairs, she started walking around the lobby, awkwardly introducing herself to random passers-by. But she found few takers. Nobody wanted to spend any more time there than they had to—not even to meet Miss Delaware.

℘ℭ℥

While famous visitors brought a bit of unexpected excitement, it was just as enjoyable for us to simply wander around the hospital.

On one of our excursions, Nadav and I found a small outdoor garden in a distant ward, which quickly became a favorite destination. The long walk gave the illusion of escape, and the fresh breeze was a welcome change from the sterile hum of the hospital's central air.

Best of all, the planters in the middle were filled with herbs, lush and fragrant. We'd go each morning to pick fresh oregano— which we'd save for lunch, wrapping the small leaves around tiny bites of chicken or hot dog to make them more appetizing.

Often, we'd return to handwritten notes from doctors who'd stopped by his room, surprised to find him gone. "You're never here!" Chitra once exclaimed with a smile after we eventually found each other. Apparently, our extended departures were unusual. I took it as a compliment.

₧₡

As spring approached, I searched for other ways to get Nadav out of the hospital—fondly remembering Nick's insistence on the healing powers of fresh air.

Getting outdoors while staying on hospital grounds was difficult, but not impossible. There was a slightly larger enclosed garden in the back of the building, past the cafeteria. On warmer days, I'd ask his music therapists if we could hold sessions outside, and they agreed: awkwardly rolling the cart outside the double doors, careful that none of the drums or instruments fell off. They'd set up shop on one of the benches, and we'd sing silly songs in the warm sun.

"Old McDonald," an old favorite, was a frequent song choice, each verse summoning a rowdy barnyard of cows, horses, dogs, and pigs. One time, bored by the usual assortment of farm animals, Nadav suggested "zebras"—which the baffled therapist somehow misheard as "sea bass." From that day on, we made sure we included a "sea bass" every time we sang, even though we could never quite decide what a sea bass sounded like.

₧₡

As the weeks went by, I got more confident in pushing the boundaries. Instead of just exploring the back garden, we'd simply walk out the hospital's front door—through the sliding doors, past security—to spend time in the small garden out front. There wasn't much to see there, to be honest, but it felt just a little bit closer to freedom. Sometimes we'd see Nadav's therapists or off-duty nurses, who'd stop to say hi, surprised to see us outside.

Every time we went out, I'd find myself gazing at the intersection at the end of the road, where a line of cars waited patiently for the light to change. The traffic would get steadily busier as afternoon turned to evening—doctors heading out, nurses changing shifts.

I get to go home at the end of the day, I'd been told by a doctor long ago. *You don't.*

As our weeks in Philadelphia turned into months, those words took on a new irony. We'd learned to adapt to hospital life, developing a peculiar set of skills that made it all bearable. But I wondered when we would ever be able to return home. We'd been away for far too long.

Chapter 39

STUCK, AGAIN

In Australia, we had simply hoped for Nadav to stay alive. In Philadelphia, we spent our days helping him recuperate.

Dr. Rome's successful procedure didn't fix Nadav's underlying problems—it just gave him a chance to recover. And as we'd learned in Australia, that was all any doctor could hope for—to give him the opportunity to heal himself.

And heal he did.

The aspergillus, so terrifying to us in those early days after his emergency surgery, just faded away. His doctors never really knew how much it had spread, but eventually, they simply stopped the voriconazole.

The nasty leg wound that he'd suffered was also on the mend, slowly but surely. Over time, the large gash whitened, then receded. Eventually, it disappeared, the only reminder a harmless-looking almond-shaped dark spot on his lower leg.

ဆာ&

We were amazed by how quickly Nadav's external wounds healed, but what was happening inside his body was even more extraordinary.

Four surgeries and countless procedures had left Nadav with an unnatural circulation and unsustainable pressures. And as we were to find out, some inexplicable force within him did not like this—and tried to fix it.

Even when cardiac surgeries are successful, the body often tries to rewire itself, seeking some sort of equilibrium. Hair-thin vessels fill with blue blood, forming new veins called "collaterals" which short-circuit the new system, subverting the surgeons' best efforts to force the blood in new directions. Sometimes they cause so much trouble that they need to be "coiled off"—a complicated procedure requiring a potentially risky cath.

And so, a winding, wispy mass of new veins had come to dominate Nadav's circulation. These collaterals represented Nadav's natural, unconscious instincts about how his circulation should work; his own second opinion on how his body should heal.

The Picasso had become a Jackson Pollock—new veins running every which way, purple blood flowing backward into his heart. His doctors had no idea how such an inefficient circulation could work. But somehow, with the help of some extra oxygen, it did.

ဆပ္ပ

At the same time, there was a more frustrating mystery to deal with.

The Fontan takedown that we'd flown to CHOP for had done its job. By alleviating the pressure in Nadav's circulation, the leakage from his blood vessels had dwindled to a dribble. Nadav had arrived in Philadelphia in mid-February with three abdominal drains. By the end of March, just one remained.

But for some reason, fluid continued to trickle into the pleural spaces around Nadav's lungs—not nearly as much as when he'd arrived, but enough to keep that drain in. And as long as that drain was there, we had no hope of going home.

It was a maddening enigma. Where was that fluid coming from? Each day, we'd look at yet another cloudy x-ray and wonder how we could get it to stop.

෫ාඟ

To help Nadav's lungs heal, his doctors suggested that he start using a special vest usually prescribed for patients with cystic fibrosis. Powered by an external motor, the vest would shake vigorously for about twenty minutes to help clear out his lungs. It looked pretty aggressive to me, but the therapists assured us that kids actually kind of liked it. They were right: Nadav did too.

To make it a little more fun, I bought a small Bluetooth speaker and put together a YouTube playlist of "shake" songs. Anything with the word "shake" in the lyrics made the cut: "Shake, Rattle and Roll," "All Shook Up," "Shake a Tail Feather," "Shake Your Booty," and—Nadav's favorite—a special version of Taylor Swift's "Shake It Off" produced by the hospital's Child Life department.

As Nadav sat there, shaking—the music booming—passing doctors found it hard not to crack a smile. The respiratory therapists, probably used to staring at the ceiling during therapies, seemed to like it too.

But the lungs, stubborn as ever, refused to clear.

෫ාඟ

Every day, morning rounds reminded us of that stubborn leak.

Starting at around 8 a.m., the medical team would assemble at one end of the hall, chattering in low voices until the attending doctor arrived. Gathering various hangers-on—residents, the nurse manager, and other specialists—they'd slowly shuffle down the hall, pushing their laptops along on wheeled podiums. Stopping at each doorway, each patient's nurse would recite the overnight report.

From our room, we'd watch the herd approach slowly, their mood changing at each stop: sometimes somber, sometimes perfunctory, sometimes animated. A laugh meant hope; low voices, problems.

We didn't worry about other patients—"compare and despair," a doctor once warned us. But the group's mood was important nonetheless. By the time they'd reach our room, it might determine whether Nadav's doctors would indulge some request, giving us the benefit of the doubt, or dig in their heels.

ঔᘏᎴ

Rounds reflected the tidal rhythms of the ward, the source of its inner gravity around which everything rotated. Dictating the pace of care, they could come early, late, or sometimes not at all. They affected our moods, our schedules, our momentum.

As rounds were the basis of day-to-day decision-making, we insisted on taking part as full participants. We rarely asked permission, and doctors almost never objected. I tended to bide my time when doctors deliberated amongst themselves, whereas Tali would jump in whenever she had something to say. But we always shared our opinions, and there was no question in my mind that we were a critical part of the medical team.

A good doctor would listen to our input, but the very best doctors solicited it. They may have had more training, more experience, but we were the Nadav experts. We knew his body best; we knew how he'd react to particular situations; and we were his unabashed advocates, lobbying hard for the things we knew were important but doctors often overlooked.

⊱⟋⟍⊰

Each night, after tucking in Nadav, I'd remind the evening nurse to have the doctors wait for me at morning rounds.

One morning I arrived to find the hall unusually quiet, the usual bustle absent. "When are they rounding?" I asked Nadav's nurse.

"Oh, they rounded already," she said. "But I can page the doctor."

I nearly popped a gasket. Up to that point, it was the angriest I'd been.

I didn't want to be at rounds just to have the doctor tell me what they were doing. I wanted to be there because our point of view was important. Not including a parent's perspective— dismissing the importance of what we knew—struck me as the height of medical arrogance.

I never quite trusted that doctor's judgment again.

⊱⟋⟍⊰

At CHOP, Nadav participated in his own rounds. His doctors came to expect this, waiting patiently as he'd come outside in his chair, or entering the room to talk if he was still in bed.

I always wondered how much Nadav understood about his own condition. We'd explain to him as best we could, trying to avoid euphemisms or oversimplifications. We felt he deserved to know what was happening—it was his own body, after all. But how much can a four-year-old comprehend?

In Nadav's case, much more than one might expect. Once, during rounds, he blurted out the word "lymphatics," leaving the young residents momentarily startled. Many of them were used to talking down to children, abandoning medical jargon for cutesy metaphors.

"Did you wear your leg huggies yesterday?" asked one particularly patronizing doctor, referring to the splints that physical therapists used to strengthen his leg muscles. "*Knee immobilizers*," corrected Nadav, rolling his eyes.

Nadav's rounds in Philadelphia always centered around his chest x-ray. The fluid leak that persisted in his right lung cast a dark shadow across silvery tissue, stubbornly refusing to disappear. Every day, we stared at that black cloud, wishing that it would pass.

The resident would usually turn the screen so Nadav could see; sometimes, with new doctors, he'd have to ask. He'd stare at it for a few seconds, intently—his doctors waiting patiently, gazing at him, wondering what else they could do to get him home.

ଚଠଷ

One afternoon, we off-handedly asked Chitra about Nadav's long-term prognosis.

It was unplanned, just one of the casual conversations we'd often have at the workstation just outside his room. But although we weren't in the family room, she was forthright and direct. She knew us well enough to know we could handle it.

"Obviously, I can't predict the future," she said. "But my best guess is that he has around six to eight months left."

Chitra's frank prognosis reflected how dire our situation really was. Even if Nadav's lung somehow cleared, she explained, he would still need a transplant to survive. And not just a heart transplant, but a heart-lung transplant—even more of a long-shot.

To me, Nadav's new circulation—the mess of collaterals that had formed, somehow keeping him alive—was a magical adaptation, a testament to his toughness and resilience. But to a surgeon, it was a minefield of the unknown, an operating-table disaster waiting to happen.

Chitra knew the truth, and her gaze told us as much. It was highly unlikely that any doctor would ever take that chance.

Chapter 40

DEALING WITH PRESSURE

After Chitra's unsettling prognosis, our focus changed. Now, the goal was not merely to get Nadav home. We needed to get him a transplant too.

We started lobbying Chitra and Dr. Rome to consider it, every chance we could. But it wasn't their decision. CHOP's transplant team—a separate department—would have to accept Nadav as a candidate for a new heart. In early April, they agreed to present him as a transplant candidate at one of their regular meetings.

Chitra and Dr. Rome were two of the calmest, most rational doctors we'd ever met—they were always brutally honest and candid about his prognosis, and despite all of the logical reasons for pessimism, I think they desperately wanted to find him some path to survival.

On the day of the meeting, we lingered around the ward, looking for them, but they were nowhere to be found. When Chitra finally appeared, she refused to talk about it. "Not today," she said, a frown on her face. "Let's talk tomorrow."

The message was clear. The transplant team had refused to put him on the list.

⍓⍓

I learned later why Chitra wasn't in the mood to talk. They'd passionately argued Nadav's case and ran into a brick wall. Perhaps the transplant team thought his case was too risky; perhaps there was something else going on. It was hard to get a straight answer—but, whatever the reason, the answer was no.

Someone told me that Dr. Rome, ordinarily so dispassionate and rational, had left the meeting so upset that he shut himself in his office, listening to classical music. We weren't the only ones devastated by the decision.

⍓⍓

By this point, we were used to hearing bad news—but this felt like the worst. Nadav's future seemed truly out of our hands. We had to somehow draw on the inner resilience we'd developed along the way—and our unshakable faith in our son's strength. No matter how bad it got, things had always seemed to work out, somehow. But the transplant seemed like a particularly difficult challenge.

I'd been doing my best to take care of myself, settling into a reassuring routine at the end of each day. After reading Nadav some bedtime books, I'd wander outside, ready for a quiet dinner, alone with my thoughts. By the time I'd said my farewells, dark had usually fallen.

I'd usually head to one of two places: a lively Mexican joint across campus, where I'd eat at the bar, or a spicy Szechuan place a bit farther away, with a quiet seat by the window. In both places, I'd order a cold beer, and sip it slowly—my body relaxing, safe from crisis until the next morning. Until then, numb to it all.

ঙ০ৎ

Our housing situation improved in the early spring when a room opened up in the Ronald McDonald House nearby. Finally, we could leave our borrowed apartment, where we'd stayed for nearly a month.

The boys liked this space better. There was a game room, and a jukebox—far more entertaining than the random collection of scattered toys in the old space. Tali and I were just happy for the luxurious pillowtop bed, and a full kitchen filled with donated food. Every Sunday morning, a visiting family or group would cook us a hot breakfast.

Calories helped Nadav grow; unfortunately, they also helped me cope. At times, stress eating was unavoidable. During the week, I developed an unfortunate taste for Frosted Mini-Wheats, which I'd found in the gigantic walk-in pantry.

Ironically, it was hard to find healthy meals in hospitals: vending machines were convenient, junk food brought comfort. In cafeterias, elegance was hit-or-miss, mushy cucumbers an all-too-easy excuse for skipping the salad bar. Better to choose a grilled cheese instead—salty, filling, predictable, reliable.

ঙ০ৎ

I dealt with stress as best I could, but the challenge of how to find Nadav a transplant was making it harder and harder for me to keep my emotions in check.

Once I lost my temper at the bedside, storming out in a fit of rage. Apparently, the nurse on duty, whom we didn't know well, had been ready to call security. When we got a copy of the medical record, months later, we found out later that the nurses sometimes logged our moods as part of their daily routine.

I once noticed that Nadav was assigned nothing but male nurses for a week and worried that I'd said something inappropriate to one of the female nurses. But when I asked the nurse manager, she just laughed; the next day, Nadav had a female nurse again.

ഇരു

The sort of anger I felt during Nadav's odyssey was never caused by hatred. I can't think of a single thing I hated during Nadav's life, except perhaps the NG tube we had to insert down his throat. But even that was a necessary evil; the tube, slimy and upsetting as it was, wasn't to blame for what we were going through. It was just trying to help, in its own way.

My body had learned to absorb all of the emotions that bombarded us on a daily basis, but every so often they'd bubble over and I'd explode in rage. Stress, tension, exhaustion—all combustible; even the tiniest frustration would light the fuse.

Whenever I felt anger, I'd let it burn a little, but I always tried to put it out before it did real harm. There were too many bridges to be burned, after all, and I vowed never to let my exasperation get in the way of Nadav's needs.

Tali and I sometimes quarreled, but our sniping was limited to the empty spaces between crises, a check valve to blow off excess steam. Our anger, expressed, was a form of communication—a cry of despair, usually aimed at someone safe, someone who could absorb it without scarring. If things got really bad, it stopped. And if Nadav needed us, we immediately buried whatever we felt, knowing that it wasn't the place or the time, and left it until later to sort out our emotions.

⁊◑ʒ

One would think that having a child in dire medical straits would bring parents together, but apparently parents in similar situations are just as likely to separate or divorce, if not more so.

During our time at CHOP, we heard a tragic story of a former patient, a little girl who had just received a heart transplant. Soon after they returned home, her father snapped—killing the whole family, including himself, in an inexplicable fit of rage. I was stunned, not because I couldn't imagine the pressure they were under, but because I felt them all too well.

But to respond by harming your family was something that I could not imagine.

I asked Chitra about it; she had known the family during their time in the hospital. I'd assumed she would feel angry, but no. "Just sad," she said wistfully, "Just sad." It was a waste, she explained, and not just a waste of a life—it was a waste of a heart. A perfectly good little heart.

Chapter 41

PUSHING LIMITS

I brought the boys to visit the hospital a week after CHOP refused to consider Nadav's transplant. It was the second night of Passover, and we looked forward to sharing a special meal with Nadav. The hospital had arranged a community Seder, and we'd eagerly accepted their invitation, pleased that the five of us would be able to celebrate the holiday together.

Passover commemorates our ancestors' miraculous liberation from a faraway land. "In every generation a person must regard himself as though he personally had gone out of Egypt," the Haggadah reminds us—words that seemed to echo our own extraordinary return from exile on the other side of the world.

We arrived to an empty room—huge trays of food at one end, the tables elegantly set with fake electric candles and white tablecloths. We thought we were just early. But nobody else showed up, not even the hospital's volunteer rabbi.

When the event coordinator stopped by to check in, we told her that it was just us. She frowned briefly but urged us to enjoy the meal anyway. "At least there's enough food!" she said, brightly.

But we'd lost our appetites, and headed upstairs early—our enthusiasm dampened by the huge, vacant space.

ଧର୍ଷ

Like the ancient Israelites, we were not short of miracles—although ours came not from the heavens but rather from within.

When he'd arrived at CHOP, Nadav had been a mess—intubated and sedated, muscles atrophied by months in bed. It seemed crazy to think that he'd ever make it back on his feet. But by the spring, he was learning how to use his legs again.

His therapists—always persistent—started by finding him a stander to strengthen his muscles. Before long, they put him on a tricycle, helmet precariously perched on his head—drains and oxygen tank held off to the side. "Push," they urged, "you can do it." And he did...slowly but surely, willing the wheels to move, ever so slightly.

Then, it was time to move his feet—first, supported under his arms, gingerly limping between the therapists' legs; then with a walker, pushed awkwardly along the floor, all by himself. And then, just holding our hands for balance, he was able to take his first steps. It was the first time he'd walked since we'd arrived at Westmead, so many months before.

Like the first words we'd heard with Gloria in Australia, I remember these steps far more vividly than those he'd first taken as a toddler. As exciting as those first steps had been, they now seemed pedestrian—a typical consequence of natural development. These felt far more remarkable, characteristic of Nadav's resilience, a force of extraordinary will.

ଧର୍ଷ

Every day after that, we'd go for a walk—tottering slowly along a red line in the hallway, the PT kneeling in front in case he stumbled, as I followed behind with his oxygen tank. Eventually, he'd be able to make it as far as the nurses' station, everyone cheering as he turned the corner: "Go Nadav! You can do it!"

A nightly walk around the ward became our bedtime routine—a little bit farther each evening, until he got too tired. He wasn't always enthusiastic, but he did it, and I felt so proud.

It was a spectacular sight to see, but as always, it still wasn't enough for his therapists. It was never enough. They put him on a treadmill in the exercise room for extra practice, hands clinging to the padded bars for support. They'd sneak him past heavy fire doors to practice walking up and down the emergency stairs.

They didn't take no for an answer. They were no-nonsense magicians.

৪০৫৪

Passover wasn't the only time the boys came to visit Nadav. I'd often bring them down on weekends, and although it was nice for them to spend time with their brother, the hospital could feel oppressive.

We'd often go for a walk together, Yaniv pushing his brother in the wheelchair—usually heading to a small rooftop courtyard in the rehab wing. It was the hospital's best play space, filled with balls, slides, and a basketball hoop—and most importantly, fresh air. They'd race around, flinging things at each other, as Nadav watched.

Their energy encouraged Nadav to get out of his wheelchair, taking the opportunity to practice walking. He especially enjoyed hiding out in a small playhouse, his various tubes wrapping through windows, twisting here and there in a tangled jumble. Sometimes he went down the slide too, gently caught at the bottom in our waiting arms.

We'd have lunch together in the cafeteria, sipping chicken soup through straws and then eating sushi afterwards ("why not?")—the boys unwrapping salmon rolls with their bare hands: raw fish with a rice chaser, their favorite meal.

Gilad and Yaniv would lobby for ice creams—but Nadav, perhaps the only boy around who didn't like it, still wasn't interested. It was a shame; so packed with calories, it was the perfect food.

What parent wishes that their kid would eat *more* ice cream?

&OCR;

For months, we asked and asked for permission for Nadav to leave the hospital grounds. But every time the answer was no. So we snuck him out.

The back of the hospital was flush against Penn's campus, a quiet corner without much traffic, and Tali knew from her college years that if you walked along the back of the hospital, making a left turn past the nursing school, and followed a paved trail up a wooded hill, you'd find a small pond filled with turtles. She started taking Nadav there regularly, pushing his wheelchair around the small dirt path ringing the pond, watching the turtles sunning themselves on half-submerged rocks.

It felt slightly transgressive, but the feeling of freedom was well worth it. Knowing that we could escape the hospital, if only slightly, was a relief. After endless days of cloudy x-rays, the fresh air gave us hope that we might eventually leave for good.

&OCR;

One day, on a whim, I decided to take Nadav to the underground parking lot to see our beloved red Subaru. (Technically, the garage was part of the hospital grounds, so I wasn't breaking any rules.) I opened the passenger door, and let him sit inside for a few minutes, enjoying a small reminder of what life was like long ago.

Seeing him there, sitting happily in his old car seat, gave me the confidence do something even more daring. A month later, when his brothers were visiting, I pulled our car up next to the hospital's back entrance—and as the boys nervously jumped in, afraid of who might be watching, Tali and I bundled Nadav into his seat, drains and all.

It was a grand adventure, the boys excitedly giggling in the back as we fastened his seatbelt for the first time in ages, and carefully pulled out onto the main road, just for the fun of it.

I drove slowly around the neighborhood, as we pointed out all of the things Nadav had never seen—the main road, Penn's campus, the Palestra gymnasium, Franklin Field. He gazed outside, emotionless; I suppose he was a little overwhelmed. But it was nice to be a family again, out for a drive—if only for a few minutes.

When we returned, we didn't say anything to the nurses, even though we wanted to share how wonderful it was, and why we were so happy. I didn't think they'd mind, really, but we didn't want to get anyone in trouble.

Later, Chitra would admit, not unhappily, that she knew something was up.

⊱⊰

After months of asking, Chitra finally granted us a day out—on July 4th. We called it our Independence Day.

Once the papers were signed, warnings issued, and monitor attached, we again bundled Nadav into the car—this time with his nurse's help. The twins sat on each side, Gilad in the middle, holding a soccer ball, and we headed off for lunch at a nearby diner. Nadav asked for a hamburger, and for a few minutes it was as if we'd escaped for good.

The next stop was a nearby playground that we'd never been to before. On any other day, this would have been an ordinary outing; with Nadav, it was a thrilling event. He couldn't climb the jungle gym like his brothers, but it was enough for him to sit on a bench and watch them play. We tossed tennis balls to him instead.

Even just seeing real dogs out for a walk was a wonderful change. Unlike the docile hospital dogs who occasionally visited the ward, these dogs were exuberant and unruly, nipping at each other, tugging at their leashes as they jumped around.

One of my favorite photos of that day shows me holding Nadav next to a "No Smoking" sign reading "Young Lungs at Play." Our sense of irony was finely tuned—Nadav's young lungs were usually supported by extra oxygen. But he wasn't wearing his nasal cannula that day, and I can't remember why. Perhaps we just wanted to leave as much of the hospital behind as we could.

The outing was fun, but it took a lot out of all of us. The boys were understandably disappointed about going back to the hospital. When we returned, Gilad played some guitar for Nadav as he rested in bed, and Yaniv read a few books, as we all settled back into hospital-land.

For now, it was as close to home as we were going to get.

Chapter 42

BITTERNESS

I t was nice to able to escape the hospital as a family. But sometimes, to be honest, I needed some time away by myself.

A mile away from the hospital was the Mütter Museum, known for its macabre collection of medical oddities. A half-hour's walk away, it was just close enough for a quick visit while Nadav napped. I wandered the exhibits, full of anatomical specimens and other random objects: organs pickled in formaldehyde, scary-looking surgical instruments, a carefully arranged collection of things that people have swallowed over the years.

There was one thing in particular I hoped to see. I had some trouble finding it amongst the ephemera, but I finally spotted it on a small shelf in a crowded hall. It was a preserved human heart—encased in plastic, sterile and static, all of its wonder long departed.

୫୦୯୫

CHOP's refusal to consider Nadav for a heart transplant had left us disappointed but undeterred, and we asked Chitra to help us explore other options. There were three children's hospitals on the East Coast that might we try, she said: one in Pittsburgh, one in Boston, and one (Columbia) not far from our home in New York.

Moving Nadav to a hospital even farther away from home would have been a logistical nightmare. But if any of those hospitals had said yes, we would have somehow made it work.

"Can you reach out to them?" we asked.

"Sure," Chitra said. "I know the people there. I can ask."

"Would it help if we wrote a note, too?" we asked. We weren't above pulling at heartstrings.

"Can't hurt," she said.

ഇഃരു

And so, we did. In the letter, we told them of the deep respect we had for the doctors we'd met. We told them of Nadav's resilience: the challenges he'd faced in Australia, and the miracle flight that had brought him back.

We thought they should know who he was—as a person, not a patient. We explained why we'd chosen his two first names. We listed the things he loved ("Curious George, eating smoked sprats, and performing catheterizations on his stuffed animals with drinking straws"). We summarized his personality ("clever, charming, cheeky, and independent").

We included two photos—one from preschool, and one from CHOP.

And we closed by telling them why we needed their help:

> "It would be a great shame for the world to lose Nadav. He is a special boy, well worth saving. Against all expectations, he has made the most of every opportunity he has been given. He deserves another chance—not just because of what he has been through, but because the world is a better place with him in it."

All of this was bundled in a two-page PDF, which Chitra forwarded along.

But it wasn't enough—at least not for Boston or Pittsburgh, who both said no.

🙰🙰🙰

Aware of our plight, one of the surgical anesthesiologists pulled us aside. "You should just sneak out and take him to Columbia yourself," she said, in a whisper. After all, although they hadn't said yes…they hadn't said no.

"What, just walk out of here—with him?" we asked, incredulous.

"Sure," she said. "CHOP can't *make* you stay. And Columbia wouldn't turn you away if you showed up in person, not a kid in Nadav's condition. They'd *have* to take care of him."

But we dismissed the idea: too crazy. No matter how strong we were, how persistent—we couldn't do it alone.

🙰🙰🙰

Nadav wasn't the only one hoping for a transplant. A few of his neighbors were on the list, including one boy on the other side of the ward, an adorable little kid whose parents were always bustling around. Tali had met his mother, and I'd said hi to the dad a few times, but we didn't know them that well.

One day we were invited to his birthday party, held in the playroom at the end of the hall. We bought along a present, a small tube of brightly colored plastic animals that Nadav had chosen from the hospital gift shop earlier that day. The boy's extended family chattered away in Spanish as they served out slices of layered Disney cake.

We didn't stay long. It was too crowded, and we didn't know anyone. (Nadav even refused a slice of cake—it was made of ice cream.) But it was nice to share in their celebration.

The next morning, a nurse pulled me aside in the hall. "Did you hear the good news?" she asked, pointing at the boy's room. "I'm not allowed to tell you what happened, but ask his mom."

It turned out that at four in the morning, long after the party had been cleaned up and all of the guests had gone home, they'd gotten a call. A heart was on its way; a transplant would be scheduled within hours.

The best birthday present ever.

℘℧℘

The little boy left the hospital soon after his successful transplant, new heart and all. It was such an inspiring experience, and it was hard not to feel pleased for him.

And yet, when I imagined the euphoria that his family felt when they'd heard the news, I couldn't help but feel a hint of jealousy. It was unlikely that we'd ever be lucky enough to feel that same triumph with Nadav. Part of me suspected that we were probably asking for one miracle too many.

I tried to wish that little speck of bitterness away, pretending it didn't exist.

℘℧℘

Of all of the emotions I experienced during Nadav's life, bitterness is still the one that makes me shudder, its inner ugliness at odds with the strength I hoped I had.

It was an emotion I usually kept in check, fearful of what it might make me. Every time I felt the slightest twinge, I trembled—a hairline crack in my inner strength. If left unchecked, I feared, it would shatter my goodness into a million sharp shards.

Every day, we trod a fine line between our world and the rest of humanity. Outside of the hospital, we were surrounded by strangers with no idea what we were going through, and no reason to care. Their lives proceeded normally; no need to temper their joy with our pain.

Usually I just ignored it, but sometimes I'd instinctively wonder whether they realized how irrelevant, superficial, and meaningless their lives seemed. And then I'd try to put that thought out of my mind. It wasn't the person I wanted to be.

∞☾☽

Those moments of bitterness only emerged every so often, in all their terrible honesty, a single glance unleashing demons within.

Take one moment that struck unexpectedly on a beautiful summer day—Tali in Philadelphia, me back home in New York with the boys. As I crossed the street, I saw a new mother in front of me, pushing an expensive pram. Walking by her side was a nanny, diaper bags slung over her shoulder.

That otherwise ordinary scene has stayed in my mind for a single reason. Instead of the happiness one usually feels for a new parent, I felt nothing but anger. *Why*, my insides screamed, *must this mother need help with something so simple as a single healthy baby?*

I'd felt that separation before, in different contexts. I thought back to the day Gilad was born, when I'd passed the packed bars full of laughter. *What on earth were they all celebrating?* I'd wondered. I felt no bitterness then, of course—just a strange sense that my happiness stood alone.

But bitterness starts with that sense of lonely difference, that you alone suffer from something from which others are exempt; that they never really know how you feel. What turns that feeling into anger is the misguided conviction that they don't care. And you really *want* to feel that way sometimes, because they don't *need* to care, and you do.

But they do care, really. Or they would, if they only knew.

ಬಿೀಇ

Yes, people say stupid things sometimes.

"Is he OK?" they'd ask, seeing Nadav at my side, NG tube up his nose and an oxygen tank swinging from the back.

How was I to answer that?

"Yes, he's OK," I could say. "His sats are in the mid-80s, he's not in intensive care, or dealing with an emergent clot—he's with his father, and all is right with the world."

Or:

"No, he's not OK," I could say. "He was born with a single-ventricled heart that's required four surgeries, his circulation is completely abnormal, and there's a good chance he won't make it."

I usually chose some variant of the first—the optimistic outlook—which is what I usually felt, and what most people wanted to hear.

But every so often, if I was in a foul mood, I'd imagine answering the other way—just so that they would feel a little bit of the pain I fended off every day.

☙❧

Humanity is what carried us along—pure generosity of spirit, an altruism that gave us buoyancy as we were swept along in uncertain waters. Were it not for the kindness of others, we might have drowned.

In early July, a child life specialist asked us if we could think of anything special for Nadav to do. We'd been at the hospital for nearly five months and explored every inch of the campus. We had been so wholly focused on food, one of us suggested that perhaps he'd like to see the hospital's kitchens. And sure enough, they managed to arrange a tour.

The three of us were whisked downstairs on a special elevator to meet the hospital's head chef, who showed us vast rooms filled with industrial mixers and giant ovens, even a special closet filled with Nadav's favorite spices. One of the guys who'd worked at the pizza station spotted us, recognizing Nadav. "Yo, OREGANO!" he yelled from across the room, a big smile on his face.

We felt like royalty. It was that sort of place.

☙❧

Tali started telling the chef about how frustrating it was to feed Nadav, asking if she had any advice about high-calorie meals.

"Oh," said the chef, "what does he like?"

"Lamb," said Tali. "He loves lamb."

"Well, we have a halal menu," she said. "It's mostly lamb. But," she added, "if he wants something special, let me know, and we'll make it."

Which is how we ended up exchanging emails like this:

Tali: [July 15, 12:08 PM] We got a copy of the halal menu and tried to order the lamb kafta over the phone but was told it's no longer on the menu. Is it possible to make him a lamb dish for dinner tonight?

Chef: *[July 15, 12:45 PM] We can do lamb chops and orzo tonight! Please just let me know what time you would like it and also your room number and I will have it sent up at that time!*

Tali: *[July 15, 1:28 PM] Thank you so much. With a few green beans please.*

Chef: *[July 15, 1:36 PM] No problem!! It will arrive around 5:45 pm. We will season the lamb chops with salt, pepper, and fresh oregano!!*

Nadav's new friends in the kitchen did their best to accommodate his tastes, no matter how picky he was:

Tali: *[August 9, 12:23 PM] Nadav has a special request for dinner… A hamburger cooked with a little garlic shallots and parsley mixed into the patty, like we do at home.*

Chef: *[August 9, 2:57 PM] Hi this request is more than achievable. The only unfortunate event is that we don't carry shallots. Would some red onion be okay?*

Tali: *[August 9, 3:15 PM] Unfortunately Nadav is not a fan of onions. Just parsley and garlic would be great. Thanks so much!!*

Chef: *[August 9, 3:44 PM] You're welcome! It is our pleasure.*

Tali wrote a thank-you note later that evening, reporting that "Nadav thought it was absolutely delicious…and ate over an ounce which for him is enormous." She added: "We are touched as always by your generosity and appreciate you giving our little guy a little taste of home."

𝕰𝕺𝕽𝕭

We often take so much for granted—our health, our loved ones, even the meals we eat.

Remembering the unexpected warmth we'd found in CHOP's kitchens, I'm reminded how much we take our humanity for granted too. The full extent of our kindness—the caring we all possess, the empathy we all can feel—is almost never seen until situations demand it.

I still feel privileged to have had a son who, by both circumstance and charm, had such an amazing capacity to reveal the goodness in the world. The irony, of course, is that were it not for his unique, inexplicable physiology—the cilia that didn't quite beat, the proteins that didn't quite twist—we may never have been lucky enough to experience it.

Chapter 43

LAST CHANCE LYMPHATICS

As August approached, Nadav's cloudy lung persisted. Dr. Rome had put in two stents, hoping that reducing his internal pressures even further might stop the leakage. But it didn't. The x-rays remained as murky as ever, and we were running out of options.

Dr. Rome was baffled; Chitra was stumped. Nobody quite knew what was leaking or why. But two other doctors, specialists in lymphatics, thought they knew what was happening. The likely culprit, they suspected, was Nadav's lymphatic system.

One of the doctors, a Russian, was quiet, and rarely spoke. But his partner—an energetic Israeli named Yoav—was always happy to chat. Yoav radiated a cheerful enthusiasm, a "don't worry, can-do" demeanor. Having heard that we were baseball fans, he promised Nadav that they'd go to a Phillies game together before the summer was over. "We'll figure it out," he said. "It will be great. We'll go. Just you see."

ॐ

Yoav was passionate about his specialty, convinced that it held the key to why so many Fontans failed. (His favorite t-shirt read: "I'm a lymphomanic.") He would lament how little doctors knew how about how the lymphatic system functioned, much less the critical role it played in a single ventricle circulation.

"Nobody understands it!" he would exclaim in exasperation. "*Nobody!*"

In the future, he suspected, early lymphatic imaging for newborns with congenital heart defects would be routine, helping doctors better determine which patients might respond better to certain approaches. If doctors knew in advance what was going on in the lymphatic system, he predicted, they might choose not to do the Fontan at all.

ଛୠଓ

Nadav's lymphatic system, it turned out, was a mess. It was like something painted by an abstract expressionist, lymph nodes missing or misplaced, vessels splattered this way and that. In retrospect, Yoav told us, it wasn't surprising that his third surgery had turned out to be so problematic.

To solve Nadav's leakage, he recommended a series of lymphatic embolizations—basically supergluing various lymphatic vessels shut to stop their flow. Tali and I were familiar with the approach; after all, a doctor at Westmead had tried a similar procedure to no avail. But the lymphologists at CHOP were on the cutting edge of the field. Their efforts over the summer helped reduce Nadav's effusions to a mere trickle.

But that still wasn't good enough. The amount of fluid leaking into his right lung was still significant enough to require a drain. Unless it stopped completely, we would never make it home.

ଛୠଓ

Things came to a head in mid-August, when Nadav's doctors asked Tali for a family meeting. I was driving down from New York, but they couldn't wait. So, I called in from a rest stop on the New Jersey Turnpike, pacing back and forth along a small patch of weathered grass.

Tali asked a few questions, calmly interrogating the doctors with characteristic detail. But their only response was a hard truth. "We've done pretty much all we can," Dr. Rome said, his voice crackling over my phone's bad connection. "And we can't stop the leak."

The bottom line was clear. They'd try one more lymphatic intervention, and that was it. If it didn't work, there was nothing more they could do.

We agreed to try it. We didn't have much of a choice.

ঌOCঙ

We didn't know any of this at the time, but Yoav and his partner apparently disagreed on what the final procedure should actually entail. One of them thought the problems stemmed from the liver; the other was convinced that they should focus on the thoracic duct. From the way it was described to us, their disagreement may have become a little heated in the operating room, possibly including finger-pointing and some rapid bursts of colloquial Hebrew.

Whatever the case, they managed to come to a compromise. They'd shut the lymphatic vessels in both places: the liver AND the thoracic duct.

We'll never know who was right. Perhaps they both were. But in the end, it didn't matter. The leak finally stopped.

By the end of the week, the x-ray had cleared up. Soon afterward, we were talking about a discharge plan.

Yoav kept his promise. Three weeks after the successful lymphatic procedure, he got the hospital to arrange a private box at Citizen's Bank Ballpark, home of the Phillies. And on a late summer evening, they went to the ballpark together—Tali and Nadav, Yoav and his family—to celebrate yet another achievement.

I didn't make it. It was my time to be back in New York with the boys, and it was a school night. I briefly toyed with the idea of driving down—we'd done crazier things—but in the end decided it would be too exhausting.

In any case, they only stayed a few innings, enough time to soak it all in and nibble on a hot dog. When I next came down, they excitedly showed me the goodies he'd been given, a red and blue Phillies backpack filled with trinkets.

It was just one more thing we'd have to pack. In less than a week—six months after we arrived—we'd finally be going home.

Chapter 44

LEAVING PHILLY

Packing up was not easy. We'd accumulated a ton of stuff over the past six months, and sorting through the piles in his room seemed an endless task. Eventually we managed to separate the things we wanted to take with us (favorite books, stuffed animals, cards from friends) from the things we'd leave for other patients (extra toys, dozens of crayons, stacks of construction paper). It was sometimes difficult to know what to leave behind—nametags, scrawled doctors' notes, leaflets from the child life department—all filled with memories, but no longer useful.

Well-accustomed to the rituals of a hospital discharge, we also packed a few boxes of medical supplies. The nurses gathered up everything around his bed, asking us if there was anything we'd like to keep. (Once assigned to a particular patient, some items couldn't be reused.) We'd ask for specific things we knew were hard to find, or prohibitively expensive—like the sticky film we used to hold Nadav's NG tube to his face, worth its weight in gold.

We had a hard time letting anything go to waste. An impressive collection of cheap thermometers still lingers in a drawer at home, batteries slowly fading, their tiny screws too frustrating to fix.

ಬಂಡ

While we were packing, we were approached by a researcher who was doing a genetic study of cardiac defects. Would we consent to genetic testing? We didn't see why not. It wouldn't help us, but perhaps what they could learn from our samples might help others.

Tali and I both scheduled blood tests. I brought Nadav along for mine, wheeling him to an outpatient clinic in an unfamiliar part of the hospital. A no-nonsense phlebotomist, obviously used to bawling, panicked children, stuck a needle in my arm and a cartoon Band-Aid on top.

Nadav watched, amused—for once, someone else was the pincushion. I put on the bravest face I could muster, a fatherly stoicism that masked my mild anxiety. I have never been a big fan of needles.

ಬಂಡ

Someone from the child life department hung a green-and-white quilt on Nadav's door, attaching a Sharpie on a string, so that it could be signed by everyone who came by. It served as a grand announcement that one of their long-term residents was finally moving out.

His nurses eagerly decorated the quilt with smiley faces and curvy hearts. But they had mixed emotions too; their smiles often overshadowed by a slight frown. "We'll miss him," they'd say, wistfully, and we'd reply: "He'll miss you too."

We spread the news to everyone we knew, including our friends in the kitchen downstairs:

> *Tali: [August 19, 1:09 PM] Thanks again for your wonderful meals. Not sure if you know but we are*

scheduled for discharge on Tuesday so we will have to cook at home!!!

The chef's response still brings tears to my eyes:

Chef: *[August 19, 2:51 PM] I think I speak for all of us when I say it has been our pleasure to serve your family. I'm glad to hear that Nadav will be discharged as I'm sure he is ready to be back home for some good home cooking as well.*

We are here to deliver experiences that enrich and nourish lives and I'm grateful that we have been able to make a difference through the food we've provided. I never underestimate the power and role that food plays in our lives, and it was a pleasure to meet your beautiful son.

How lucky we were! How many people leave the hospital thinking how much they'd miss the food?

ဆာၚ

For old times' sake, Tali and I spent our last night at the Irish pub we'd visited that first week in Philadelphia, the one with the Rocky poster near the bar. We lifted a glass in an exhausted toast, somehow granted another unexpected step on the long path home.

The next day, it was time to say our final farewells.

Someone had suggested we take Nadav's wheelchair home with us, but Tali refused—she didn't want to give him any excuses not to walk. So, we found a little red wagon, to make it easier to bring him downstairs; and sat him inside with the few remaining bags. Wheeling him down the familiar halls for the last time, we said our goodbyes.

There was some sadness in leaving, like saying goodbye to a house full of close-knit cousins. We had been there nearly half a year, the weather shifting from bitter cold to the heat of summer. Inside, the temperature stayed constant, the rhythms of the hospital protective and comforting.

And then it was time to go, our red Subaru having been packed earlier in the day.

❧

A nurse had promised to help us out, but when I pulled the car up to the rear entrance, she was nowhere to be found. It wasn't a hardship, but I remember being a little disappointed that she wasn't there.

But looking up at the building we'd come to know so well, I realized that it was no longer ours. Leave the nurses for those who needed them, I figured. Thank goodness we don't need to be here anymore.

It was time for us to finally head home.

Proper.

HOME AGAIN

Chapter 45

HOME, PROPER

I f we hadn't done the trip so many times before, I would have been nervous to drive home with such precious cargo in the back seat. The last time Nadav had been on a highway, he'd been in an ambulance. But even though I was at the wheel, our trusty Subaru would take us home. It knew the way.

We merged onto the service road leading from the hospital to the Schuylkill Expressway, toward the Walt Whitman Bridge and New Jersey. The on-ramp was always cluttered with billboards—car dealerships, clothing, casinos. But this time, I noticed a new sign out of the corner of my eye.

"YOU NEED TO SEE THIS!" it urged, next to a snapshot of the Sydney Opera House. "AUSTRALIA FROM $1,865 – AIRFARE INCLUDED."

ജ

Nadav sat in the back seat with his favorite friend—a stuffed monkey—at his side. They gazed out of the window together, watching the world go by as we zoomed north on the New Jersey Turnpike.

I put on "Shake a Tail Feather" from the Blues Brothers, one of Nadav's favorite songs on the "shake party" playlist and turned it up so Nadav could hear. He smiled, singing along quietly, waving the monkey in time with the music, so his friend could dance too.

I can't imagine what Nadav must have been feeling at that moment. But even if he wanted to tell me, I'm not sure if he would be able to find the words. He was too young; I was probably too old. He was the cardiac kid; I was just the dad.

But his smile said it all. It was pure delight, an unbelievable accomplishment—and we felt nothing but pride.

ℰℐℬℛ

We stopped for lunch at a favorite diner just off the Turnpike, halfway home—the same place I'd take his brothers whenever we drove down to Philadelphia. Connoisseurs of chicken broth, Gilad and Yaniv considered the soup there to be as good as their grandmothers'. And they always insisted that we sit in the "lounge" near the bar and a row of TVs. Soup and sports, a heavenly combination.

When we arrived with Nadav, the lounge was empty. It was just the three of us, eating together in freedom for the first time in almost nine months. Nadav happily slurped his soup through a straw as Tali and I gazed at each other, amazed we'd come this far.

In all our times there, we'd never met this particular waiter. But he must have sensed it was a special occasion. When it came time for the check, he smiled, and told us it was on the house.

ℰℐℬℛ

We arrived home in the late afternoon, to an empty apartment. (We'd arranged for the boys to stay with my parents to make things easier.) I carried him upstairs, feeling his soft skin next to mine—and opened the door, finally welcoming him home.

Nadav sat on his bed for a few minutes, looking around at the bedroom; spent some time at his small table in the kitchen, taking it all in; and played with some Legos on the floor, familiar toys he hadn't seen in nearly a year. And then, after a bath, it was finally time to sleep. It had been a long, crazy day.

But first, we read a book in the biggie bed. Together.

ಶಂಛ

t was nice to be home. And—to tell the truth—a little scary too. Over the next few days, thousands of dollars of medical equipment filled our apartment. Oxygen tanks, NG tubes, a CPAP machine—all delivered by a friendly technician named Gabriel, our new guardian angel.

Whenever a new shipment arrived, we opened the boxes like eager children, making sure everything was right. Were the tubes the right size? Did the syringes fit the needles? And why on earth did they send so much gel? Nadav's brothers loved the boxes, too, using them as flimsy bumper cars until the cardboard bent too much to push.

The most important thing was making sure Nadav had a steady supply of supplemental oxygen. We'd arranged for an oxygen concentrator to be delivered to our apartment, along with extra tanks for when we headed out. They came in various sizes, each a trade-off between duration and weight.

One day, I stopped by a firehouse to show Nadav that the firemen needed oxygen too. They had fun comparing tanks: theirs were worn and dirty, dusty gray; Nadav's were green and shiny new.

The ends of the oxygen tubes hung over Nadav's ears, holding a cannula that gently pushed oxygen into his nostrils. Sometimes, we'd accidentally put it on backward—leaving the oxygen to blow gently past Nadav's face, tickling the tip of his nose as it disappeared into thin air.

Every medical device has its own tricks, and once Gabriel taught us some little things that made it easier—*attach this to this; turn this; better to do this*—the oxygen concentrator was simple enough to master. We had no trouble conjuring it to life; and eventually its steady hum faded into the background, like the subway trains that rumbled deep below our building.

୫୦୯ଷ

Now that we were home, it was important to turn our attention to things other than medicine. Once again, we had to leave the hospital behind and rediscover what it meant to lead a normal life.

All three of the boys were again sharing the same room; bedtimes were routine, aside from the low hum of Nadav's CPAP machine; and during the day, things were chaotic as ever.

Tali was determined to not let anything stop Nadav from having the same experiences as his brothers. Even before we came home, she'd started documenting and arranging the specialized care he'd need. And she had already made up her mind that Nadav would spend the fall like any other five-year-old.

He was going to go to kindergarten.

Chapter 46

KINDERGARTEN

We'd lived across the street from a public elementary school for years. But we'd only visited it once, four years before, when we were trying to decide what school was best for Gilad.

Crammed into a stifling hot cafeteria with dozens of other anxious parents, we'd been welcomed by a stern warning from a frazzled staffer. "The first thing you need to know," she said loudly, trying to project her voice off the ceiling and around the room, "is that there is *no parking on the street.*"

It wasn't a great first impression, and we ended up sending Gilad (and later, Yaniv) to another public school a little farther away. But it was our zoned school, and when Nadav finally returned home after his nine-month medical odyssey, it became his.

৪০৪৪

By law, the Department of Education has to accommodate any child with a disability. But that didn't mean that it would be easy. ("If they give you a hard time," one hard-nosed mom warned us, "just threaten to sue 'em.")

Bracing for the worst, we set up a meeting with the school staff—the principal, assistant principal, psychologist, parent coordinator, two teachers, and a paraprofessional. They sat around a cramped table, putting on airs of relaxed eagerness. But I suspected most of them were secretly terrified. To us, who'd seen him at his worst, Nadav looked fine. But I doubted that any of them had ever seen a child so ill, much less take responsibility of caring for one.

Pleasantries quickly turned into negotiations. Who would take him to the bathroom? How would he get upstairs? Unflinching advocates for our son, we parried policy with persistence; a stubborn strength that came from five years of bending the world to our will. He is going to go to this school, we said in as many words. And you are going to help make it happen.

At one point, we reached an impasse. I can't remember if it was about toileting, or his oxygen tank, or whatever; it wasn't going to work, and the dam was about to burst.

And then his teacher—who hadn't said a word to that point—leaned over, across the table, and met our eyes.

"Listen," she said, "we're human."

It was a statement of fact, but also a promise. To my ears, it was a commitment as firm as a wedding vow.

I knew then that we needn't worry. He was in the right place. They cared, and they would make sure everything would be OK. They were human.

℘℘℘

Mary, his teacher, was worth her weight in gold; a heart as large as the sun, and all of the right instincts.

"Let Nadav come on the second day," she said. "That will give me time to introduce him to the kids, away from the first day craziness."

As it turned out, Nadav caught a cold, and didn't start until two weeks later. In the meantime, Mary helped the class understand what to expect. She explained that his heart didn't work properly, but that otherwise he was like anyone else; she described his oxygen tank, and his cannula, and his NG tube; plainly, directly, honestly.

She put his name on the door, along with everyone else's, written on a smiling green frog.

ৡ০জ

Mary knew the secret strength that children have—and that adults too often lack—a remarkable ability to look past the surface, without implications or inference, and see things for what they are. She understood that kids needed to know the truth; that fear came from not knowing.

Adults see an oxygen tube and think: this tube means that your lungs are in such bad shape that you can't breathe properly. It means you're in trouble; you might even die. That knowledge brings us fear.

But explain to a child that a tube gives you oxygen, and they'll understand that's what it's for—helping you breathe. This knowledge—that the tube serves a useful purpose—is a source of comfort.

She was a wonderful teacher.

ৡ০জ

The next day, when it was time for school, Tali and I took Nadav across the street together. We parked his stroller in the yard (it was still difficult for him to walk long distances) and I saw an old friend with his wife. They'd just dropped off their kids too.

"First day of school," I beamed, an oxygen tank slung across my back. "Could you take a photo?"

Other kids streamed by, full of manic energy Nadav couldn't match. While they skipped and bounded up the stairs, he took each step slowly, carefully, gripping the handrail with one hand, and mine in the other. When we eventually reached the classroom, it was marvelous to see him there—no longer a patient, but a normal kid on his first day of school.

We figured that given his lack of strength, Nadav might go to school a day a week, or perhaps a few hours a day. But that first day, with Tali at his side, he stayed until the bell rang, and at dinner, he was the happiest I'd seen him in a long time. "Do you want to go back tomorrow?" Tali asked, already knowing the answer. He went back the next day, and the day after, and the day after that; each day a quiet triumph.

Still, when he went to school, one of us would always stay home, just in case.

🙞🙜

Perhaps the most nervous person in the school was the nurse. She'd probably been looking forward to a boring year of skinned knees, and was suddenly responsible for a world-champion cardiac kid. She called us often, apologetic every time; just a little concerned; just keeping an eye out.

"Don't worry, everything's fine," she'd say. "But could you just come over and check that his oxygen is working?" Or, "He's looking a little tired, could you come take a look?"

I'd come to her office, and sit down, and ask Nadav to come over and tell me what was wrong. I knew that no matter how tired he was, if he could walk across the room, he was OK.

He'd walk over, every time. And I'd give him a big hug, and a kiss, and tell him to have a great day in school.

On the rare occasions when the nurse from Yaniv's school called, we must have seemed like terrible parents. He had a headache? A scrape? A fever? Whatever. We had more important things to worry about.

ಐೞ

Mary was right. Those looking after Nadav were "human" in the best sense of the word. His para patiently fed him tiny scraps for lunch, singing songs to convince him to eat just another bite, just as we had in the hospital. His therapists were full of excited updates, high-fiving him as he left for home, his infectious charm contagious as always. One even built him a special chair out of reclaimed wood, so that he could sit with proper posture and not get too tired.

Nadav had a hard time with stairs, so whenever the class visited the library on the second floor, we came by to help out. It was lovely to see him with his classmates. They'd bring him books, help him hold crayons, give him hugs. One curly haired girl named Charlotte sat next to him every day, especially sweet; we met her mother, and thanked her profusely. But we both knew there was really nothing for us to thank her for. Her daughter was just being a kid and a friend.

ಐೞ

One evening we went across the street for parent-teacher conferences. There wasn't too much to discuss—we were already in daily contact with most of the people caring for him—but it was nice to meet some of the other people in his life.

I met the art teacher toward the end of the evening, just as he was packing up, and introduced myself as Nadav's dad. He smiled, offering his hand. "Thank you for choosing to send him to public school," he said. Even though it hadn't occurred to us to send him anywhere else, it was nice to hear.

Nadav wasn't a burden; he was a gift.

Chapter 47

COLUMBIA

While we were glad to be home, the medical equipment that filled our apartment was a reminder of how tenuous things really were. Nadav's circulation was working, somehow, but it was putting an intense strain on his heart. And as Chitra had warned us, his physiology was ultimately unsustainable.

Columbia was our last hope, so as soon as we could we tried to get their attention. After all, we'd made a magical connection to CHOP when we found ourselves stuck in Australia. Why should this time be any different?

We relied on word of mouth to make our case. My sister knew someone who worked in Columbia's pediatric cardiology department—we wrote to her. A friend's father was on the hospital's teaching faculty—we wrote to him. Each time, we sent a copy of our letter:

> *"As parents who prefer reality and honesty to blind faith, we are well aware that any procedure will likely present considerable risks, especially given Nadav's unique physiology. We believe that Nadav is worth those risks, and hold out hope that there is some medical option that might help him."*

Something must have clicked, because just after Nadav started kindergarten, Columbia finally agreed to see him. There were no guarantees, they stressed. But it was a start.

It would be our fourth hospital in as many years. Once again, we'd have to learn a new set of rhythms, a new cast of unfamiliar faces. Once again, there was no playbook, no plan. Just the opposite: three of the East Coast's leading hospitals had already told us there was nothing they could do for our son.

We made an appointment to meet Nadav's new cardiologists—hoping that we'd somehow find a way to thread the needle again. Perhaps they might even agree to consider Nadav for a heart transplant. But it was just as likely that they'd turn us away.

☙CB

Everything about the first appointment was odd and unfamiliar. But it was more the strangeness of a new space than anything else; the medical team turned out to be friendly and compassionate. The cardiologist gave Nadav a brief examination, but there wasn't much more to learn—he already had all of his medical records from Philadelphia. "I'll present him at our weekly staff meeting," he told us. "And then we'll take it from there."

By the end of the week, we had our answer—another disappointment. They didn't consider Nadav to be a candidate for a transplant, not in his current condition.

But the cardiologist wanted to keep seeing him, thinking that they might be able to improve his circulation with a series of caths. If they could coil off some of the pesky collaterals that were putting such a strain on his heart, he reasoned, it might make things better. And after that—if it worked—what else might be possible?

It was still a long shot. Each catheterization would be tricky, with considerable risk. Given his condition, the anesthesia was worrying enough, never mind the intervention. We all knew what this meant: there was a real chance he could die on the table.

It was a risk we were prepared to take, and—thankfully—Nadav's new cardiologists were too. We agreed to schedule his first procedure for mid-November.

Tali and I had made the same choice every step of the way: put Nadav in the best position to pull through, and trust that he would.

All we needed was one more miracle.

ಬಂಳಿ

By this point, Tali and I had become experts in most aspects of his medical care—not just the surgeries, the medicines, and the dense medical jargon that described it all, but the avalanche of paperwork that inevitably cascaded from our mailbox onto the kitchen table in the aftermath of any medical procedure.

Much of Nadav's medical equipment was expensive, especially if insurance was paying. The bills we received seemed like ledgers, starting with some outrageous amount at the top, only to be sliced down by lines and lines of discounts, adjustments, and insurance payments. Each line represented some sort of hidden negotiation; each participant getting their share. But I didn't mind who was getting rich, as long as it didn't make us poor.

I had always feared being blindsided with a huge, unexpected expense—only too aware of the many horror stories surrounding America's health care system. But since we were lucky enough to have solid medical insurance—which covered pre-existing conditions and had a reasonable out-of-pocket maximum—we no longer worried about who would pay for it all.

Nadav spent nearly eight full months in the hospital in 2016: two months in Westmead, six months at CHOP—not to mention our outpatient visits at Columbia. Our insurance company paid out millions of dollars to care for him that year, covering everything from his flight home to the gauze his nurses wrapped around his wounds each day.

As the air ambulance coordinator had told us when we first spoke:

Y'all are very lucky.

෨෬

Even though we were glad to be home, I still felt a little melancholy. I found myself missing the places we'd left behind, and the friends we'd made along the way. And so, months after we left Westmead, I prepared a package with some special gifts for the people who cared for Nadav while he was there.

For Glenda, we found a *hamsa*, a Jewish talisman whose shielding hand is thought to bring its bearer health, peace, and good fortune. For Yishay, we ordered a custom New York Mets t-shirt with the number 14 on the back, for the hours she'd spent operating on Nadav. For the rest of the ward, we sent an album packed with photos.

For Nick: a small, hand-crafted keychain, clasping a cast-silver model of a Gulfstream jet.

෨෬

We didn't realize that at the same time Westmead was trying to send us a gift as well. The Australian nurses had checked Nadav's charts and realized that he still had some heart beads remaining. They tried to mail them to us in the States, stamps carefully pasted in the upper right corner of the package, but used the wrong address. "They came back in the post," one of his nurses wrote, apologetically, "via many countries, I suspect."

When they finally found their way to our mailbox, we opened the package to find the familiar glimmer of colored glass—including a pink crystal heart, for Nadav's discharge nine months before. And in a separate, tiny purple mesh bag, they'd added another special memento, just for us—a small silver airplane, looped at one end so it could be threaded onto a string.

A nice reminder, I thought, of the types of miracles we'd needed, even now.

Chapter 48

BACK TO NORMAL

It was strange and wonderful to have all three boys home again. We busied ourselves around the city as best we could, dragging oxygen tanks wherever we went, rediscovering all of the simple pleasures we'd taken for granted before our fateful trip Down Under.

Even something as ordinary as a trip to the grocery store could bring delight. The boys' favorite spot was the meat section, twins cruising around in the shopping cart, Gilad lifting ten-pound briskets over his head like a strongman.

In the seafood display, we spotted a familiar fish packed in ice—SEA BASS, $13.99 a pound. I sent a photo to his music therapists at CHOP, suddenly missing the laughs we'd shared in the hospital garden. But we appreciated our freedom nonetheless.

80CB

Our calendar was packed that fall, family outings interspersed with medical appointments: "New Victory Tickets," "Nadav PT," "Young People's Concerts," "Service Check for CPAP."

I'd forgotten how busy we were, perhaps because the things we did paled in comparison to the life-or-death events of the previous year—or simply because I hadn't gone through and organized all of the photos we took. With everything going on, it was hard to find the time.

Sifting through them now, I see so many things that have disappeared from my memory:

— A Halloween pumpkin we carved, decorated with some of Nadav's extra medical supplies: oxygen cannula stretched around the face; NG tube threaded through its hollow nose; syringe stuck in a diagonal above one eye.

— The boys standing outside our polling place on Election Day, little "I Voted" stickers pressed to their chests. When I asked them who was going to win the election, Nadav—ever the contrarian—confidently announced: "Trump."

— A video of Nadav reading his homework, carefully sounding out each word, correcting Tali when she mistakenly said, "Last page." "No," he said, "two pages left"—holding up two fingers as proof.

Looking through those photos, I found many others too—the five of us bowling; visiting the Museum of Natural History; Nadav cuddling on the couch with his cousin at a Hanukkah party—but after a few minutes I had to stop. The happy memories that rushed back, overshadowed by all the medical drama we'd experienced along the way, were too overwhelming.

&oc&

A few weeks after we returned home from Philadelphia, I'd noticed that the New Zealand rugby team—the world-famous All Blacks—were coming to Chicago in November to play a match against Ireland. We'd been to cricket and soccer matches in Australia, but never rugby—and so on an impulse, I bought two tickets. Never mind that we were in New York; perhaps we could find some way to use them. That old travel itch, I suppose, was tickling at me.

As November approached, I decided that I'd take Gilad. If we left early enough on a Saturday, we could get there by midday—the game didn't start until three in the afternoon. And it would be a surprise: I told the boys I had to go to Chicago for a meeting, saying nothing about the real reason—until 4:30 a.m. that Saturday, when (bags surreptitiously packed) I shook Gilad awake in his bed. "It's time to go," I whispered.

"Mnmmmrfnf," he mumbled, eyes closed. "What is it?"

"We're going to *Chicago!*" I whispered.

"But I'm not *allowed* to go," he groaned, in a daze; until he realized I wasn't kidding, and then, slowly—a mischievous smile emerged beneath his bleary eyes.

৪৩৪৩

We ate breakfast on the plane, and I opened my computer. "We're going to watch a movie," I said. "A movie about Chicago." Yes, I was prepared: I'd brought along *The Blues Brothers*. What else would we watch on a flight to the Windy City?

Truth be told, the movie probably wasn't appropriate for Gilad. There was more cursing than I remember, probably far too much for a nine-year-old. But every time Jake or Elwood said something inappropriate, Gilad just looked at me with smiling eyes. After all, as he'd already reminded me, he went to public school—he'd heard it all before.

The day turned out to be a great success. We visited the fan area in the parking lot before the match, where Gilad played a bit of touch footy, receiving the ultimate rugby souvenir—a bloody nose. He won a scarf, a hat, and a little cardboard sign reading "TRY!" which he vowed to wave every time the All Blacks scored.

Our seats were in the very last row of the upper deck. We could barely make out the action down below, which might have been just as well; the Irish trounced the Kiwis in an unexpected upset. Nobody threw a pint of beer at us. But it was great fun anyway.

After the game, the crowd streaming out into the chilly night, we found a pizza place, packed with fellow fans. (Gilad, ever the New Yorker, insisted on thin crust.) The next morning, after a huge breakfast, we visited The Field Museum of Natural History; and then back home on an early-evening flight, in time for school the next day.

It was great to be on the move again.

ଽ୦ଔ

Two weeks after we returned from Chicago, we returned to the hospital for another procedure. But this time the patient was Gilad, not Nadav.

After a routine checkup, Gilad's ENT had told us that the tiny tubes that drained fluid from his ears had fallen out and needed to be replaced. Otherwise, he warned, the buildup could cause painful ear infections. This wasn't a big deal—Gilad had already had two similar operations, both common childhood procedures. By now they seemed almost routine.

For us, accustomed to much more complicated and difficult hospital visits, it was not a particularly stressful experience. I drove him to a clinic in Brooklyn at the crack of dawn while Tali stayed home with the twins. We'd be home in time for a late lunch.

હ⟩⟨જ

I was perhaps the most relaxed parent there, glad to be dealing with a low-stakes procedure for once.

Gilad's doctor diligently pointed out the various risks before asking me to sign the consent forms. I knew all too well how much could go wrong, even with the longest of odds; but strangely that knowledge granted me a certain calm. Compared to what we'd gone through with his brother, the chance of anything unexpected was infinitesimal.

I signed the forms without a second thought.

હ⟩⟨જ

We spent the time waiting for the procedure taking silly videos with my phone's camera. A nurse arrived, giving Gilad an anesthetic that she warned would make him "goofy"—and sure enough, his facial expressions grew ever more contorted, our shared silliness giving way to a series of demented gurgling giggles that had him in stitches.

I watched the video while waiting for him to come out, and it was one of the funniest things I'd ever seen. When he emerged from surgery—perfectly fine, no surprises—I showed it to him, laughing. But the giddiness of the anesthesia had worn off. He was clearly embarrassed and made me swear never to let anyone see it.

He'd grown to an age where he was old enough to care what others thought; old enough to be embarrassed by the sort of silliness that we once shared without regret.

Chapter 49

THE SECRETS OF
THE UNIVERSE

A close friend, after hearing our story, told me that we had "learned the secrets of the universe."

It wasn't true, of course. At best, we might have been more aware of them. The mysterious ways in which the body forms and grows, giving life. Not that things go wrong—but the amazing ways in which they go right. And when things *do* go wrong, the body's extraordinary capacity to compensate and heal.

The miracles we'd seen in our journey around the world rekindled the wonder that I'd felt when I first learned of the tiny feather-beats of embryonic cilia, laying out their magical paths of proteins. The collaterals Nadav had grown were equally astonishing; each tendril a riddle that hinted at some greater unknown.

Gilad's sniffles invoked no such wonder. They seemed too trivial to be of real concern—and after his twin brothers were born, even more so. Some kids are just prone to ear infections, I reasoned. Nothing to be too concerned about.

But as we were soon to learn, they were intimately connected to his brother's devastating condition—a revelation that left me reeling.

ஐ‍ଔ

T hat fall we received a genetic report based on the blood
samples we'd given at CHOP. Dense with jargon, it
revealed that Nadav's condition was, in fact, genetic. His
defects were caused by a mutation in the H5 gene that prevented
his embryonic cilia from functioning properly.

Mutated H5 genes were known to cause similar issues in
other children. There was even a proper name for it: Primary
Ciliary Dyskinesia, or PCD. But although there were plenty of
other kids with a similar condition, there was something remarkable about Nadav's specific mutation.

It had never been reported before. It was unique.

ஐ‍ଔ

Of course, that strangely formed gene did not suddenly appear
out of thin air. It came from us.

Nadav had not simply inherited a mutated H5 from a single
parent; he'd inherited *two* mutated H5 genes, one from each of
his parents. Tali and I were both carriers.

And the mutations we carried were exactly the same.

Completely, perfectly identical.

Never before reported, never before seen.

"I suspect you had a common ancestor, about four or five
hundred years ago," the genetic counselor said when she told us
the results. A fork from which our family trees had diverged,
many generations ago.

ஐ‍ଔ

Here is where I should say something profound about falling
in love with this particular woman—this particularly wonder-

ful woman—how I knew, once we met, that we were meant to spend our lives together; and how that connection unknowingly reunited a centuries-old mutation that would reintroduce itself to the world by screwing up our beloved son's heart.

I wouldn't change any of it.

What other choice did we have? Had we known, would we not have married? Or perhaps, would we have decided not to have children? Might we have cherry-picked, rolling the dice until we formed perfect embryos, free of any complications?

But then we would be missing our sons. Sons we loved. Sons who, for better or for worse, belonged to us.

No, I preferred to accept this as our path through life. Better to trust that it was fate, *beshert*—meant to be.

ॐ⋇ॐ

But that wasn't all.

Since we were both carriers, each of our children had a one in four chance of carrying on the mutation. And so, we had Nadav's brothers tested. Yaniv wasn't a carrier, but Gilad was. Like Nadav, he'd inherited a mutated gene from each of us.

Suddenly Gilad's short NICU stay, constant congestion, and frequent visits to the ENT made sense. They were caused by the same genetic issues as his younger brother. But while Nadav's condition was perhaps the worst possible outcome of a mutated H5, Gilad's was one of the mildest, causing little more than clogged sinuses and a constant runny nose.

Gilad took the news well—he seemed proud to share weird genes with his beloved brother. When he was a little older, he would give a talk to his entire grade about the condition they both shared. "To you, I seem like a normal sixth grader," he told the assembly—confidently, confidentially cool: "But actually, I'm a mutant."

℘ℭ℞

Who knows what tiny twist of fate, what mislaid protein—might have determined which of our sons would be born healthy; which would be born with a persistent cough; and which would be born with a broken heart?

In the future, I suspect, some of these mysteries may be revealed. Until then, they remain in the realm of the unknown—a product of whatever unseen, moving hand that swirls our fate. We are left to ponder the extent to which we are able to determine our own destiny, to intrude in the natural processes of life and death; haunted by a suspicion that, in the end, we ultimately have no control.

I suppose all we can do is try to accept the limits of our own humanity, and somehow make peace—however tenuous—with those perplexing forces we know nothing about.

I never found this easy. From the moment Nadav was born, I knew I might have to come to terms with his death. Faced with this persistent existential dread, I had learned to search for the awe in the unknown, hoping that life's many wonders might somehow mask its inevitable terror.

Chapter 50

CATH

I t was mid-November, little more than a year after we'd stood in the Qantas terminal at JFK, waiting for that fateful flight to Australia. Our long, improbable circle around the globe had finally carried us home, nine months late. But in many ways, we were back where we started.

Yet another hospital, yet another procedure. This one—our first cath at Columbia—was neither part of a carefully curated plan, nor borne of emergency need. There were no studies indicating it might work, nor cautious odds based on the tiniest of samples. It was a long shot, based on something between a hunch and a hope.

Like we'd heard so many times before: if it didn't work, there was nothing more the doctors could do.

ళ్లుు

Arriving at a new hospital was always an adjustment. We'd arrived at Mount Sinai as expectant parents facing a terrifying diagnosis; we'd staggered into Westmead as disoriented travelers dealing with an unexpected crisis; we'd landed triumphantly at CHOP as grateful refugees, one step closer to home.

We fought our way into Columbia, desperate pilgrims on a quest for one more miracle. We clung to the unlikely belief that the doctors there could somehow prune away the inefficiencies of Nadav's imperfect circulation, somehow making it possible for him to get a new heart.

One more hospital, one last chance.

ဘာဝ

Adjusting to a new space was not easy. Columbia's meeting rooms were unfamiliar, the hallways confusing—even the hand soap had a strange smell. The boys didn't feel comfortable there, either. The playroom had a pool table, and special programs for siblings, but they wandered around sullenly, longing for the video games they'd become accustomed to at other hospitals.

Unlike the security personnel at CHOP, who held a gentle kindness beneath their stern veneer, the guards at Columbia were obstacles—not friends. The children's hospital was connected to the adult hospital—farther north, closer to the subway—and as the winter weather got worse, it was tempting to use the adult entrance to avoid the slush.

For some reason, this was forbidden, as I found out when I tried it one snowy day. "Where do you think you're going?" a guard snarled at me, unmoved when I told him my son was in the children's cardiac ICU, just down the hall. He just pointed at the front door, as if I'd committed some heinous crime, and asked me to leave.

But the cardiology staff did their best to make us feel welcome when Nadav was admitted for his first cath in mid-November, and the procedure seemed to go well. The interventional cardiologist had managed to coil off one of the main collaterals, slightly reducing Nadav's pressures without significant impact to his vitals.

It was a good start. If we could continue to successfully tie off collaterals, his circulation might return to some sort of balance. At the very least, it would reduce the strain on his heart.

&OC8

The day after the cath, as Nadav recuperated, we were invited to a special parents' tea in the cardiac ward. The gathering was generous and lovely—volunteers in pink vests serving home-made cakes and dainty cookies to exhausted parents, many of whom checked their watches nervously, leaving with polite thanks after a few minutes. I'd decided to take a short cookie break while Tali stayed with Nadav down the hall. Thankful for the respite, I was in no rush to get back.

Some of the volunteers were parents whose children had once been patients in the cardiac ward. One introduced me to her daughter, who'd received a heart transplant a decade before, and now seemed in perfect health. We chatted for a long time about what it felt like to have been a patient; how thankful she was to survive; her hopes and dreams for the future. (I think she was planning to go to med school.)

It was an effortless, wonderful conversation. Talking with her made it easy, even obvious, to imagine that we might have the chance to emerge unscathed, freed from the constant tragedy of a broken heart; to imagine that everything could be OK, because she was; that amongst all of the death and despair, there was at least one mother able to watch her daughter grow up.

And then, silently, a nurse leaned over my shoulder.

"Please come with me," she whispered. "Your son is coding."

Stunned, I got up, excusing myself. Back to reality.

And—once again—blindsided by the unexpected.

ഇഗ

Hospital emergencies are classified with colors, most of which describe unimaginable disasters: bomb threats, active shooters, hazardous waste spills. A few times, we'd heard loudspeakers announce a "code red," accompanied by flashing strobes and high-pitched whistles—but they always turned out to be false alarms; nuisances, not disasters.

A patient emergency—an acute change in condition, requiring immediate attention at the bedside—is technically considered a "code blue," according to the charts posted on nurses' stations. But in practice, it's just "coding," no color needed.

For doctors and nurses, "the patient is coding" means come quick, and don't panic. For parents, it's a gut punch, a blindsiding *thwack*. Don't interrupt the doctors rushing in the halls—just pretend to be calm, as your heart sinks into the floor.

ഇഗ

By the time I'd reached Nadav's bedside, the crisis was over. Half the staff seemed to be jammed into the room, watching the monitor tensely; but I could tell that whatever happened had passed.

Tali explained what had occurred. She'd turned on Nadav's chest vest to clear his lungs, just like we did every afternoon at home, but he hadn't reacted well, his heart rate plummeting. The nurse panicked, sounding the alarm—but once Tali turned the vest off, he'd quickly recovered.

It probably isn't a good idea to do the vest, Tali said.

The doctor on call agreed, obviously relieved. But as the room emptied, she still gazed at the monitor, just in case.

⊰⊱

The crisis was a sudden reminder of the delicate balance that kept Nadav alive—and how precarious our path had been. Years from now, I suspect, pediatric transplants may well be routine. Perhaps they will simply grow new hearts from stem cells—or even just print them, mighty muscles built to order—and be done with it. No more endless surgeries, wrenching the body's circulation into unusual circuits, waiting for another's tragedy to make a new heart magically appear.

The procedures we take for granted today—the BT shunt, the Glenn, the Fontan—will be remembered as necessary, but barbaric; the resulting trauma, even for those patients lucky to survive, tragic and avoidable.

The volunteers at tea parties will be survivors, not parents; and every year, their mailboxes will be filled with Valentine's postcards.

⊰⊱

We breathed a sigh of relief when Nadav was discharged a few days later. But we were eager to return to the hospital, hoping to keep up the momentum.

We had wanted to schedule the next cath in mid-December. But it kept getting delayed—first, because of a miscommunication, and then again, because the interventional cardiologist wanted to wait for another specialist to assist.

At times, I secretly missed being an inpatient—to live as a resident rather than a visitor, granting us an insider's view of the hospital's ever-churning gearbox and giving us some influence over its inner workings. It was hard to get things done from afar, without the power of eye contact and the rhythm of daily check-ins—especially since his new doctors still didn't really know him.

But we were happy that we'd coiled off one collateral, at least. Hopefully there would be many more.

Chapter 51

CHANGING SEASONS

Fall brought with it the High Holy Days, always a reflective and emotional time for Jewish families—especially ours. Each day seemed laden with meaning: from the second day of Rosh Hashana, the twins' Hebrew birthday, when we read the story of Abraham's near-sacrifice of his son Isaac—to Yom Kippur, the Day of Atonement, when the book of life is closed, our fates sealed for the coming year.

Observing the holidays once again exposed a chasm between us and the rest of the world—a separation especially stark on Yom Kippur, when Jews fast from sundown to sundown. In the afternoon, we'd walk back home for a quick nap in suits and ties, passing all sorts of people doing what they normally do— moms pushing strollers; kids on phones; workers with double-parked trucks.

It was strange to pass these people. They inhabited a parallel universe in which this was just another day, going about their business while our world stood still.

୫୦୯୫

One of my clearest memories from that fall came during a silent prayer, part of the Yom Kippur evening service. The congregants stood, swaying slightly, while Nadav sat fidgeting in his chair. After a few minutes, obviously bored, he started to sing:

"Tzedakah, tzedakah, tzedakah,
That is what we give..."

You're not supposed to talk during that prayer, but nobody got annoyed. It was hard to ignore the magic of the moment; a perfect interruption on a day focused on personal reflection and repentance. My grandfather, who never minded children's interruptions, would have been tickled to hear it.

🕉

As the weather cooled, and Thanksgiving passed, a celebratory spirit filled our neighborhood. As Jews, our traditional obligations had been fulfilled earlier in the fall; now, we found ourselves surrounded by Christmas. Stores played catchy carols, green and red bunting hung from streetlamps, the sidewalks filled with fresh fir trees for sale, their sweet scent wafting into the cool air.

Given our faith, Tali and I were ambivalent about these celebrations. We weren't against them, but the traditions weren't ours. And since the Christmas spirit was so pervasive, we felt a need to remind our kids why we didn't celebrate the same things their friends did.

Often this took the form of rhetorical questions. "Why don't we have a Christmas tree?" I'd ask as we walked down the street—to which the boys would reply, as if on cue: "Because we're Jewish!"

But Nadav, as always, was a little different. "Why don't we have a Christmas tree?" I asked him once, on the way back from school. I was a little taken aback by his matter-of-fact answer: "Because it's not Christmas yet!"

He was secretly Christian, his brothers joked when they heard the story. Gilad suggested that we change his name from "Nadav" to "Ned."

෨෬

Like the angel we brought back from Nadav's first surgery, we did welcome one Christmas tradition into our home.

A close friend of mine had been part of an *a capella* group in college. After graduation, she'd married someone in the ensemble, and together, they moved to our neighborhood. Each year, they invited their fellow singers back for a reunion, and they'd celebrate by caroling around the area.

It was too cold for us to go out, so I invited them to come by and sing for us. They arrived close to the kids' bedtime, filling our small apartment with shivers. To warm them up, I poured small shot glasses of vodka, and introduced them to the boys, who were uncharacteristically shy.

Before the singing started, I half-jokingly asked if they knew any non-Christmas songs.

"Not many," one answered apologetically. "But it should be OK. Jesus was Jewish when he was born, wasn't he?"

We'd never played Christmas music before, but it didn't matter. Their beautiful harmonies—so different from the lilting melodies we'd sing when kindling Hanukkah candles—still filled our apartment with light. And after some extra vodka shots, they bid us farewell, laughing as they tramped down the stairwell and back into the cold.

๛

Christmas songs were noticeably absent from Nadav's school holiday show, which had been carefully choreographed to be as nondenominational as possible. No Santas or menorahs to be found; just a lot of gold stars and a heaping of fluffy fake snow, the songs vaguely evoking themes of light and happiness and togetherness.

Nadav's teachers saved us a seat in the front row, so that we could see him up close. His class sat together on risers in three straight rows, right in front of the stage—with Nadav on the lowest riser so that he wouldn't have to negotiate the stairs. They waved their arms around in a semi-synchronized routine, as coordinated as five-year-olds can be, their eyes searching the room for some glimpse of their parents' faces.

I've replayed the scene many times since, on my phone and in my mind: Nadav keeping up as best he could, nodding his head in time with the music; his classmate Charlotte finding her mother, and then, grabbing his arm, noticing us—there we were! And, finally, his look of recognition, so pleased that we could be there together.

๛

And then—January, and a new year.

The winter cold was inescapable, or perhaps that's just how I remember it. Having traversed the hemispheres twice in the past fourteen months, we'd almost forgotten what real cold felt like.

Each time we went out, I'd worry that Nadav wasn't warm enough, especially if we had a particularly long way to go. In our neighborhood, walking was far more convenient than taking the car; if we drove, we'd have to circle for hours looking for a parking spot. So, we often chose to brave the chill.

One outing was particularly frustrating. Nadav hadn't been feeling well, and his doctors wanted him to get a blood test—suggesting that we do it in a lab closer to home rather than schlepping all of the way to the hospital. The nearest lab was a half-mile away, not too far—so I bundled him up in the stroller, looped his oxygen tank over the handles, and set out into the slush.

∞∞

What should have been an easy trip turned into a nightmare. The lab we were heading to had moved, and by the time we'd reached the new location the staff told me that they no longer took our insurance. So after some frantic Googling on my phone, we tramped over to another location, another fifteen minutes away.

The lab was on an upper floor, in an old office building; completely empty except for two phlebotomists on call. We arrived in a mess.

The woman who drew the blood was welcoming and warm, but as I unbundled Nadav, careful not to tangle his NG and oxygen lines, I realized that she'd never had to deal with a child in his condition. She gently looked at his small arm, searching for a vein. "It's not easy, but it can be done," I reassured her, silently worrying that she wouldn't be able to find one and shuffle us off to yet another location.

It had always been difficult to draw blood from Nadav, and we'd had some excruciating draws in the past. Sometimes the phlebotomist just gave up, suggesting that someone else try. There was one cardiology fellow at Mount Sinai who somehow managed to get it right every time, and when all else failed, he'd be summoned to help. Eventually we got into the habit of just calling him first.

She had to stick him twice, the first time not drawing nearly enough blood. But during the second draw, gently rubbing his arm, she eventually managed to fill half of a second vial. "That's enough, I think," she said. We were done.

I felt terrible, having put Nadav through that ordeal. Later, I wondered if we should have just gone to the hospital. The blood was important, but Nadav's health was too. And I wondered if what we went through—just for a few drops of blood—had really been worth it.

⁜ℂℇ

We heard the results of the blood test the next morning. Some of his levels were low, so his doctors suggested we bring him in for observation, and a possible transfusion. It didn't sound great, but we'd heard worse.

We asked his pediatrician where to go. Should we take him to Mount Sinai, his original hospital, or to Columbia, where his new cardiologists were planning another procedure in a few weeks?

"Go to Columbia," she said. "If anything needs to be done, they'll be prepared for him; they'll know what to do." So, I walked him to the car, and drove uptown.

Chapter 52

PRIDE

For most families, going to the emergency room is probably pretty scary. But not for us. We knew how nurses worked; how doctors thought; why machines beeped. Most importantly, we'd come to know its pace—when to be patient, when to push. Things took time.

A friendly nurse settled Nadav into a bed, wrapping a plastic band around his wrist. The ER doctor introduced herself, gave him the once-over and ordered some blood tests. Nadav and I sat together, telling silly jokes, just being together. Tali was at work, so I called with an update: they'd decided to give him a transfusion as soon as possible, to help replenish his red blood cells. Nothing we hadn't seen before.

Nadav's teacher sent an email during the day, wondering how he was doing. I'd forgotten to let them know he wasn't coming in to school, so I sent a smiling photo of him, thumbs-up. "We're in the hospital," I wrote. "Not feeling well, nothing major. Hopefully he'll be well enough to see everyone tomorrow."

Tali arrived in the late afternoon, having left the boys at home with my mother. The doctors had decided to keep Nadav overnight; upstairs, they were preparing a bed. But no transfusion yet. Something was holding it up.

෴

Want dinner? I asked. The hospital was in the middle of a bustling Dominican neighborhood; we'd discovered a fantastic roast chicken place a few blocks north, and I had a secret craving for some plantains and spicy green sauce. I was there and back in half an hour, the aromas filling the ER. Tali carved pieces for Nadav with a plastic knife, weighing them on the little scale, and we quietly munched together, just the three of us.

Still no bed; still no transfusion. But it was time for me to head home—it had been a long day. Tali would stay overnight with Nadav, and we'd regroup in the morning.

"I love you, Abba," Nadav said.

And I put my hands on his head, as I did every night at bed-time, and whispered the traditional blessing:

May the Lord bless you and keep you
May the Lord shine his countenance upon you,
and be gracious unto you
May the Lord look kindly upon you, and give you peace.

Adding, as I'd started doing since we returned home, some extra lines:

And a good night's sleep
And a happy day tomorrow
With your Abba
And Ima
And brothers
And classmates
And friends.

I kissed him on the forehead, gave Tali a hug, and headed home.

ഗ്രൗ

It was nearing midnight by the time I got home, the boys fast asleep, my mother drowsy. Exhausted, I was ready for some dumb TV. Sinking into the couch, I opened a beer and took a sip. And then the phone rang.

Tali called me: calm, controlled, upset. "He's coding," she said.

Then some mumbles away from the phone, some distant doctor's voice. "It won't do any good," Tali said; I wasn't sure to whom. "He's not going to make it," she said. She knew.

His heart had stopped.

They tried to resuscitate him; our DNR from Australia had lapsed. But Tali knew it was useless.

"Just stop," she said. "It's no use. It won't work. Just stop."

"I'm coming," I said.

I don't remember what she said then, but it didn't matter. It was clear. He was gone; it was over.

ഗ്രൗ

I couldn't leave Nadav's brothers alone in our apartment, but my parents weren't answering their phones; it was the middle of the night, and they'd gone to sleep. I had to drive over to their house, let myself in and pound on their bedroom door to wake them up.

"It's Nadav," I said, in tears. "Nadav's died. You need to come over and look after the boys."

ഗ്രൗ

I drove straight to the hospital, numb. Our old Subaru helped me along, retracing the route along quiet streets, empty and deserted. Each red stop light jolted me from the thoughtless distractions of the road, reminding me that he'd died, and forcing me to consider what it meant.

My greatest fear had always been that I'd have to tell his brothers. But somehow, after all we'd been through, that didn't scare me anymore.

৪৩

I found Tali with Nadav's doctors in an empty room, sitting in silence.

"I'm sorry," said the cardiologist.

They left us alone.

৪৩

As a parent, you live for moments of pure pride. First steps, first words; bar mitzvah, graduation; marriage, grandchildren. Many of those things, as I'd suspected, we'd never be able to experience with Nadav.

It is a terrible thing to know when your son is born that you will probably outlive him. But as our time together had taught me, this is true only if you measure life in years. We learned to measure life in miracles.

When I held him in my arms that night, I felt all sorts of emotions—sadness, pain, grief. But the most overwhelming thing I felt was pride.

I felt as much pride in Nadav's five years as any parent feels in a lifetime: a special, vivid feeling that I consider myself fortunate to have experienced, over and over again.

Chapter 53

SUCH A THING AS NOTHING

Ironically, on the night Nadav died—when we needed a social worker most—there were none to be found. Nobody on site; nobody on call.

The nurse in charge, visibly shaken, asked us if we'd like to speak to a rabbi. Knowing we were Jewish, I suppose she thought it was the next best thing.

Eventually they got someone on the line, a child psychologist, half-asleep and incomprehensible. It turned out to be the most awkward call of my life; listening to someone we'd never met, barely audible on a crackly connection, mumbling something irrelevant, when all we needed was someone to guide us through the logistics of death.

But there was nobody else. We were on our own.

૭૦૦૪

We arrived home at some ungodly hour, spent and dazed—knowing that in a few hours, when dawn broke, the boys would wake up, and I'd have to tell them what had happened.

Tali and I had a lot of practice in dealing with bad news. More than a few times, we were warned that Nadav might not have long to live. At least twice, we were told point-blank that he wouldn't make it. Sometimes we heard nothing at all, leading us to fear the worst.

The news that your son may die soon is a difficult thing to hear. But it is an even harder thing, I think, to tell. Throughout Nadav's life, my greatest fear was how to tell his brothers that he had died. Whenever things were at their worst, I could only think of what I'd have to say to them—not knowing how I'd ever find the words.

Now that that time had come, I somehow found the courage to do what I'd always feared. The past five years had forced me to confront vexing questions of my own existence, of my own mortality, of the delicate wonder of life's mysteries. But it also taught me how strong and smart kids are; how resilient they can be, even more so than adults; and how much they deserve our honesty—especially when it comes to things that we do not truly understand ourselves.

And so, I trusted their strength—and told them the truth.

৪০৫৪

When I was Gilad's age, we'd take annual family vacations to a farm in the Shenandoah Valley, in western Virginia—especially precious because of the time I'd spend alone with my dad. In the evening, when my younger siblings were tucked into bed, we'd have time to ourselves with no distractions. The two of us would head outside to the porch, dimly lit by a hurricane lamp in the rural stillness, cool breezes wafting in from the dark hills around us.

Outside, we'd plug in his beloved four-band radio, and gently angle the antenna, exploring the world. He'd fiddle with the dial until we picked up the BBC World Service on a short-wave band, its faint signals bouncing off the ionosphere—bearing the unmistakable chimes of Big Ben over the Atlantic. And then he'd let me switch it to AM, where we could find local baseball broadcasts from as far away as St. Louis or Chicago, a dreamlike sojourn to cities I'd never seen before.

One evening, we lay on our backs on a gently sloping hill, my arms folded beneath my neck to keep my head above the autumn dew. The sun had set, and we were gazing at the stars, far brighter in that dark sky than the narrow sliver of haze we were used to back home. "We're looking backward in time," my father explained, a concept that blew my mind. The light from those glimmering dots had traveled so far that the stars themselves might no longer exist.

ಌಛ

"What's between the stars?" I asked my father.

"Nothing," he said. "It's empty space."

That couldn't be right. There must be *something* there, I reasoned, and told him so.

"No," he said. "There's nothing there. Nothing at all."

"*There's no such thing as nothing*," I insisted, filled with a brash stubbornness; and repeated it over and over again in the days that followed, as if to make it true.

ಌಛ

Every time I raise my eyes to the heavens, and look at the stars, I'm reminded of my father's words: *there is such a thing as nothing*. It was a lesson that took a long time to learn, and one I still struggle with. I still find it terrifying to think that we are surrounded by nothingness, spanning the immeasurable expanse of the starlit sky.

I wished that it weren't so, that nothingness did not exist; and had I lived in a different era, I might have been raised to believe it. The ancient Greeks rejected the emptiness between the stars, believing the heavens were filled with *ether*—a necessary element breathed by the gods themselves. Newton, too, bristled at the idea of a cosmic vacuum, reasoning that starlight must require some medium to carry it along.

Even now, quantum physicists are dreaming up ideas that could reconcile this contradiction. Perhaps they might eventually explain how the energy of the universe interacts with empty space. But these theories, too complicated for me to grasp, offer little comfort.

৪০৫৪

My own objections rested on a simple fear of death. My father had lost his own father when he was sixteen, a massive heart attack on a Friday night, a sudden loss that lingered with him always. Growing up with the ever-present shadow of my own father's mortality, I could not accept the suffocating, inevitable reality of an empty void.

But when Nadav died, I had to admit that my objections did not matter. I no longer felt obliged to explain the mysteries of fate; I would never understand them myself. All I knew was the truth.

"Your brother has died," I said.

Confirming, against my will, the inexplicable nothingness that spans the universe; the empty darkness that surrounds every shining star.

Chapter 54

SHIVA

In the aftermath of Nadav's death, we once again found strength in our traditions. The rituals of Jewish mourning guided us through the process of death as surely as Nadav's doctors had helped us navigate his life.

Every tradition had a spiritual explanation; but I found that behind every custom was a good dose of common sense, centuries-old guidelines to help mourners navigate their grief. They allowed us to set aside inexplicable questions of life and death, and deal with the immediate realities we faced.

We followed the prescribed sequence, guided by ritual. The body must be buried as soon as possible (no need to linger on the shock of the death) in nothing more than a simple wooden casket (no need to be stressed by any unnecessary financial decisions) after which you find yourself amidst friends bearing food (cooking being the last thing on your mind).

Perhaps the most comforting tradition was the insistence that as mourners, we were surrounded by others, lending support as best they could. Nobody, of course, knows quite what to do, or say—sometimes causing odd, tangential conversations; at other times, prompting awkward silences. But as someone later told me, "the important thing is to be there." No matter what was said, it was good to feel other hearts beating in the room.

୬୦୦୪

The memorial service was packed, full of friends and family and doctors and teachers, everyone holding some small memory of Nadav in their hearts. Afterward, they filed past, an endless stream of familiar faces, his life passing before us in a blur.

At the end, hanging back until everyone had left, was the family we'd met in those first weeks in the Mount Sinai NICU. We'd stayed in touch over the years, visiting them often as our kids grew. The two sets of twins would all play happily, sword-fighting with long balloons or chasing each other around the yard.

I'd managed to hold back tears until that point—but we cried together when we saw each other, alone in the empty hall. Even though their son was still alive, they shared our pain. The father gave me a hug I'll never forget; tears streaming down our faces; clinging tightly, as if he was afraid to let go.

To this day, it always makes me happy to see their children—especially their son—the parents' dedication reminding me so much of the strength we once took for granted.

୬୦୦୪

For seven days after Nadav died, friends and family filled our home for the *shiva*, the traditional days of mourning. It seemed like everyone we knew had come, even two of Nadav's favorite nurses from CHOP, who'd driven all the way up from Philadelphia. We were so touched that they'd made the effort.

Each evening, by dinnertime, the apartment would empty out. One shouldn't turn away visitors to a *shiva*, but the rabbi had the smart idea of setting recommended visiting hours so we wouldn't be overwhelmed. By the end of the day, the whole experience felt utterly exhausting.

On the third day, we attended Shabbat services in the synagogue I'd grown up in, where the rabbi offered some remarks about Nadav in his morning sermon. "Nadav was blessed," he said. "He had the opportunity to travel around the globe, touching people's hearts everywhere he went. He consecrated the world."

ℭℂℓ

Although our traditions have brought me much comfort over the years, they can also trigger deep and difficult feelings, bitter ironies that I struggle to understand.

Each year, on the twins' birthday, we read the same Torah portion—how Isaac, the son Abraham was prepared to strike down, was saved—and I'm reminded, pointedly, that our son was not. The passage, which once gave me hope that all would go well, now fills me with an aching pain.

I am not a Torah scholar, and I'm ashamed to admit there are large gaps in my knowledge. In fact, it wasn't until after Nadav died that I came across the story of his biblical namesake—Moses' nephew, the son of Aaron, the high priest. Once again, the parallels to our own Nadav were astonishing: the biblical Nadav was struck down in his youth, without warning—consumed with his brother Avihu by a divine flame.

The Torah explains that the brothers perished because they improperly prepared an offering to God—an honor reserved for the high priest. Some rabbis say they were led astray by inflated egos and shameless pride. But other interpretations are more forgiving, suggesting that Nadav and Avihu's unauthorized sacrifice was not necessarily a sin. Instead, what they sought is something that burns within us all—the human striving for transcendence, the desire to make some connection with the divine.

It is human nature to wrestle with the blurry spaces at the edges of our understanding. Our own lives are just the latest chapters of an ancient tradition, each generation confronting the same contradictions—searching for some meaning, trying to make sense of it all. At some point, however, we must accept that there are some things we will never understand.

It is up to us whether we are left with a sense of frustration or awe.

ഇരുൻ

Our week of mourning still held one last moment of wonder.

On the last night of *shiva*, as the last guests were leaving, we heard the doorbell ring. An unfamiliar woman stood at the door, clutching a plastic bag, flustered and apologetic.

"I know it's late, and you don't know me," she said. But she explained why she was there. She was friends with some of Tali's friends in Australia, who felt terrible they couldn't be there with us. So, they sent her instead. She'd driven almost two hours on their behalf, simply to pass on their condolences.

I was astounded that she'd made such an effort, driving so far to console total strangers. She wasn't even Jewish. But what happened next sent chills down my spine.

"I felt I should bring something, so I picked out a bottle of wine," she said, opening the bag. "I'm not sure if it's appropriate, but I saw the label and thought it felt right."

This woman had never met us before; she knew nothing about us, or Nadav, or our crazy journey, and yet in her hands was a bottle of Hope Estate Shiraz, vintage 2012. It was the same Australian vineyard we'd visited in the Hunter Valley months before, glugging plonk, full of giggles, before disaster struck.

I was amazed at the coincidence. Throughout Nadav's life, my brain had always sought out patterns, hoping that they would give me strength in uncertain times. But this one left me reeling. I had no idea what it might mean.

"It said 'Hope,'" she explained, tentatively, baffled by our reaction. "I saw it and figured, we always need some hope, right?"

Chapter 55

BLESSINGS

To mark the end of the seven days of *shiva*, mourners are encouraged to leave their homes and take a walk around the block. For us, it was yet another reminder of the healing properties of the outdoors. Tali and I walked to a nearby park, and sat briefly on a small bench, listening faintly for memories in the cool winter air.

Soon it would be time for me to return to work. Condolences were still flooding in from many of my colleagues, and a co-worker asked if I wanted a company announcement to be sent out. I wasn't sure how to answer—how public was our grief?—but finally mumbled something along the lines of "Sure, why not?"

It was the best decision I could have made. The announcement was artfully written, and when I returned to the office, everyone knew what had happened.

Well, almost everyone. There were still some awkward moments, like the casual acquaintance who asked off-handedly, "How are the kids?" He must have missed the memo, but I didn't correct him. It was a conversation I didn't need to have.

೮೦೮೩

I got a few heartfelt notes from Jewish co-workers who recognized Nadav's Hebrew name and decided to reach out, even though we didn't know each other. Knowing that I'd still be in mourning after returning to work, they offered to arrange a *minyan*—the ten-person quorum necessary for mourners to recite the daily prayers. But I demurred. It was a kind gesture but unnecessary, given the number of congregations within a few blocks of our office.

"In that case," one wrote, "we will make sure you don't go alone."

So, every day for a week, around lunchtime, I'd meet a stranger in our building's lobby. They'd introduce themselves, we'd shake hands, and on the ten-minute walk to the local synagogue I'd tell them our story.

By the time we reached the *shul*, they'd inevitably have tears in their eyes. And so, I'd find myself comforting *them*: assuring them that his short life wasn't a tragedy, but a blessing; how much I appreciated their company; and how lucky I was to be able to share him with them, my shining lights of kindness.

ഒരു

I t is a tradition to give to charity in memory of a lost loved one; and so I decided to count up the loose change in Nadav's old *tzedakah* box, rolling the coins in paper sleeves. I promised the boys I'd multiply the amount by ten and give the total to charity in Nadav's memory.

Gilad's first reaction was disbelief. "We could get an Xbox for that!" he gasped, insisting that that's what his brother would have wanted. But we discussed it over the next few weeks, considering all sorts of worthy causes, and finally decided to give part of it to his old school, to plant a garden in his memory.

JAMES G. ROBINSON

ဆဝ၆

When we returned to the school the following spring, the building was as familiar as ever. The friendly guard at the front, who'd welcomed us with a big smile when we dropped off Nadav each morning, took a minute to place our faces. We hadn't seen him in ages; perhaps it was odd for him to see us without Nadav. But after a flash of recognition, he welcomed us in.

The school had decided that Nadav's garden would be housed in a small wooden planter, filled with the herbs that he loved. It was a lovely spring day, and although we still ached from his absence, it was gratifying to see his teachers and classmates again—five-year-olds excitedly digging little holes in the dirt, dropping in assorted plants and herbs, patting down the soil on top.

Heading back to the school's entrance after we'd planted the garden, we paused to talk to the security guard at the front desk. Tali asked how he was doing; we weren't quite ready to say goodbye.

Only in New York would an African-American gentleman answer with the Hebrew word for the Almighty. "*Hashem*," he said, pointing upwards with a smile. "*Hashem Gadol.*"

ဆဝ၆

Later that summer, whenever we'd see a ripe cherry tomato emerge in the school garden, Yaniv would pluck it off— helping himself to a favorite treat.

Amongst my many swirling emotions, I couldn't help but feel a strong sense of unfairness—for his classmates, those lovely, innocent souls, who had to be told about their friend's death; and for their parents, who had to do the telling. I hoped that they would have the courage to be honest, to trust their children's strength. But I also felt terrible that they were put in that position.

I had known since Nadav was born that I would probably have to confront his death. And for the past five years I had wrestled with that knowledge, twisting and turning it, trying to make sense of it. To think that when that stone dropped, its ripples would push outward, bringing grief to people we didn't really know—I couldn't help but feel some guilt.

At the end of the school year, a few parents put together a yearbook. It had a special page just for Nadav, and quotes from all of his classmates about how much he meant to them. It made me feel better to know that they could handle our loss too.

Chapter 56

US

A few months after Nadav's death, Tali and I found our-selves at a support group for grieving families, surrounded by other parents whose children had recently died. One family had lost their daughter suddenly, unexpectedly: healthy and safe one day, gone the next. I could not for the life of me imagine what that must be like.

And yet they looked at us the same way, with the same hor-ror. To live life knowing that your child's death is a distinct pos-sibility...that one day you'll have to say goodbye? As we told our story, I could feel the other parents shudder.

I tried to explain to them that it was not a misfortune for us to have shared Nadav's life, short as it was. It was not even a trag-edy to wrestle with the possibility of his death. It only reminded me how lucky we were to experience him, and all of our chil-dren—three brightly shining gifts, the greatest of blessings.

Tali later asked Yaniv if things would be better if his twin hadn't been born, allowing us to avoid the sadness of his loss. His answer radiated the unique wisdom of an eight-year-old. "We might have been healthier," he said. "But we wouldn't have been as happy."

৪০৫৪

We met many extraordinary people during our journey, many of them far removed from our life in Brooklyn. They all fell in love with our son—and yet Tali always said, a little wistfully: "I wish they knew him before."

This is the Nadav I remember:

— His curly hair, light brown with a streak of blonde at the top. Our family barber always wanted to cut it, but we never let him.

— His eyes, deep and knowing; gazing studiously at the camera; behind them a remarkable, unhurried calm.

— His dancing—gentle, not frantic—rocking back and forth against the fence at a minor-league baseball game; lost in his own world on the dance floor at his cousin's *bat mitzvah*.

— His laugh, heard in the background of one of my sister's recorded songs. She'd once invited our boys to come to the studio to listen in on a recording session, and as they tried to keep quiet, the microphones picked up one of Nadav's unsmothered giggles. She left it in.

৪০৫৪

Those moments are long past. All that is left are fleeting memories of the happiness we felt together when our boys were young.

I suspect that all parents must feel a similar sense of loss. Each passing year reminds us that our children will never again be newborns, or infants, or toddlers. Those special years are gone forever, except in our memories: the discoveries they made, the pride we felt, the ways their lives were fresh and new—a blank canvas, yet to be imagined.

ະ⊙Ƈȝ

The following winter, in the midst of the holiday season, we joined a few friends for a brief vacation at a kitschy resort a few hours away from our home. The neighboring amusement park was closed on Christmas, so there were good deals to be had on rooms—and as our friends had promised, the indoor waterpark was more than enough to entertain the kids.

They clambered over plastic dolphins in the pool, wrestling each other into the warm water; slid down two fairly exhilarating slides; and looked longingly at the adults-only hot tub near the windows, overlooking the snowy parking lot outside.

It was a fun day, and afterward, we collapsed into bed, exhausted.

ະ⊙Ƈȝ

As usual, we shared the room's two queen beds with the boys—Yaniv (who kicked) with Tali; Gilad (who rolled) with me.

With all that kicking and rolling, we were used to some sleepless nights. But nothing compared to what happened at three in the morning—when Gilad woke up, writhing in pain.

"My ear!" he whimpered, pressing his hand to the left side of his head, on the verge of tears. "It HUUUUUUUURTS!!"

It woke me up, of course, and Tali too. It was clear to both of us what had happened—all that splashing earlier that day had triggered an unusually painful ear infection. And of course, we hadn't brought anything at all that would help—no Tylenol, no ear drops, nothing.

ಬಿಀೞ

Tali went into the bathroom to check her phone, looking for a 24-hour pharmacy nearby. There weren't any. There was a children's hospital, though…

"Is it crazy to go there?" she asked. "Just for their pharmacy?"

"Yes," I said. "Completely crazy." Not going anywhere near a hospital for an ear infection.

"Why don't we check to see if they have any children's Tylenol at the front desk?" I suggested. "There are tons of kids here. They must have something."

So, Tali pulled on a sweatshirt, and some jeans, and headed downstairs to ask.

ಬಿಀೞ

I was left to console Gilad, still silently bawling. And then—just a few minutes after Tali had left—the answer popped into my head. We had an emergency kit in the red Subaru, parked just outside. There had to be some Tylenol in there.

I checked; and there it was. Hallelujah.

Full of pride, I headed down the hall to tell Tali, before she disturbed any sleepy receptionists.

ಬಿಀೞ

Tali was standing in the empty lobby, lights dimmed, surrounded by endless stretches of carpet, the hotel breathing its gentle hum. She'd just convinced a security guard to open the gift shop and was waiting for him to find the keys. She looked beautiful.

We stood, both completely calm. I showed her the red emergency kit. She whispered, explaining where the guard had gone.

In that instant, we stood together, remembering all of the nights we'd spent in hospital-land. For me, it was as romantic a moment as we'd ever shared: just the two of us, together, in an empty lobby, as the world slept; feeling the strength of each other's presence; sharing another medical crisis—averted, yet again.

ᒍᑎ

The children's Tylenol worked. Gilad fell asleep, and Tali soon after, her soft breaths joining Yaniv's gentle snores. But I could not rest.

My mind spun, pondering the mysteries of life, and love, and how things end. I lay awake, surrounded by magic and emptiness in equal measure. And I realized how lucky I was to once more have that brief glimpse of how we'd been, together, at our best.

ACKNOWLEDGMENTS

I am deeply grateful to the many people who have helped make this book a reality.

My friends at *The New York Times*, particularly Shane Murray, offered indispensable support during Nadav's life and continued flexibility in the aftermath of his death. I am especially thankful to my many newsroom colleagues who encouraged me to write about our experience: a long list that includes (among many others) Jodi Rudoren, Jodi Kantor, Susan Chira, and Hanna Ingber—and most of all Monica Drake, who commissioned the Travel article that convinced me that our experience might resonate with others.

I am indebted to many mentors who have inspired me during my career. Mike Shatzkin helped me navigate the world of book publishing. Pat C. Hoy II taught me the art of essay writing. Michael Shapiro, my partner at the Columbia School of Journalism, not only insisted that "you need to write this" but also provided a master class in the art of long-form narrative nonfiction.

Many people helped with the process of writing. Josh Robin, a first-class mensch, opened his Rolodex when I needed it most. Anders Hofseth suggested I use Scrivener to draft the book, keeping me organized. Alex Wright and Maaike Bouwmeester generously offered a quiet place to write, as did Scott Adkins, Erin Courtney and the staff of the wonderful Brooklyn Writers Space.

Two extraordinary editors—Cissi Falligant and Jane Rosenman—offered perceptive advice on early drafts of this work. Brett Wean, one of the most talented storytellers I know, shared insightful feedback on a later draft. Roberta Thorndike helped polish the finished manuscript.

Rabbi Adam Baldachin provided many thought-provoking observations on issues of tradition and faith. Susannah Heschel graciously granted me permission to quote her father for this book's epigraph.

The incomparable Alice Martell believed in this book and helped it find a home. Debra Englander and the staff at Post Hill Press—including Ashlyn Inman, Conroy Accord, and publisher Anthony Ziccardi—made it real.

It goes without saying how much I appreciate everyone who has helped us through the long journey of the past decade: friends, family, doctors, nurses, strangers. To the countless people who cared for us and Nadav, thank you from the bottom of my heart.

The most special and heartfelt thanks go to my wife Tali and our two surviving sons, who (each in their own way) steadfastly supported me through the difficult and often painful process of writing this book. It is never easy, but we are very lucky to have each other. I love you all so much.

CHARITIES

We are forever grateful to the many organizations who were there for us when we most needed it and continue to provide invaluable assistance for others in similar situations.

For a complete list, please visit
morethanamemoir.com/charities

The greatest kindnesses, of course, cost nothing.

BOOKPLATES

For a free bookplate (autographed by the author) please visit **morethanamemoir.com/bookplates**